The future of marketing

■ ■ ■ ■ ■ ■ ■ ■ ■ ■ ■ ■ ■ ■

FINANCIAL TIMES
Prentice Hall

In an increasingly competitive world, it is quality
of thinking that gives an edge – an idea that opens new
doors, a technique that solves a problem, or an insight
that simply helps make sense of it all.

We work with leading authors in the fields of
management and finance to bring cutting-edge thinking
and best learning practice to a global market.

Under a range of leading imprints, including
Financial Times Prentice Hall, we create world-class
print publications and electronic products giving readers
knowledge and understanding which can then be
applied, whether studying or at work.

To find out more about our business and professional
products, you can visit us at www.business-minds.com

For other Pearson Education publications, visit
www.pearsoned-ema.com

Pearson
Education

The future of marketing

Practical strategies for marketers in the post-internet age

C. N. A. Molenaar

FINANCIAL TIMES
Prentice Hall

An imprint of Pearson Education

London • New York • San Francisco • Toronto • Sydney • Tokyo • Singapore
Hong Kong • Cape Town • Madrid • Paris • Milan • Munich • Amsterdam

PEARSON EDUCATION LIMITED

Head Office:
Edinburgh Gate
Harlow CM20 2JE
Tel: +44 (0)1279 623623
Fax: +44 (0)1279 431059

London Office:
128 Long Acre,
London WC2E 9AN
Tel: +44 (0)20 7447 2000
Fax: +44 (0)20 7240 5771
Website: www.business-minds.com

First published in Great Britain in 2002

ISBN 0 273 65497 7

British Library Cataloguing in Publication Data
A CIP catalogue record for this book can be obtained from the British Library.

10 9 8 7 6 5 4 3 2

Typeset by Land & Unwin, Bugbrooke
Printed and bound in Great Britain by Biddles Ltd, Guildford & King's Lynn

The Publishers' policy is to use paper manufactured from sustainable forests.

About the author

▪▪▪▪▪▪▪▪▪▪▪▪▪▪▪▪▪▪▪▪▪▪▪▪

Prof. Dr C.N.A. Molenaar (1949) is an authority on the use of information technology in the area of marketing. He specializes in the strategic deployment of both automation and the Internet for the commercial pursuit of organizations. By combining academic knowledge and research with consulting experience he has been able to differentiate opportunities and optimize their application.

Cor Molenaar is Professor (occupying an endowed chair) of e-Marketing at the business administration faculty of the Erasmus University in Rotterdam. This is a part-time post. The main sponsors for the chair are the Achmea insurance company, Sun Microsystems, Energis and ATOS-Origin. The DMSA (the Dutch Direct Marketing and Sales Association) was initiator and is chairman of the Stichting Leerstoel e-Marketing.

Cor is also director of the strategic consulting agency *e*XQuo Consultancy in Oosterbeek, near Arnhem. The agency advises organizations on the use of the Internet and information technology in marketing. Its customers are large, internationally oriented organizations. Prior to this, Cor was the director of Ogilvy&Mather Dataconsult in Amsterdam for ten years. In this position he was responsible for, among other things, the setup and management of helpdesks for KLM (Flying Dutchman) and Philips (customer services).

Since May 2001 he is also an (associate) partner for Peppers & Rogers, an international marketing consultancy firm located in norwalk (CT) USA. In this function he is a member of the strategic board and responsible for business development in Europe.

Cor has published several books on database marketing, sales and marketing automation and future developments, including *Het einde van de Massamarketing* (1993) (*Interactive Marketing*) and a thesis on 'New Marketing, toepassingsmogelijkheden van informatietechnologie binnen marketing' (1997) ('New marketing, deployment of information technology in marketing').

Cor Molenaar is a much sought-after speaker at national and international congresses. He has given speeches at almost all the prominent marketing congresses, such as the Direct Marketing Congress at Montreux, the Dutch Direct Marketing Congress, the National

Marketing Congress and the Congress of the Direct Marketing Association in America. The Speakers Academy in Rotterdam coordinates all speaker programmes.

Cor Molenaar
cor@cormolenaar.nl
cor@exquo.com

Contents

List of figures

List of tables

Foreword

If you picked up *The Future of Marketing* thinking it would be a thrilling read, taking you on a whirlwind tour of all the marvellous and utterly revolutionary e-technologies now flooding the world's business landscape, then you guessed wrong. Cor Molenaar makes it immediately clear that he for one does not believe the new economy is revolutionary at all. Rather, it is evolutionary – it is the natural consequence of an ongoing, iterative process, accelerated a bit by new technologies, yes, but evolutionary nonetheless.

Stripped of hyperbole, this new global economy can be seen for what it is: A more or less inevitable response to a series of transformations, some large and some small, that began shortly after the end of the Second World War and reached a crescendo around the turn of the millennium.

Of all the many transformations that occurred in the second half of the 20th century, the two with the most direct impact on marketing strategy were social and technological. In general, consumers all over the world developed a greater sense of empowerment coupled with higher expectations. The enhanced sense of self and the desire for achieving a quality lifestyle were both enabled and reinforced by continuous improvements in communications and information technologies. There are only a few places in the world where you can't buy a colour TV, a PC or a cell phone. ATMs are ubiquitous, and if the wizened craftsman in the remote tropical village you visit doesn't accept American Express, he surely takes MasterCard or Visa.

So it should come as no surprise that managers and executives all over the world are wrestling with the ever-growing demands of technology-empowered customers. Cor, as we do, believes the answer to meeting these demands lies in developing practical Customer Relationship Management (CRM) strategies.

In fact, one could argue that CRM has already become the *de facto* standard for competing in this customer-centric economy. It's safe to say that business organizations lacking basic CRM capabilities will find it extremely difficult to attract, retain and grow profitable customers. They will also find it difficult, if not impossible, to manage an increasingly decentralized and more highly skilled workforce, resulting in lost productivity, widespread inefficiency and higher employee turnover rates.

Fortunately, for all the challenges posed by a customer-centric economy, there are even more opportunities for sustained growth and profitability. With a practical CRM strategy in place, business organizations can focus on meeting the actual needs of their customers, retaining their customers, and growing the value of their customers. This approach results in superior customer loyalty, greater efficiency and higher margins. It also tends to immunize the organization against price-based competition and downward pressure on margins.

Indeed, there can be little doubt that when properly implemented, CRM strategies have the potential to supercharge an organization's effectiveness. Perhaps this is one reason Gartner Group predicts that spending on CRM technology will grow at a rate of between 30% and 35% for the next several years.

But it's important to remember that CRM is a strategy, not a suite of technology solutions. Practical, workable CRM strategies cannot be purchased and installed like software modules. CR strategies must be developed, embraced and implemented across the entire organization. We're seeing more evidence every day that even the most carefully planned and well-implemented CRM programmes can be brought to a screeching halt if channel partners and distributors aren't included in the process. Or if middle-level executives, charged with putting these new technologies to work, aren't first clued in on the overall vision of the customer-centric firm. Or if salespeople are asked to use their new tracking tools to cultivate relationships, but the sale compensation structure continues to pay disproportionately for new account acquisition.

The inability of management to comprehend, at least initially, the scale of difficulty involved in any CRM strategy is the leading reason that 80% of CRM initiatives are deemed failures. In our series of books on one-to-one marketing strategy, we have stressed the need for careful planning and realistic expectations. We have also emphasized the need for setting achievable goals. Our mantra has always been to take things one step at a time, build gradually, and learn from your mistakes.

One lesson we have learned is that while CRM strategy requires significant up-front thinking, nevertheless it can't be developed in a vacuum. Your e-strategy must be tested, measured, refined, re-tested and validated in practice.

Under no circumstances should CRM *strategy* be confused with CRM *technology*. In their haste to automate as many sales and marketing functions as possible, some business organizations risk sacrificing the 'personal' touch necessary to nurture and develop customer relationships. But there's no hard and fast rule in CRM saying that customer relationships must be automated. Instead, customer relationships can and should be *enhanced* and *enriched* by automation, but not necessarily *replaced* by automation.

Automation strategies and customer development strategies should not be viewed as separate, or even conflicting, activities. Technology gives a firm the ability to augment the traditional qualities and benefits sought by customers from their suppliers – familiarity, convenience, good listening, prompt responses. We have found that the most successful companies do not use technology just to promote efficiency and productivity. Rather, these firms use increasingly sophisticated technology to assist them in an ongoing process of creating deeper, stronger and *more humanly personal* bonds with their customers.

As Cor points out, most customers still prefer the 'personal' touch when they need help making a purchasing decision or solving a problem. From a CRM perspective, the customer care function is a vital piece of the sales and marketing continuum, providing invaluable opportunities for the organization to learn more about the needs of its customers.

Yes, customers do have genuinely human needs within the context of any business relationship. And there are a host of legitimate business reasons for catering to those needs. But a truly customer-focused business must define those needs carefully and determine which ones are most likely to have the greatest impact on the customer's relationship with the business.

Any company that values long-term customer relationships will learn quickly that customers want four basic things:

1 They want you to know who they are, and remember them from one event or transaction to the next, no matter what part of the selling organization is engaged.

2 They want you to remember what they need, or what their specific preferences are.

3 They want a reliable way of communicating with you.

4 They want you to provide a product or service that meets their specific needs.

From the perspective of the supplier or selling organization, these specific customer desires map easily into the four steps an enterprise must take in order to develop and manage 'one-to-one' customer relationships:

1   identify your customers;

2   differentiate your customers;

3   interact with your customers;

4   customize for your customers.

An organization devoted to increasing customer loyalty and unit margins by improving its long-term relationships with its customers must sooner or later grapple with each of these relationship-building steps. And each step is composed of a variety of different tasks and sub-tasks, many of which can be handled more efficiently and accurately by computers than by humans.

So the question isn't so much, 'How can you use technology to *automate* a relationship?' as it is, 'How can you use technology to *strengthen* a relationship and make it more valuable over time?'

The answer, of course, depends less on technology than on the structure and organization of a company's sales and marketing efforts. If the sales force is organized around customer needs, and if it is rewarded or incentivized consistently for increasing the value of existing customers as well as for acquiring new customers, it will rapidly discover the advantages of a well-designed sales force automation tool.

The same holds true for the marketing department. If it understands that its role isn't just to create demand for a line of products but also to determine the needs of specific customer sets, then it will quickly perceive the value of an automated system for collecting, organizing and analyzing customer feedback.

All of this, naturally, circles back to the bedrock premise we share with Cor: customers play the central role in the new global economy, and customer relationships are created and developed through strategies that are enabled by technology, but not ruled by technology. This is good news for business leaders with the capacity to strategize, and bad news for anyone still cherishing hopes of a 'quick fix'.

Cor's emphasis on good, old-fashioned discipline is an excellent antidote to the heedless enthusiasm of the 1990s, in which various technologies, and particularly the Internet, were too often seen as perpetual motion engines for generating cash. Alas, we have all grown wiser since
 days.

The Future of Marketing to you as a virtual roadmap for
usiness. Cor's vision is clear and unambiguous. In a
g economy where the customer has the upper hand, an

organization's success or failure will depend largely on the strength of its customer-centric vision and the strategies that flow from that vision. To be sure, technology will play an important role, but its role will not be decisive. In the final analysis, careful planning and exemplary discipline are far more likely to decide the outcome. This book will help you walk the winding path to success without getting lost along the way.

Don Peppers
Martha Rogers, PhD

Introduction

▪▪▪▪▪▪▪▪▪▪▪▪▪▪▪▪▪▪▪▪▪▪▪▪

With the customer in mind

At the beginning of every millennium there is always a sudden drive to initiate change. The beginning of the 21st century has been no different so far. A desire to do things differently spreads across the world and companies and consumers behold all new opportunities in amazement. Internet and interactivity have become synonymous with the concept of change.

Once more man occupies centre stage, both in his private life and at work. Man is quick to adapt to change and can see the advantages of transparency, communication and individuality. Companies have to adjust to a totally different way of doing business. The consumer has to gear himself to the fact that patterns and roles will blend into one another and that the boundaries between working life and private life will become blurred. Shopping and relaxing will almost become one and the same. The choices once made with reference to organizational form, structure, products and services and even markets will have to be reassessed. The world has changed and through technology the world will change even more. Areas such as automation, finances and marketing, which were at first distinct specialities, will converge and strongly influence each other. Specialities will merge, affect each other and become closely related. Working groups and project groups will have to be multidisciplinary and management decisions will have to be made on a multidisciplinary level.

Employees are better informed than ever and perhaps even more involved in what goes on in an organization. What is certain is that employees are closely involved with the customer and the relations an organization has with the outside world. Technology enables us to access information in many areas, to better substantiate our decisions, and to maintain relations with customers, employees and other business partners in a different way. This is the root of all change as we know it today.

These new opportunities (changes) are often presented as a revolution. E-commerce, one-to-one marketing and customer relationship management (CRM) are today's vogue words. But a vogue word does not imply a revolution. It implies changes, facilities and new opportunities that lead to organizational changes and to changes in the relations between organizations. The old way of doing business was based on the spoken word and on knowing each other. 'An honest man's word is as good as his bond' clearly indicates that business is based on trust and on the spoken word. You only do business with someone you know and trust. In fact, nothing has changed. It is curious that these basic values should stay the same. Customers want to do business with companies they know and which show that they attach great importance to their clientele. Customers prefer the personal touch when they want help on purchasing items. They want support on how to use products. They also want to be regularly informed of new developments. New developments, such as customer service, call centres, loyalty programmes and newsletters, are being presented as a revolution, but in fact they amount to nothing more than doing business the old-fashioned way, just with new tools.

Because of the consolidation of the past 50 years, many of the basic classical elements of doing business have been neglected. Technology took the lead and the basic need for trust and interaction received little attention. Present technology developments, however, are based upon the basic principles of business, putting the customer first.

People do not change

People may not change, but technology does. After all, technology empowers organizations to change and technology changes the relations between people and organizations. People no longer have to go to work; work can also go to people. We no longer have to go shopping; the shopping can be done from home. Suddenly the home and the community are important again. We can organize our business and private matters from our own home. We can reassess our private lives, redefine the division of roles with regard to our work and our private lives, our partners and our children. There is no longer a strict division between home and work, between studying and work and between business and private life. These aspects of life are melting into one another and influencing each other. Life is suddenly about the correct way of dealing with all challenges and all opportunities. This is not new either; after all, our ancestors were doing this in the 17th and 18th centuries too. Husband and wife worked together; the home and work were one. People lived in communities and together they looked after or taught their children.

The young took care of the old and the strong looked after the weak; together they took care of each other. This still happens, only in a different way, on a different scale, and technology offers even more possibilities than before. Still, technology really only facilitates what was possible before. Thus, once again, there is no revolution.

Organizations are changing

In the past, the storekeeper came to your door, everyone was completely up-to-date on what went on in the village, and people were entirely schooled in their own trade by peers and masters. The elderly helped the young and the young helped the old. Social structures were strongly entrenched in communities, social groups and cultures. This cannot easily be changed by technology. Still, there have been some changes. People are not just aware of what is happening in their own environment, they also know what is going on in the rest of the world. They know and want to talk about it, which is possible. It is possible in person (be it small-scale), by telephone (be it in real time) or via the Internet. Whether it is exchanging information or just 'chatting', in principle, people continue displaying the same behaviour, only facilities change and because of this so do scale and opportunities. 'Technology facilitates change.'

On an organizational level, a similar picture emerges. In the past, organizations were independent entities, with a real leader at the helm. A boss who knew exactly where the company was headed, a man of vision and spirit. Often he also invested his own money in 'the business'. Organizations were small and transparent and everyone was closely involved. This changed in the 20th century. Organizations grew and their market coverage increased. Organizations no longer focused on small village communities but on a region, a country, even the world became a commercial stage. Marketing also became important, especially after the Second World War. There were no longer any shortages, everything was plentiful. The challenge of production demand shifted from production to sales. Businesses were manufacturing for an unexpected demand, eager to tap into unlimited markets. The entrepreneur wanted to know more about the market and later also wanted to know more about his organization and customers. People wanted to compete and were asking themselves how they could be better and more successful. People chose to focus on core competencies and made deliberate choices to achieve customer loyalty, to motivate employees and to keep shareholders happy. The complexity of doing business increased, as did the challenge to respond to all those changes. There were opportunities and threats for businessmen and women and opportunities for employees.

Society is changing

The old social structures were shaken by no less important changes. People were better educated and schooling became accessible to everyone. Men no longer had absolute power in politics and business. Women not only became full members of society but also had their own ambitions and preferences, their own outlooks and interests. They were recognized in their own right, and became self-supporting and independent, emotionally as well as economically. Moreover, because of increased mobility, together with telecommunications and greater transparency, it was far easier to try your luck elsewhere. People travelled the world in search of work, freedom and security. Regional boundaries disappeared, cultural boundaries faded, and technical boundaries vanished. Once again, people were compelled to re-examine choices made in the past, bringing about further important changes.

People were suddenly allowed to migrate up the social ladder instead of horizontally only. A painter could become a director and a talented bricklayer's son could become a professor. It was all down to recognizing, developing and using your talents.

Organizations no longer had to restrict themselves to the product once chosen. It was possible to expand the diversity of production and to do more business than ever before. You could go onto the world market if your own country proved too small. Organizations grew far beyond their original natural boundaries. They also started looking for gain in places that were previously inaccessible. Manufacturing was concentrated in low-wage countries and companies were established in countries that were favourable in tax terms. Knowledge was acquired from countries and universities with the best know-how. People simply looked for the best possible way to grow and to compete.

It was only organizations and people that went in search of new opportunities and made new choices – countries also searched to re-establish their borders and conditions for existence. Technological developments afforded opportunities for far-away countries such as Finland,

Ireland and Taiwan. In addition, the concentration of industry created scope for specialization. Silicon Valley is perhaps the most typical example of the trend that encourages industries to 'find each other and strengthen each other'. Governments can help stimulate and facilitate this.

Technology facilities change

The world is in motion, markets are dynamic and people are changing. Old choices are being reassessed and again people are looking for the best way to coexist or live together. People suddenly know a lot more and are a lot more aware of what is going on. The restrictions imposed by old country borders are a thing of the past. It is possible to communicate anywhere and everywhere. People are just a phone call or an e-mail away from anyone in the world. People have a wealth of knowledge, freedom and social opportunities. These are the social changes of the past decades, changes that did not have their origin in technology, but that found a partner in technology and allowed us to respond more quickly and vigilantly.

Technological development ran parallel to social and economic changes. The opportunities afforded by technology will incite entrepreneurs, directors and people even more to think about what they want and what is possible. It remains a process of choice, both in terms of use and possibilities. People must not let themselves be led by each new technological opportunity – after all, this would be no more than following a trend. It is important to have an insight into what is happening and why, to delve into the patterns of market evolution, the patterns of technical evolution and the patterns of social evolution. These patterns influence each other and determine future developments. There is evolution in all these areas.

This book will focus primarily on evolution in marketing, on how business was first done (aimed at the masses), which opportunities technology offers (knowing and facilitating the customer), and which changes this can lead to. What must an organization do to anticipate changes and which opportunities and threats does this constitute? This should be seen as a coherent model between outlook and realization, between marketing, organization and technology.

The book will discuss the various areas of evolution from a strategic point of view, starting with the decision model, which can be used to determine both the focus of an organization and the opportunities provided by sound customer relations. This model is based on four different approaches to market orientation, by which it is possible to determine any organizational and marketing changes, as well as the use of the Internet. It is an orientation model for the use of marketing tools, the realization of marketing activities, and the use of the Internet and the changes that may result. Next, we will look at the role of the Internet in more detail as well as the available options with reference to the use of the Internet. What can you do with the Internet, how can it be used and what changes will result? In practical terms, its use is adjusted and changed on a daily basis. Subsequently, we will discuss background, outlook and choices. The models and areas of application will be merged into a strategic cubic model, a cube that provides a basis for the strategy of organizations, the choices in marketing, and the opportunities and demands of the Internet. It will shape the future of marketing.

Finally, the book will focus on implementation and realization. Structures and models will be brought together in such a way that they will provide the opportunity to understand what is really going on. They will be discussed in concrete terms, partly academic, but always based on practice, with many examples of the use of the Internet and its use in practice. After all, theory explains what happens in practice. Hence this book. It aims at interaction between theory and practice. It will give managers and directors something to hold on to in the face of what has to be done and, moreover, it will inform you of what has happened (in terms of strategy, the Internet and marketing), where we stand and how you can gain a competitive advantage. Based on the orientation of a company, the interaction with customers and the deployment of technology, the 'future of marketing' is decided by the turbulence of markets and the strategy of market leaders. More than ever before will the customer be in control.

Profound discussions with my students at the Erasmus University have led to an understanding of what is really happening now and to a critical approach to the use of the Internet. Young people view these developments realistically. Working with my customers has inspired me to approach the use of the Internet and any resulting changes on the basis of actual problems. Thanks to the formulation of problems in real terms, the opportunities provided by technology and the clear perspective of young people, it is possible to bridge the gap between theory and practice. I expect that this will provide a basis for the strategic decisions of many organizations. It is because developments are evolutions that it is possible to predict the future and to make logical choices.

1

■■■■■■■■■■■■■■■■■

The Internet has changed your world

He who waves aside all changes as 'hype' will certainly have peace of mind, but no future.

The future belongs to the new economy; old norms and values no longer apply in this future. The Internet will change the world and consumers will e-mail, WAP and surf. Companies will buy on virtual market places and will take a different approach to dealing with customers, personnel and consultants. The whole world is in turmoil and everything in it is changing at an incredible rate. Desperately, company managers try to keep up with all the changes, to string along. Sometimes they would rather wait and see which way the wind blows. Small start-up companies have the option to stop in their tracks and start again. Large, financially powerful companies on the other hand can simply buy a new 'dot com' company and secure the knowledge they need. Investing, interpreting and learning the rules of the game, the compelling need to change is intensifying. These are the kinds of problems that company policymakers are faced with on a daily basis.

The world is being taken by storm. The figures speak for themselves: in 1995 there were 10 million Internet connections, in 2000 there were already 375 million. This expansionary growth is expected to reach 490 million by the end of 2002 and 740 million by the end of 2005 (see Table 1.1). Such an exponential increase in growth rate can also be seen in Europe. Certainly in view of the number of commercial Internet connections, the penetration of 60% and 100% in 2005 shows that the need to have a commercial Internet connection is put on a par with the need to have a telephone connection. This is irrefutably an irreversible process.

Table 1.1		Number of Internet connections by the end of 2000	

No.	Country	Number of Internet users (millions)	%
1	US	135.7	36.2
2	Japan	26.9	7.18
3	Germany	19.1	5.10
4	UK	17.9	4.77
5	China	15.8	4.20
6	Canada	15.2	4.05
7	South Korea	14.8	3.95
8	Italy	11.6	3.08
9	Brazil	10.6	2.84
10	France	9.0	2.39
11	Australia	8.1	2.16
12	Russia	6.6	1.77
13	Taiwan	6.5	1.73
14	Netherlands	5.4	1.45
15	Spain	5.2	1.39
	Worldwide	375	100

Source: eTForecasts

Developments in the Netherlands

In the Netherlands the growth in the number of Internet connections has been no less turbulent. At the beginning of 1999, less than 30% of the population had surfed the Internet.[1] In January 1999, only 13% of the population used the Internet on a daily basis. In March 2000, however, this figure had already risen to 22%. By the end of 2000, it was expected that 2.7 million Dutch men, women and children would be using the Internet on a daily basis. Additionally, the number of people who use the Internet only occasionally is also increasing rapidly. At the beginning of 1999, 28% of Dutch people aged 16 and over occasionally used the Internet. By 2000 this had increased to 5.1 million (41%). There is, however, a noticeable difference in Internet use between the Randstad (urban agglomeration of western Holland) and the rest of the Netherlands (see Figure 1.1).

In the Netherlands, 2.7 million people are active on the Internet on a daily basis. The majority are (still) men, with a total of 1.8 million, as opposed to 840,000 women (see Table 1.2). Nonetheless, women are becoming more active. In the US, the number of women active on the Internet has already superseded the number of men; however, they use

Figure 1.1 *Internet use in the Netherlands*

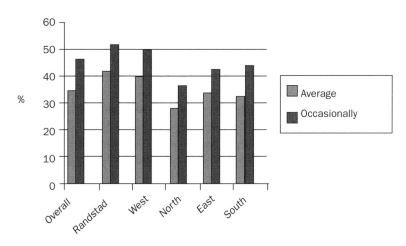

Source: Internet in the Netherlands 2000

the Internet less intensively, which makes it look as if they are lagging behind the men.

Table 1.2 *Ratio of men to women on the Internet and time spent on the Internet per month*

Country	Male Internet users	Female Internet users	Average time spent on the Internet per month	
			Men	Women
US	49.25	50.75	9:54:57	8:18:26
UK	60.86	39.14	5:52:51	3:46:57
Australia	54.87	45.13	8:01:41	5:57:08
Ireland	55.20	44.80	5:18:42	3:21:59
Singapore	57.57	42.43	7:23:38	4:30:18
New Zealand	52.33	47.67	8:46:29	6:00:07

Source: Nielsen/netrating May 2000, The ratio of men to women on the Internet in May 2000

We can also perceive differences in acceptance in different demographic groups. Here age is not the most important criterion for determining the differences between users, although it is a fact that the elderly use the Internet less frequently. However, this is by choice. For the elderly

As soon as the elderly recognize the advantages of the Internet, they use it a lot and also become active surfers

to use this medium it has to fulfil a certain need, it has to serve a certain purpose and it has to fit in with certain behavioural patterns. Often this medium does not satisfy these criteria, which is why the elderly appear to lag behind. This matches their way of life. However, as soon as the elderly recognize the advantages of the Internet, they use it a lot and also become active surfers. They play games and take part in the sweepstakes on the Internet. Senior citizens are active mailers, they read the weather reports and browse the news sites. This behaviour indicates that the elderly have the time and see the Internet as a pleasant way to pass this time. In addition to games, (general) information is an important source[2] (see Table 1.3).

Low income is a critical factor in accessing the Internet. The lower income group lags behind for economic reasons and therefore constitutes a problem group.

Table 1.3   *The elderly on the Internet*

Activities of the elderly on the Internet	Intensity
Surfing	Very active, very frequent
Games	90% regularly play games and take part in sweepstakes
Buying	30% occasionally buy something on the Internet
E-mail	95% regularly send and receive e-mail
Other	70% regularly read the weather reports
	57% look for special offers
	56% read the news sites

Source: Greenfield Online, July 2000

Acceptance

The medium of the Internet was accepted very quickly, and so we have arrived at the core of the present discussion. Acceptance was especially quick among the younger generation, who were happy to reap the benefits of unlimited and interactive communication. They accepted the medium with all its facets, unhindered by prejudice or preconception. Young people had the advantage of having grown up with the computer.

They had heard about the archaic Pac-Man by Atari, but grew up with the Nintendo, the Gameboy and later the Playstation. They accepted this new medium as it happened. They did not and do not need books on how it works, nor do they read manuals or acquaint themselves with the rules of the game. They just dive in and learn hands-on. If they encounter problems, they discuss them with each other and the problem is solved. And so a communication structure developed parallel to this technology, based on direct contact and interactivity.

It is therefore no coincidence that the mobile phone is developing in line with the acceptance of the Internet. At first the two technologies seemed to be developing separately, but we should have known that they would converge, a coalescence of two different kinds of development and two different types of technology. Computer technology has its limitations, as does mobile communication technology by the sheer fact that it is focused on speech transfer. Demand creates supply and in the next few years combining both technologies and their uses will be a great challenge to technology, to marketing and to organizations.

Young people have grown up with the possibilities of interactive technology. They have fully accepted the new demands, customs and inherent opportunities into their everyday lives. The process of acceptance did not go as smoothly for the older generation, however. After all, the 'older' generation had to cope with existing modes of thought, existing customs and existing structures. As people get older they also become less carefree, because of their knowledge and experience and also because of the responsibilities that cannot be ignored. Responsibility comes with age, as does the awareness of the consequences of change. It is like being shackled by knowledge, custom, thought patterns and perhaps even culture.

New technology has a lot to offer, but it must also have added value. Technological changes or improvements must fulfil a need, solve problems or make life more pleasant. If this is not the case, technology will not be (readily) accepted. This is the reason behind the 'wait and see' attitude many people have towards the Internet. 'What use is it to me personally, to my organization and possibly to the society I live in?'

This also applies to mobile telephony and the Internet. Office workers quickly discovered the advantages of e-mail and the efficiency it offered. Workers, for example, suddenly had a quick way of conferring with each other. For offices it was just a small step to accept the Internet. At the beginning of the 1980s it was already possible to transfer data between workplaces because of networks and databases.

Later the advantages of LAN (local area networks) and WAN (wide area networks) were added to those of e-mail. Server technology, as promoted especially by Hewlett-Packard and Sun Microsystems, was imitated after the recession in the early 1990s by big players like IBM. Decentralized data processing, client-server concepts and data systems were seen as an integral part of the (data) infrastructure of an organization. Employees learnt to work with this technology and to use it efficiently. The possibilities offered became integrated with our normal activities. Also the changes that were brought about by new reporting methods, new methods of analysis, new presentation tools and techniques and finally the delights of a new generation of word processors were easily accepted. People recognized their usefulness and did not even dwell upon the resulting changes. A PowerPoint presentation has become just as normal to companies as having a cup of coffee in the break. The fact that only five years ago people still worked with overhead sheets and an overhead projector is almost unbelievable.

Changes and developments

The changes brought about by the acceptance of this new office technology happened almost unnoticed. The secretary's job changed and the manager's job changed. Managers started typing their own letters, made their own reports and presentations and started handling their own post (e-mail). They were suddenly carrying out work that had previously been carried out by less qualified personnel (the secretary). This was not only more efficient, but information was also available more quickly and could be consulted and interpreted without the intervention of others. The secretary became a PA (personal assistant) and started carrying out more specialized work. This division of tasks took place almost unnoticed.

Technology facilitated this change. Inter-company and inter-departmental relations started changing in the same way. Computer systems became an integral part of the organization. It is no longer possible to imagine companies working without computers, even if these are used only for word processing or bookkeeping. If there are so many computers in all these organizations, why then do we not let these computers communicate with each other? This is, of course, a logical thought. The development of linking computers to a central server (networking) became especially important in the mid 1980s. This was, however, difficult to realize because of the technical problems caused by the differences in hardware and software, which was often written specifically for one type of hardware or operating system. But there were also organizational problems. How could a company simply link its computer systems with all the risks involved? It was unthinkable. How could a company remain independent when fully linked to the systems

The development of linking computers to a central server (networking) became especially important in the mid 1980s

of other companies, such as vendor companies? How do we protect our knowledge, our independence and our data? And if everything is linked, copying or hacking is also easy. The new opportunities forged by technology and the changes in the market (different relations between competitors and different cost structures due to, among others, manufacturing in the Far East) prompted organizations to further stimulate this development. Companies started developing ways to link systems, to make software systems compatible, to transport data and to record data automatically. In the 1980s a lot of time and study went into electronic data interchange (EDI), which could be seen as the forerunner of data transport via the Internet. By making systems compatible and agreeing data protocols, two organizations could send data to each other. Scanning allowed data to be recorded automatically and the advent of EAN (electronic article numbering), with a unique barcode for each product, made it possible to link stockkeeping to purchasing activities.

The development that accompanied the uniformization of systems and data was accelerated by new hardware and software developments. Routers (like those made by Cisco) allowed messages to be sent to and from different computer systems. New programming techniques like 'object-oriented' programming not only enabled organizations to structure and use data differently but also enabled system-independent programming. Because of the development of the programming language JAVA and programming in HTML (Hyper Text Markup Language), it became possible to run programs on different computer systems. The early 1990s offered ideal opportunities for a new infrastructure. And then there was the World Wide Web, a new Internet development.

World Wide Web

The Internet already existed as a data network used by universities for the exchange of information, which enabled them to share knowledge. The idea to also apply this technology outside the academic world was born from the gateway linking these university computer systems. In view of the huge diversity in computers and systems, a technique was sought that would offer access via servers linked to a 'backbone' (Internet). Linking computers to servers and servers to a backbone reminded developers of a web. The scope of this web was unknown. Just like with a spider, the size and appearance of the web was subject to continuous change.

The first plan was based on a data network that could be used by universities, schools, libraries, the civil service and the business community alike. The big breakthrough came several years later, when Netscape and some time later Microsoft came up with a browser, which provided very user-friendly access to the World Wide Web (WWW). Because of the competitive battle between Netscape and Microsoft, acceptance of the World Wide Web was accelerated, in the private sector as well. Microsoft, however, initially did not see the potential of the World Wide Web. It was a data network for government authorities based on server technology and routers. Microsoft owed its existence to personal computers (Windows-based) and application software. The world of civil servants, servers and routers was not really Microsoft's market. It was not until Netscape succeeded in linking the personal computer to these servers with user-friendly software (navigator) and the Netscape 'Navigator' opened up opportunities for the private sector that a different market suddenly emerged. Microsoft almost lost the battle of the 'browser' and decided to give away its browser 'Explorer' for free with Windows. This not only ensured that Microsoft became an important player overnight and a market leader shortly after, but suddenly every computer user could have direct access to the Web.

Next followed a competitive battle between telecommunication companies. Most of them had just been privatized or, as in the US, had just been freed of market leaders (AT&T). A battle broke out about consumers, about new applications and the possibilities of the telecommunication network. Telecoms companies (see Figure 1.2) did not only set up Internet service providers (ISPs), which made use of the telephone network, but they also stimulated them to provide more and more services. It was 1998 and the battle of the websurfer had started.

Figure 1.2 *Planet Internet, an Internet service provider, an initiative by KPN Telecom (KPN also owns, for example, Planet Internet, Het Net and World Access)*

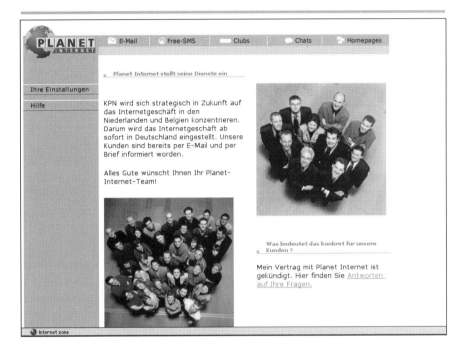

Development phases

Six phases (see Table 1.4) can be distinguished based on the technological development of the Internet. These phases are determined by what is technologically possible and by users. The overview shows that the Internet was developed specifically for transferring and sharing sources of information, which is why this application was ideal for research and thus very applicable to academia. When use of the Internet became more frequent, the need arose for more facilities and greater speed. This need ran parallel to the development in organizations and in the computer industry. After all, the 1980s stood at the threshold of the personal computer, data systems, databases and server technology. It was against this background that a backbone was developed for data transmission, for which computer systems were linked together permanently to serve a generic data platform. Logically, these were the technological possibilities of the Internet and how it was used at the time.

Table 1.4   *Development phases of the Internet*

Phases	Timing	Features
1. Experimental networking	1965–1980	Technology-driven
2. Discipline-specific research	1980–1985	ARPANET, linking researchers from all over the world, building on-line communities
3. General research networking	1985–1991	NSFNET program. Exchange of information and access to remote resources within the world of education and research. Launching a backbone network base for further growth and usage
4. Privatization and commercialization	1991–1999	Expanding backbone services far beyond the research communities, linking organizations and facilitating commercial transactions
5. High-performance computing and communication	1995–2002	Advancing the computing infrastructure for science and engineering research by supporting access to high-speed networks and supercomputers. Technology transfer developments
6. National information infrastructure	2000–	The I-way, extending networking everywhere and enabling new consumer applications. Convergence of computing, entertainment, telecommunication by using the Internet network, cable, TV and information provider industries

Source: Summary by Kalakota, Ravi and Whinston, Andrew (1996) *Frontiers of Electronic Commerce*, Addison-Wesley, pp. 89–123

In the early 1990s this development went into a new phase because of the World Wide Web, new generations of software and hardware, and the variety of commercial opportunities the Internet was starting to offer. During the 1990s the Internet became available for a large group of companies and users. New applications that could also be used for commercial purposes were developed specifically for these new groups. By the end of the 1990s there were many changes. The Internet was no longer used just for existing business processes and working methods but had become the basis for an increasing number of other applications. This sparked a process of change for many organizations and many markets for which the recent developments were just the beginning.

Applications

According to Kalakota and Robinson,[3] Internet applications can be divided into five areas:

* *From individual to group communication* – in addition to systems that support decision making, this area includes chatting, tele-meetings, mailing services and bulletin boards.
* *Data transmission and delivery services* – e-mails, EDI services, news groups and multimedia applications.
* *Databases* – access to databases and sources of information, file transfer and search functions.
* *Data processing services* – all kinds of software services, such as statistics, simulations and games.
* *Facility services (sharing)* – sharing printers, faxes and computers.

In fact, the applications described above are all based on the possibilities the Internet already offered in the 1990s (fourth and fifth phase of the Internet). Tools and techniques were developed on the basis of these possibilities and commercialized or employed in (commercial) organizations.

Internet generations

In addition to the six phases outlined in Table 1.4, the use of the Internet can be divided into three generations.

The first spans the Internet as a data infrastructure. This generation lasted well into the early 1990s. The Internet was used by government authorities, such as defence, and by universities that saw a chance to share information, an application which was especially important as it provided ardent support for the Internet. Many students and teachers were able to share each other's knowledge and sources of information. This led to the foundation of the present applications of the Internet. Of course, the first-generation Internet had its limitations (see Figure 1.3). For example, the possibilities for sending information were still very

Figure 1.3   *The first-generation Internet: a network of computer systems*

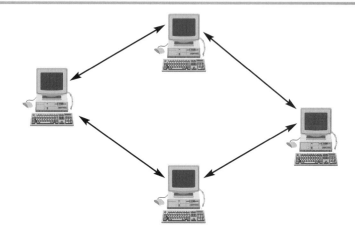

limited, the software was not yet user friendly and there was no simple way of linking systems.

But that was not imperative: it was more or less a closed network between universities.

All this changed when:

● a real backbone started to develop;

● easy access became available – the browser provided a user-friendly way of surfing from site to site;

● society changed and the Internet was accepted as a medium that fitted in with this change (just like mobile phones).

The second generation (see Figure 1.4) is merely the forerunner of the third generation. The third generation will facilitate the use of the Internet with more applications (images). Internet access will no longer be limited to the computer, but will be achieved through other devices, such as a WAP (wireless application protocol) telephone or a palmtop computer. This means that the process of change will be accelerated and that applications will become more advanced.

The third generation will facilitate the use of the Internet with more applications (images)

Figure 1.4   *The second-generation Internet: servers and computers linked to an information backbone*

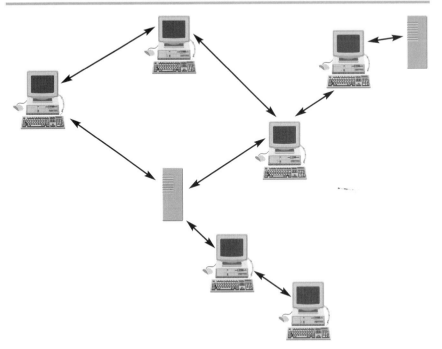

The classification of generations is based on the functionality, the users and the possibilities of the Internet. This line of approach distinguishes the generations outlined in Table 1.5.

The present focus is still on the second generation of possibilities and Internet applications. However, this generation merely represents the onset of change. The foundation is being laid with system-specific functionality. As soon as the user can choose which device is best suited for which application and when, there will be eminent changes and the infrastructure will become crucially important. This infrastructure will form the basis for commercial processes and for the relations between organizations, people and authorities, and will cause the commercial and competitive playing field to change. In order to gain an insight into these changes and to respond to the opportunities, it is necessary to place them within a framework of change and thought patterns. As we can see, the development of the Internet is not a revolution but an evolutionary process that can be divided into phases or generations. Each new phase or generation builds on the possibilities created by the

Table 1.5 *Internet generations*

Generations	Possibilities	Users
First generation (up to about 1993)	Data transmission and access to external sources of information	Research, education and universities
Second generation 1993–2001	• Data facilities • Communication facilities • Transaction facilities • Collective use of applications (among others entertainment)	Organizations, private individuals, new service providers, such as Internet Service Providers (ISP) and application sharing services and commercial suppliers
Third generation 2001–	• Data, speech and image transmission (convergence) • Far-reaching multimedia applications. This application supports a multi-device approach. The Internet (or the Internet structure) can be used together with a multitude of devices, from PC to TV and mobile phone (WAP and i-mode, a Japanese mobile (Internet) application)	An advanced infrastructure for images, sound and data. In this way all suppliers and consumers can become Internet users without being restricted by distance, location or other physical barriers

previous phase or generation and makes the most of experiences and existing limitations (see Figure 1.5).

A parallel can be drawn between the Internet generations described and the application of technology. At present the change from a multi-point connection via a backbone construction to a third-generation multi-device platform is in full swing. This multi-device platform will greatly influence the daily lives of consumers, managers and employees. Not only will it lay the foundation for a universal infrastructure, but the resulting possibilities will be unprecedented (see Figure 1.6).

Uses

The way an organization uses the Internet will also influence the way it operates. Changes in the way goods and services are sold lead to increased efficiency and reduction of costs, resulting in bigger profit

Figure 1.5   *New dimension Internet applications*

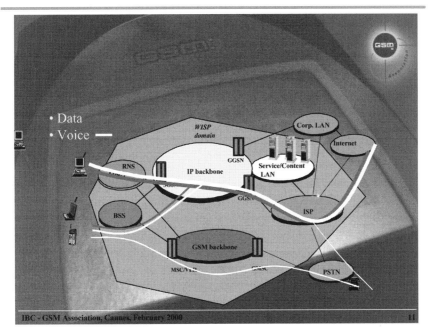

Source: IBC–GSM Association conference, February 2000
Third-generation infrastructure – an ordinary link between the Internet backbone and a computer and a mobile link between the Internet backbone and a modified telephone using the GSM network. Transmission of speech and images is also possible, which means that there may be several infrastructures

margins even if the price stays the same or increases because of an improving level of quality. The way the Internet is used also leads to more products and services without requiring more resources (people), for example selling software that can simply be copied by customers (more sales, no costs). This particular use, i.e. increasing sales without having to increase resources, has led to the development of new economic principles.

Economic growth is no longer related to an increase in the number of vacancies or deployment of other resources. The ambition to expand one's reach through the World Wide Web has led to a different definition of market ('global') and to a different market potential. It requires incredible effort to reach this larger market. This increased effort goes hand in hand with much higher costs, which in turn result in longer lead-time. This has led to the formulation of the principle that higher initial investment is required to reach a large market and

Figure 1.6   *The commercial opportunities of the Internet*

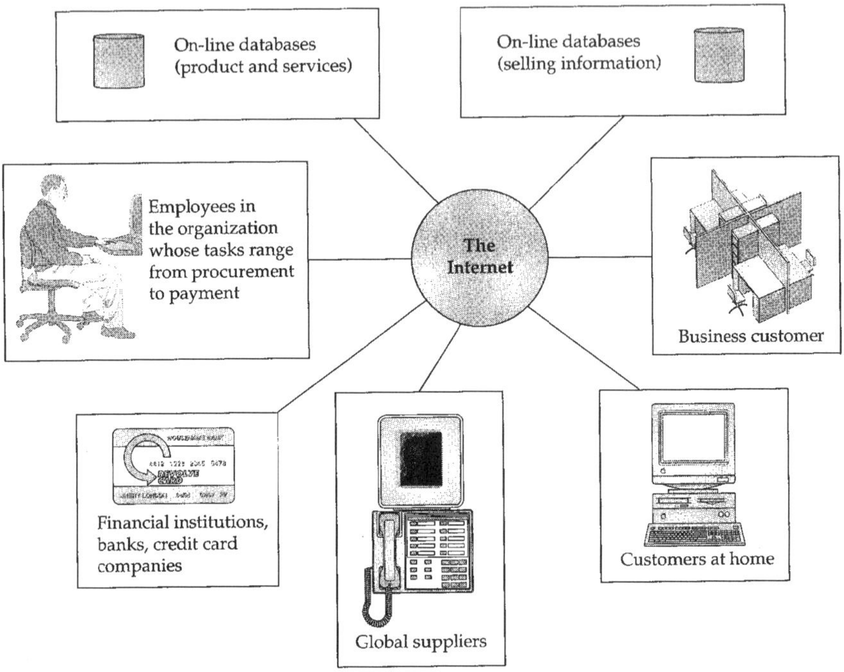

On-line databases (product and services)

On-line databases (selling information)

Employees in the organization whose tasks range from procurement to payment

The Internet

Business customer

Financial institutions, banks, credit card companies

Global suppliers

Customers at home

Source: Kalakota, Ravi and Whinston, Andrew (1996) *Frontiers of Electronic Commerce*, Addison-Wesley, p. 131

approach many potential customers before profits can be made. This investment in market coverage should lead to an exponential growth in sales and profits in the future. Because of this initial investment, the break-even point lies further into the future for the new economy than for existing markets and structures. This fact is one of the principles of the new economy. Companies are focused on future profit and on approaching potentially large markets. This is in fact nothing new, but intrinsic to the size of the market and the necessity to develop an infrastructure. Examples from the past, such as the construction of the railway network and the electricity network, are actually comparable situations.

The example of the electricity network speaks to the imagination especially because it happened only recently. Edison not only had problems convincing people that electricity was an important invention, he also had difficulty finding investors who were prepared to put their money into a new infrastructure. Even when he had proven on a small scale in New York that it could work, he still had to try to interest new investors in his invention. A lot of things also went wrong during implementation. Initially, it was a job that required great accuracy and had to be supervised (by Edison). It was not until he was able to transfer his knowledge to others that the job went more quickly. The overhead cables presented the second implementation problem. There had been several accidents, with passers-by knocking and hurting themselves on open electricity cables, before these were given a protective layer and secured in such a way (to the tops of buildings or in the ground) that they no longer presented a danger to passers-by. To start with, the construction of an electricity network required huge investments – the infrastructure had to be completed before it was possible to actually realize any turnover based on the supply of electricity.

> **It is difficult to convey an inviting concept in an appealing way so that potential customers will start buying and come back for more**

The above situation is also applicable to the Internet. First, companies must invest in a commercial infrastructure: the market. They must also reach potential customers. This can often be achieved by putting in a lot of marketing effort. However, marketing effort is intangible. Consequently it is difficult to convey an inviting concept in an appealing way so that potential customers will start buying and come back for more. The time it takes to reach this objective determines its success. The idea that it is not necessary to make a profit in the new economy is correct, but only for a very short period. Companies must invest before they can sell. The question is to what extent and for how long companies are prepared to invest. It is essential that the goods and services invested in have a money trigger and that they create a necessity or a desire to come back and buy more. This is what determines the success of an organization on the Internet (see Table 1.6).

Structure of Internet applications and facilities

There is a distinct difference in the way we approach the Internet and the way we apply it. This dichotomy consists of an infrastructural part

Table 1.6 Specific Internet-related products and services

Core facility	Directly related products/services	Dependent products and services
Internet infrastructure	Internet service providers Telecommunication providers	Routers, modems
Tools	Software, hardware, PCs	Browsers, e-mail
Add-ons	Virtual markets, virtual shops, virtual communities	Databases, data systems

Internet serves as a basis for the development of specific services and specific products.

and an application part. Edison's electricity infrastructure is visible, tangible and essential to the supply of electricity, which powers light and the use of equipment. These are all examples of applications. It is not possible to make money on electricity until there is an infrastructure. Companies can use this infrastructure to make money on tools and on 'add-on' products, such as lamps, fuses and, in a later stage, vacuum cleaners and refrigerators. This comparison also holds

Figure 1.7 The structure of the Internet

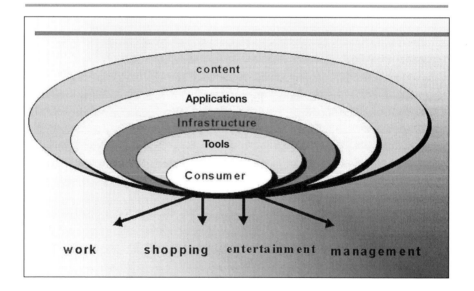

for the Internet. The opportunity to make money lies in facilitating the infrastructure (cable companies, telecommunication companies), developing services for the infrastructure (such as ISPs and search engines), tools for the use of the infrastructure (such as browsers and portals) and finally, specific equipment and applications that exist only because of the infrastructure (e-commerce).

Figure 1.7 represents the structure of the Internet and its uses, with the infrastructure at the core. *Infrastructure* is still strongly focused on the telephone network, although part of the infrastructure is already based on cable and mobile networks. Adjusting the infrastructure to accommodate broadband applications or via ASDL (asymmetric digital subscriber line) techniques will also allow the infrastructure of the telephone network to be used for transmitting moving pictures. As a result television could start playing a more important role in Internet access, albeit only for specific (image-oriented) applications.

Applications could be constructed on the basis of the possibilities provided by the infrastructure, such as sites, shops, portals and communities that are worthwhile accessing via the Internet.

Content very much determines Internet traffic and the number of visitors to a site. All applications should have content. What's on offer and what can you do on the Internet? Content also determines how much time is spent on a site and how often people return to the site (stickiness).

Before you can access the Internet you will need a *device* such as a personal computer or a TV. The availability of these devices and the user's experience with them has up to now been an important factor in the use of the Internet (especially in the restrictive sense). The computer has always been the most important device for accessing the Internet. In England, however, it is already possible to send e-mails by television, and the development of digital TV is facilitating access to the Internet and the use of Internet applications. Furthermore, devices such as the telephone (mobile) and electronic palmtops will lead to the Internet being used in a different way and to developments of applications specifically for these devices. Third-generation Internet use is focused on multi-device support (access to the Internet with a variety of devices).

Consumers play a central role in the acceptance and use of the Internet. Which purpose does it serve and which added value does the consumer perceive? The use of the Internet can generally be subdivided into four different areas: working, shopping, entertainment and managing.

Working

The various applications used for communication are important to working behaviour. The possibility to log on directly to certain suppliers or to certain sources of information and the availability of specific applications all lead to changes in working methods. Not only will division of tasks change between a secretary and a manager, as described above, but the place of work will also change. Going to the office to work is becoming much less of a necessity. Thanks to the possibilities of communication via the Internet, the need to communicate face to face has become less important. It is now possible to communicate with others any time and anywhere. This development cannot be seen separately from the development of the mobile phone. These needs and possibilities mutually influence each other. The Internet, and e-mail in particular, is data or text-based, while mobile telephony is speech-based. It is not totally far-fetched that these two applications will converge. SMS (short message service) messages can be seen as the first initiative in this direction. These can be created 'on the computer' of the telecom provider (e.g. KPN or Libertel) and mailed via the Internet to the owner of a mobile phone. The message is received and read as an SMS message. In the same way, it is possible to listen to e-mail messages by telephone or voice-mail messages on the computer.

The way the consumer is affected with reference to work is that they are no longer tied to a physical workplace or place of residence. In fact, the place of work could be the same as the place of residence. It is possible to keep in contact via voicemail or e-mail or by logging on directly to the system at the office. The physical place in a central office thus becomes a place for meetings and social gatherings. This application will lead to changes at work (no fixed workplace), changes in the management of people (more results-oriented and less time-oriented) and to a change in working environment (a workplace at home). Employees will decide whether they have to come to the office or whether they can carry out their work elsewhere. People will look for harmony in their place of work, which will be partly at home, partly at the office and perhaps even partly on the road. This is a big change for organizations, i.e. no longer seeing work as being related to a fixed workplace.

Due to the possibilities of communication via the Internet or mobile phone we no longer know where someone is. People will have to be critical in their choice of workplace and go to work only if contact with other people is deemed necessary or considered important. Finally, the social function of a workplace could become a reason for going to the office. In fact, offices will be used primarily for meetings and social contact. People will go to the office or 'to work' only if work cannot be carried out elsewhere, i.e. to use office facilities that are not available at home, or if the work needs to be carried out in a central place (production or construction workers). Other employees will increasingly weigh up the pros and cons before making a conscious decision. As a result they will be able to plan their time more efficiently (no more time travelling to and from work and no more interruptions at work) and be more productive. This, too, is one of the hallmarks of the new economy. This change in behavioural pattern could, among other things, solve the vast traffic problem both on the ground and in the air.

the Inte.... mobile phone we no longer know where someone is

Shopping

The same sort of changes can be found in shopping behaviour. The need to go shopping will disappear now that it is possible to buy on-line at home. Items can be ordered via the Internet and delivered to a person's home. People can search, select and buy via the Internet. This does not mean that stores will disappear, only that it will no longer be necessary to go to the store to do your shopping. The way people will use the Internet for shopping (searching, comparing, orientation) will depend on personal needs and preferences and whether or not they will actually want to buy on-line.

The big advantage of the Internet is that people can quickly and easily orientate themselves on offers that are not restricted by existing boundaries or time. However, while the physical restrictions have disappeared, people miss seeing, feeling and smelling, the character-istics that are so typical of real shopping. In addition, people who buy on the Internet have to wait for their goods, whereas shop-bought items can (usually) be taken home straight away. Social and personal contact between people is also an important reason for having a store. After all, we must not forget that the items ordered also have to be delivered to our homes, which means that someone has to be at home when the goods are delivered or that there have to be facilities for home delivery.

The Internet does offer a choice where shopping is concerned, but it is the consumer who decides whether or not it is a good choice and whether or not to take advantage of it. This immediately determines the condition of existence for the stores of today. However, because people will weigh up the pros and cons of Internet shopping, shopping and buying behaviour will also change. Existing stores must be aware, even more than before, of why customers shop and why they go to the store.

Shopkeepers must clearly work at the raison d'être of their stores, namely expert advice, the presence of items, the social character and the local function of the shopping centre. If shopkeepers anticipate this, it will clearly be possible to meet customers' needs despite the changes in buying behaviour. Shopping via the Internet will then just be an additional way of meeting the needs of certain groups of customers. Many customers will always be drawn by physical basic values.

Entertainment

The Internet will also bring changes in the field of entertainment. It is possible, for example, to play games on the Internet, on-line, with a group of other people, or download games from the Internet and play them at a later time on a different medium of your choice (computer, mobile or other device). Finally, there are specific applications, such as chatting, community sites and hobby clubs, set up for recreational purposes.

The concept of playing at home together with others who are also at home somewhere is what makes this application interesting to many users. The possibility to chat via the Internet is a social activity that fits in well with people's behaviour. The need to have contact with other people and to exchange information can now also be achieved in a non-physical way. People can chat in news groups or with certain communities that are based on special interests or behaviour. The Internet is merely a facilitative medium that replaces personal contact. Behaviour itself, however, does not change – it is inherent in human nature.

Managing

Finally, the fourth consumer activity allows consumers to manage all sorts of matters such as finances or time. Specific financial sites, such as quicken.com and smartmoney.com, can manage customers' investment portfolios, give them advice on investment, or allow them to use or download all types of financial planners. There is also an option that will keep customers up-to-date on specific news. They can subscribe to newsletters or an alert service (if something changes you will hear from us). They can also use the Internet to carry out certain activities on-line that were previously done off-line, such as on-line banking (see Table 1.7). Developments in the field of on-line invoicing and payments are also leading to greater efficiency.

Table 1.7　　　　　　　　　　　　*Examples of functional uses of the Internet*

Internet layer	Example
Consumer/user	The Internet user and personal use
Device	Personal computer, notebook, telephone, television, PDA (palmtop)
Infrastructure	Telephone network, mobile network, cable
Application/use	Sites, communities, portals, search engines
Content	Information, communication, transaction
Process	Infrastructure, information supply, communication and transaction handling

These four key areas of Internet use show that the Internet is encroaching upon consumers' daily lives. It suddenly allows them to make choices that were not possible before and to weigh up the 'real' activities that can be supported virtually (communication and information supply) against activities that can be carried out 'virtually' (such as buying on the Internet). The weighing up of real activities against virtual activities and the split between virtual processes and real processes is the essence of the use of Internet and the basis for change. This applies to both consumers and organizations. Organizations have to reassess their working methods, their processes and their approach to the outside world, customers and suppliers.

The Internet and competitive conditions

The influence that Internet can have on organizations stems from the possibilities it provides for facilitating processes in a different way and maintaining relationships with the outside world. The use of the

Figure 1.8   *Competitive forces that lead to changes in market conditions*

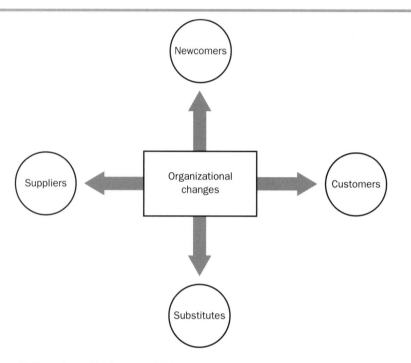

Source: M. Porter, *Competitive Strategies* (1980) Free Press, New York. The central block depicting market conditions has been adjusted to indicate the effect of organizational changes on competitive relations

Internet can influence the way in which organizations operate. This can be outlined by means of Porter's competitive model (see Figure 1.8). Applying the Internet in the right way can reinforce the five competitive forces differentiated by Porter.

The influence of the Internet is noticeable in all five areas mentioned. At the moment everyone's attention is focused on the changes that affect customers, the reason being that this is visible and concerns everyone. People who visit the Internet can (nearly always) directly consult consumer sites; after all, the aim is to reach the consumer. This is not so for business applications. In such cases the Internet mainly facilitates existing business relationships.

People who visit the Internet can (nearly always) directly consult consumer sites; after all, the aim is to reach the consumer

These sites are not freely accessible and are often not known to parties not directly involved. They are usually specific to an organization, to a certain industry or to a limited group of companies. Therefore, there is little need to advertise such sites, which sometimes gives the impression that businesses are not very active on this front. This is, however, not true. An example is the development of market places where parties maintain relations with other parties in the supply chain or collaborate with similar companies. In particular software providers such as Ariba and CommerceOne expect to see great prospects for such market places, as do the many that have invested in these shares. Software company SAP has even set up a separate organization for this – mySAP (mySAP.com) – which develops and facilitates market places and can interface with existing (ERP – enterprise resource planning) systems.

Relationship with customers

This is the change that is visible in the field of marketing. The customers have a choice in what and where to buy. They can first orientate themselves and find information on the Internet as part of the buying process before they decide where to buy. As a result the customer is far choosier, but also better informed (more assertive). In addition to a rich choice of suppliers in normal shops, people can now choose from a large number of suppliers on the Internet. It is possible to compare prices and products and to take factors such as service and support into consideration. The consequences for suppliers are:

* an independent consumer who makes careful choices;

* a customer who can choose from a multitude of suppliers;

* a customer who will no longer let himself be bound to one particular supplier – as a result customer loyalty will diminish in favour of the possibility of making selective and careful choices;

* the supply and suppliers' market is becoming more transparent, as a result of which prices will start levelling out. It is important for suppliers to have a competitive advantage over other suppliers by having a good product and by rendering good services for a reasonable price (as perceived by the customer).

These are the developments that are taking place in the customer relations structure. The Internet can also cause change in a customer's buying behaviour. Customers will no longer go to only one supplier but rather to a group of suppliers, who fit in with the customer's behaviour or approximate the customer's preferences. Offers can be found on special shopping sites on the Internet, for example, communities that appeal to consumer groups with special interests or behaviour. Examples of such communities are sports sites, like sportal.com and behavioural sites, like travel.com.

In addition to the behaviour and interest-based sites, suppliers can collaborate on the basis of a specific function. This involves portals. A portal is a gateway to the Internet or to a certain source of information on the Internet. In the eyes of the customer, this portal is an important factor to being active on the Internet. Many ISPs, such as Planet Internet and World Online, want to serve as portals. This will enable them to attract advertisers who want to reach the portal users. Search engines can also fulfil a certain portal function for people looking for particular sites on the Internet. The most familiar example is Yahoo!. In short, communities are more customer and behaviour-based, whereas portals are more supply and demand-based. In both cases, the market structure changes, as does the way in which companies do business. A supplier can choose to 'go it alone' on the Internet or to link his site to a portal or community. Finally, a supplier can decide whether he wants to be visible only on certain sites (via banners or icons) or whether he wants to link up with certain sites at process level. In this case it is possible to offer a product or service the moment the visitor to the site buys something or retrieves certain information. For example, the moment someone books a trip, they are presented with the option of taking out travel insurance. This method of doing business is called 'affiliate marketing'.

Relationship with suppliers

Organizations can also choose either to enter into a closer relationship with suppliers or to reorganize their purchasing activities. This choice strongly depends on the type of item concerned and the degree of interdependence. If organizations have a unique product, they will try to form a strong affiliation with suppliers, which will enable them to streamline their purchasing and production process and therefore make it more efficient. The various types of 'just in time' management show the effect of this type of collaboration. Stocks are minimized and suppliers are informed about production and remaining stock via the production system. In this way organizations can determine themselves when to replenish stocks. It should also be possible to link computers or cash desks to give suppliers an insight into companies' stock levels. As soon as the stock has reached minimum level, suppliers could make new deliveries. The supplier could, for example, be warned by an alert function when the stock falls below a certain minimum level. The delivery, the conditions and the method of payment would all be agreed beforehand. Although this method of collaboration was possible in the past by directly linking computer systems or by agreeing certain protocols, such as with EDI, it is the use of the Internet in particular that is stimulating this development. After all, it is not necessary to make many technical agreements thanks to the universal character of the Internet. This means that many organizations can adopt the Internet without any intervention in their information supply or systems.

In addition to direct agreements between organizations, companies can agree to carry out purchasing activities together. The advertising world has had media buying agencies since the early 1990s. These agencies buy TV advertising space and advertising space from newspapers and other media (such as posters and open-air media) on behalf of advertising agencies. Because of their combined purchasing power, agencies can agree lower prices and enter into better agreements with suppliers about times and placement. In other words, it is possible to exercise more buying power and more power on the whole. The same can be achieved in 'virtual' market places, where companies can enter into agreements about collective buying of products and services. The virtual market place combines the purchasing requirements and enters into price agreements on behalf of the parties concerned. Several market places have been set up, for example for car components, computer components and also by grocery stores (such as Ahold) for the purchase of foods. In this way companies exercise power over manufacturers and, as a consequence, change power structures and market conditions. The fact that this buying power is not limited to local borders indicates that this is a global change. This will affect agreements and pricing between the purchasing party and the manufacturer, especially in professional market places where we find the larger companies, and will result in lower costs, which will be passed on to the consumer.

The manufacturers' reaction will no doubt determine the degree to which these market places will give rise to lower costs. At present only Unilever has adjusted its strategy in anticipation of new market conditions, by being even more focused on a limited number of strong 'global' brands. Closer cooperation between manufacturers and companies and between companies and consumers will also allow manufacturers and consumers to cooperate more closely. This will bring about new structures and patterns. The Internet will facilitate these changes (like VMI, Vendor Management Inventory Systems).

Newcomers

If existing boundaries between companies and countries are starting to disappear, it means that companies can go in search of other markets for their products and services. These markets could differ in geographic location, or the target group could be different, as could the sales technique used to approach the market. As a result of services being offered via the Internet, borders are disappearing and customers are buying from sources that best meet their specific requirements. Amazon can deliver its books and CDs to anyone anywhere in the world. The need to have a book or, even more so, the need for music is so universal that it is easy to sell across the border. A customer's choice is based on either price or convenience (CDs), or on range, provision of information and convenience (books). This may not be as easy for other items, but if consumer demand is to be subjected to globalization, local markets will become less distinct as their specific characteristics disappear. This will lead to foreign newcomers to other markets. Amazon is a good example of a newcomer that has changed the book trade in dozens of countries. At the very least local booksellers have adjusted to the fact that the consumer can buy foreign books just as easily and a lot cheaper straight from another country (from Amazon or Barnes and Noble).

> **As a result of services being offered via the Internet, borders are disappearing**

A similar change can be seen in financial services. It is easier to buy shares on the US stock market (Wall Street or Nasdaq) via Fidelity or Charles Schwab than via your own bank. The information provided by newcomers is often better and more complete. This means that market conditions and structures of countries will change and that service providers will have to reconsider their competitive strength. (Who could have predicted that Sony would offer banking services successfully!)

Substitute products

The supplier translates customer requirements into products and services. But a proper look at the opportunities offered by ICT (information and computer technology) and the Internet will reveal that companies have sales opportunities and ways of contacting customers that did not exist before. This in itself indicates that there is a need to assess whether organizations would still sell their products and services in the same way if they were forced to make new choices. The logic of past choices has often been superseded and organizations are looking for another way to sell their products and services using modern technology and anticipating present-day customer requirements. An example is selling insurance products in supermarkets. Customers still regularly go to the supermarket, whereas they may no longer go to the bank.

Searching for new sales channels in response to the change in behaviour and the emancipation of customers is one of the challenges facing suppliers. If organizations no longer strive for product loyalty but instead for loyalty based on personal contacts, they will increasingly react to associated customer demand. In this way it is possible, together with other parties, to provide customers with a total package that is consumer binding and also provides facilities and services. For example, concepts such as 'the home' offer a total package of house-related services, from insurance to gardening and security. In this way an organization can take advantage of shifts in customer psychology due to social and technological changes.

Organizations will also be adjusted on the basis of these four external competitive forces (see Figure 1.9). They will enter into an increasing number of partnerships with other parties who will take over certain functions of the organization. We have indicated that purchasing activities can be transferred to market places, but it is also possible to consign financial activities to an independent entity that will be responsible for managing the cash flow of an organization. Furthermore, the effects of linking systems, changes in purchasing and new customer relations will influence organizational structures and the authority of various departments (see Figure 1.9).

Figure 1.9

Influence of the Internet on competitive powers

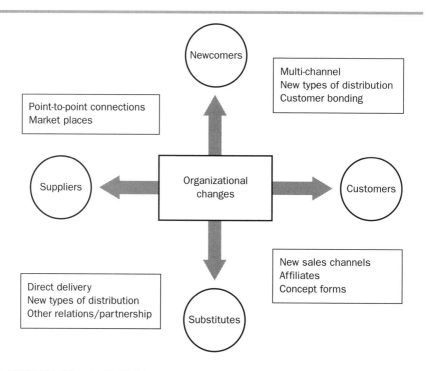

Summary

The implementation of the Internet leads to changes in both consumer behaviour and organizations. The Internet transcends a mere technological infrastructure. Thanks to its increased versatility, its effect on business and life in general will be even greater. From the angle of infrastructure, however, it will not often be evident that the Internet facilitates these changes. It will look as if the new 'devices' and visible tools, such as notebooks, televisions and mobile phones, facilitate these changes. Applications will be developed and accessible using one or more of these tools as and when it suits the user. The Internet and its applications will become more global in character, whereas the focus of support for consumer behaviour will be on the individual. Weighing up what is culture-specific against what is structure-specific will become important to organizations. It will determine the extent to which their product or service will be successful in certain markets.

An infrastructure is being created within the new economy and companies are looking for new markets and customers. This requires a lot of investment, especially in marketing, and sometimes leads to the tendency to think that 'new economy' stands for loss. Yet nothing is further from the truth. The new economy has to generate profit, but everyone realizes that it is necessary to invest before it is possible to realize a profit. But the question is, what should a company invest in and for how long should it be prepared to continue investing in the development of a new market? There must be a 'path to profit' for each new venture, a scenario clearly focused on profit. Market dynamics and economic growth then determine the time it takes to reach the break-even point. Economic developments and experiences with the new opportunities of, for example, the Internet and global marketing show that in the eyes of the investor this 'path to profit' should clearly be quicker than the time it has taken most companies to date.

Notes

1 *Source*: Internet in Nederland, Internet Databureau, the Internet monitor figures of Intomart have also been incorporated.

2 Greenfield Online survey in July 2000.

3 Kalakota, Ravi and Robinson, Marcia (1999), *e-Business, Roadmap for Success*, Addison-Wesley Longman Inc.

2

■■■■■■■■■■■■■■■■■■

Finding your e-market

Carrying water to the sea is pointless. That is why many managers concentrate on the tidal movements only. The changes observed are qualified as external factors.

'Marketing' is the discipline that studies the relationship between an organization and the market(s) it serves. Marketeers observe and analyze market demand. They look at the way in which a certain market demand is catered for by the organization, and establish the level of harmonization between demand and supply. Market research, marketing communication and distribution are the key areas in which marketeers are experts. However, due to the changes seen in many markets and far-reaching technological developments, past choices made by organizations in the area of marketing are not necessarily still valid today. Today, it is not the markets that are of central concern: modern marketeers are increasingly focusing on individual customer behaviour (see Table 2.1). Similarly, it no longer suffices to target one's marketing efforts at local, domestic markets: today's market place spans the globe.

Along with these changes, many of the traditional marketing strategies and instruments are changing. Organizations are compelled to re-examine whether the choices made in the past are still effective, and whether new marketing tools, such as the Internet, could be useful and should therefore be used. At the same time, the traditional marketing approach lacks a reference frame to support this decision-making process. A mere review of the current marketing activities and marketing instruments is insufficient. In 1997,[4] marketing developments were first organized in the form of an orientation-based marketing evolution model (see Figure 2.2). This model enabled organizations to decide what changes were

> **Organizations are compelled to re-examine whether the choices made in the past are still effective**

necessary in relation to possible use of the Internet. As such, the orientation model provides a strategic framework for guiding the changes and decision-making processes with respect to the use of Internet applications.

The basis for marketing communication was established in the 1950s. Advertising – the 'art of influencing consumer groups' – was developed in the ensuing decades. Today, creativity is still regarded as the linchpin of the advertising industry. Where this concerns mass communication, focused on large, homogenous groups of potential customers, this is an understandable view.

Table 2.1 *Survey of evolution in marketing and marketing orientation[5]*

Period (indicative only)	Marketing management philosophy	Prevailing marketing orientation
1950–1970	Classic marketing concept	Orientation on transactions, product features and product values (brands)
1970–1983	Social marketing concept	Orientation on target groups and other interest groups
1983–1994	Market-driven (target groups)	Orientation on target groups and individual communication
1994–1998	Individual customer relations (customer belongs to homogenous target group)	Customer orientation with services and modular product
1998–	Individual customer relations based on the needs and wishes of the individual customer	Customer-focused orientation, focused on individual wishes/ network orientation and interaction with customers and suppliers

Source: Molenaar, C.N.A., 'New Marketing', 1997

As world economies prospered in the 1950s, there was a strong growth of effective demand. Computers were introduced in the same decade, along with many new forms of distribution, such as the supermarket concept.

Together with the development of new techniques in the area of production and distribution, and new forms of communication, came the need for uniformity, recognition and assurance. In the first two decades after the Second World War, there were many developments that can still be seen in marketing today. The market was the focal point in a company's approach to products and sales policy, and the foundations were laid for a range of new marketing instruments.

Today, many companies continue to analyze current and potential markets on the basis of the traditional reference frame: product, price, place and form of promotion. Thus, principles of Philip Kotler, seen as the most influential economist in shaping the modern approach to marketing, are still firmly entrenched in the minds of modern marketeers. These principles, in short, hinge on a market approach that is based on specific product/service combinations, focused on a specific market or target group. The traditional marketing instruments demonstrate at once that the focus is, quite essentially, on product supply.

This approach first began to take shape in the 1950s. Rapidly improving living standards and equally fast-rising consumer demand made organizations aware of the effectiveness of a supply-driven marketing strategy. By approaching the market on the strength of the organization's specific abilities, and creating a product supply in accordance with those abilities, it was possible to control and guide the sales process.

Commercial policy, from thereon, was built on a relationship with the market, different marketing forms, and the possibilities of the traditional marketing instruments. Focused importantly on market demand, the new approach continued to be firmly rooted in existing organizational structures. There was a product or service to be marketed. On the basis of customer preference and the possibilities of the organization, the product or service could, to some extent, be adapted to suit market needs. Likewise, product positioning and communication were harmonized with target group expectations.

Central to the strategic choices taken in the area of marketing were the now-traditional marketing instruments, product, price, place and promotion – the same instruments that served as the foundation for Philip Kotler's theory, and the same instruments that still assume an important role in marketing and customer relations today.

Product

A product is a combination of certain physical elements and service elements, which can be sold as a separate entity. As such, services are also regarded as a product. A product can, however, consist of three components: 'a physical component', which is tangible, a 'virtual component' which is intangible (service, warrantee) and a 'perception element': what do the buyers think they're buying?

These three components together form 'the product'. Based on the classical marketing theory, a great deal of attention is paid to the physical product and corresponding features. These product features determine the character of the relationship to be developed with the intended market and market players. Technological advancement enabled manufacturers to make the various product features increasingly efficient (large variety of car types, large array of PC designs, etc.). Similarly, it became possible to manufacture certain products increasingly efficiently for smaller target groups. Because this reduced the supplier's market reach, a more intense marketing approach was needed on behalf of smaller groups, a development that gained important momentum in the 1980s. And although Kotler's principles were still the standard, a more differentiated marketing policy became increasingly important.

Price

What is the best price strategy? A universal strategy or a strategy that differentiates between different markets and/or market segments? Should a market price simply be calculated on the basis of cost price plus profit margin, or can the price be used to instil an expectation of quality in the buyer? Or could it serve to create a competitive advantage over the competition, by following a deliberate, competition-related pricing strategy?

Price is directly related to a specific product and to the targets of the organization. In traditional marketing theory, price has an important function in communicating with the target group, and in enabling a supplier to either stimulate or slow down demand. Furthermore, a pricing strategy can help attain the desired market position, the objectives of the organization, or a certain product perception in the buyer's mind.

Should the sale price be based on your products and services, with the cost price serving as the basis for the sale price (cost price plus profit margin)? Should you follow

For many organizations, a pricing policy is an important instrument in lending shape to their marketing strategy

the market in setting your price, or take a more conscious and pro-active price strategy, e.g. market price surplus or creaming-off strategy? For many organizations, a pricing policy is an important instrument in lending shape to their marketing strategy. It can influence demand, it can raise the threshold for newcomers in the market (lower prices reduce profit potential), or lower that threshold (high prices, high profit potential).

In practice, price appears to be an important communication instrument in the buying process, as most consumers will relate price to quality. Expensive brands are equated with quality; cheap products tend to raise low expectations. The traditional marketing theory clearly relates price to a specific product or service. The objective of reaching a transaction is beyond discussion. Turnover figures are in most cases the chief criterion by which success is measured, regardless of how they were achieved.

Place

Mostly, the place where a product is bought is fixed by physical and local circumstances. A local store or a national supplier determines where the purchase takes place. The place of sale – like the price – generates associations in relation to the buying process. An address in 'PC Hooftstraat' in Amsterdam, or on 'Fifth Avenue' in New York will generate different expectations than a retail outlet in your local shopping centre. The consumer expects to buy a different (better) product at the former, and is prepared to pay more for it. The place of purchase – mail order distributors aside – is traditionally associated with a certain physical location. Hence, distribution channels and shopfloor arrangements are traditionally considered as important elements in the promotion process.

Immediate interaction between the prospective buyer and the physical product, typically, has been one of the key factors traditional marketeers have relied on. The presence of the actual product or corresponding service influences the buying process. Because impulse buying is on the increase, many sales promotions and point of sale specials are designed to stimulate that moment. The consumer can see, feel and smell the product, and – if he wants to – he can even take it home. Therefore, the physical sales location is an outstanding opportunity for selling a product or a service, and adds quality to the buying process. In times of prosperity, when spending behaviour is freer, the purchase moment will be spontaneous rather than premeditated, therefore buying behaviour will be more impulsive.

Moreover, customers today are increasingly convinced that bad products are simply not sold any more. The customer-retailer bond is strong enough to instil an almost blind faith in consumers that the products sold by a particular shop are always good. Shopfloor sales promotions, in many cases, are designed to stimulate that confidence and thus consolidate the bond. In 'business-to-business' environments, the value of physical communication visibly increases. There is clearly a need to gain the client's trust by relationship building and loyalty programmes. Relationships can be intensified and consolidated by moments of physical communication, e.g. at trade fairs, exhibitions and seminars, and by offering incentives in the form of skyboxes (a business lounge in a football stadium) and incentive travel. Knowing and trusting each other is considered as important in business today as delivering the right product or service. The new electronic forms of bonding – e-mail, the Internet and the extranet – support the process of building trust. People are looking for new harmony in relationships. The Internet has brought important changes in relation to the place of sale as a traditional marketing instrument. Therefore, the role and value of the place of sale as a marketing instrument requires regular reassessment.

Promotion

The final link in the traditional marketing instrument chain is promotion. In most cases, a sales promotion will focus on mass communication and mass communication instruments. Sales promotions can be grouped in terms of 'above the line' activities, designed to persuade mass audiences, and 'below the line' advertising, designed to stimulate sales directly. The latter form of promotion is mostly used for short-term sales strategies that are intended to influence the buying moment. Sales promotions, direct mail, telemarketing and guerrilla marketing belong in this category. Mass communication (above-the-line) is aimed at influencing customer perception, the objective being to create a 'top of mind' position. The developments surrounding the Internet will affect both long-term promotion objectives and short-term actions. Today, mass communication is increasingly used to draw visitors to a specific site, while more focused promotions are used to stimulate actual sales.

The Internet does not dispense with the need for mass communication. However, the role and function of mass communication is changing towards influencing target group behaviour, and inducing target audiences to visit a specific site. In this way, mass communication contributes importantly to brand and image building. The crucial difference with traditional mass communication lies in the fact that, with the latter, the basis was always the product itself, whereas today the product is used to stimulate brand awareness and to persuade potential customers to visit the company's Web site. Where the classic approach was about stimulating brand recognition and generating product associations, in the Internet era the distributor has, in effect, become the brand, for example, Amazon.com or ebay.com. This development is encouraged by the trend of brand concentration among manufacturers such as Unilever.

The four traditional marketing instruments are summarized in Table 2.2.

As the Internet is accepted as a new (marketing) medium, the traditional marketing instruments will prove their worth in a number of ways. At the same time, the focus in marketing is shifting away from the transaction moment towards the relationship-building process. This shift reflects the changes that are taking place in organizations' marketing orientations. A company's marketing orientation determines to a large extent how the Internet can be used effectively and how the traditional marketing instruments are best applied. As such, a marketing orientation can serve as a strategic framework for deciding how to use the above instruments, and to guide the process of changing marketing policies and organizational structures.

> **A company's marketing orientation determines to a large extent how the Internet can be used effectively and how the traditional marketing instruments are best applied**

Strategy

The vision of marketing has developed from a sales-oriented, traditional marketing concept to a marketing approach with strong social undertones, whereby the dominant orientation has shifted from target groups towards interest groups. In the 1980s, particularly due to the

Table 2.2 *Basic value and core competency per marketing instrument*

Marketing instrument	Basic value	Core competency
Product	Consists of a physical element, a service element and a perception element. Product features are important criteria for communicating with the market. Technological developments enable features to be added and better product	Product qualities and product values differentiation
Place	Physical location enables direct contact between product and potential buyer. The buyer visits the selling place to see, touch, sense, and often to buy the product	Local presence. The relationship with the shopkeeper or physical place of sale is an important factor in the decision to buy
Price	Price is a perception of product value and quality. Price also indicates practical value and exclusivity	Price is the most important source of information in relation to product perception and brand positioning
Promotion	Focuses strongly on products and product features. Instrument for communicating with markets or target groups. Promotion forms include direct promotion to reach potential customers, point of sale promotion, and mass communication	Product-based, target-group focused. Often used to support product perception and generate product associations at the moment of purchase and during use, e.g. an aftershave user feels irresistible to women when using the product

introduction of computer technology in marketing communication (laser printers), there was strong emphasis on direct communication. In the past decade, marketing efforts have moved more towards individual customer relations and alternative forms of distribution. In the process, an increasingly large array of communication instruments has been developed to support the marketing effort. In addition to shopfloor promotions and account management, direct mail, coupons, telephone promotions and, more recently, Internet advertising have been used.

How and to what extent the various options are usable will depend on the organization's marketing orientation. The marketing orientation provides an indication of how customer-oriented the organization is. Customer orientation is reflected in the extent to which a company's marketing strategy and organizational structure are adapted to meet the needs and wishes of individual customers. This can be appraised by looking at various elements, e.g. structure of the organization, level of interaction with the customer, business processes, and organizational culture. In essence, an organization's marketing orientation already provides an indication of how the Internet could be used, and the strategy to be followed with regard to e-commerce.

Table 2.3 *Schedule of marketing orientations*

Marketing orientation	Internally focused	Target group focused	Customer focused	Network oriented
Focus	Product	Target group	Relationship	Synergy and teamwork
Product	Standard	Target group focused/service elements	Customizing/ personalization	Direct interaction/ customizing
Distribution	Via distribution channels	Via selected channels	Multi-channel Strong emphasis on direct communication	Direct communication and close cooperation
Price	Cost price plus profit margin as basis for the market pricing	Target group compliant	Relationship-indicative (lifetime value)	Open-book calculations Risk-sharing
Promotion	Mass communication	Target group communication and direct communication	Direct communication	Direct interactive communication
Sales process	Distribution channel support	Prospect oriented	Account management	Cooperation
Organization	Hierarchical	Matrix of business units	Strong front office with customer teams	Network organization
Internet	Information medium Limited applicability	Information and communication medium	Strong focus on transaction	Infrastructural

Source: Molenaar, C.N.A., 'New Marketing', 1997, p. 97

The differences outlined in Table 2.3 immediately provide an indication of the limit conditions of the marketing orientation, and the scope it offers for customer interaction. The chosen orientation implies that strategic choices were made in relation to the market model. What market(s) are to be approached, and how?

Internally focused orientation

An internally focused orientation characterizes organizations that operate through distribution channels. The focus in the organization lies on the internal structures and processes. Organizations like this concentrate their attention on manufacturing products, which are marketed through the distribution channel(s). Product features and qualities to a large extent determine their market potential. Essentially, it is this kind of internally focused marketing orientation that typifies the traditional approach to marketing, as adopted by many organizations in the 1950s and 1960s. It was also this type of orientation that served as the casting mould for the marketing theory and marketing instruments described earlier.

The markets in which this group of organizations move are characterized by relative stability. These markets are generally not very dynamic, and customer demand is fairly homogenous. Examples of this are the fuel market and the market for soaps and detergents. Customer bonding relies on product loyalty, and customer relations are built and maintained by the distribution channel. The marketing strategy is reflected in the structure of the marketing department. A marketing team is led by a marketing manager/director, and supported by a distribution manager (supply chain manager), a product manager and a communication manager.

If the organization produces goods and services for the mass market, it will probably have a single distribution channel, a (product-based) brand strategy and a mass-market approach to marketing. There are no direct customer contacts; communications at customer level are restricted to the distribution point. Rather, the supplier will concentrate on delivering a good product for the right price and pushing those goods in the direction of the distribution channel. Communication with the market relies on mass communication techniques (influencing buying behaviour by product perception) and consolidating the relationship with the distribution channel. There will be considerable efforts in the area of market research to enable the organization to respond better to market needs. In organizations where an internally focused orientation is followed, the traditional marketing instruments and principles are valued highly. (See Table 2.4.)

Table 2.4   *Application of marketing instruments with internal orientation*

Marketing instrument	Application
Product	Limited variation. Product is made to serve a mass market or specific target group
Price	Largely determined by the market. Suppliers must comply with going prices and competition. Limited options for independent price strategy. Cost monitoring is a priority, since cost control is one of the few options for increasing market share (i.e. increase profits)
Place	Depending on the objective, i.e. market share or share of turnover within specific target groups, distribution will be selective or intensive
Promotion	Mass communication and promotions, focusing on influencing sales at the buying moment (sales promotion). Direct communication is product-based, not interactive or individual
General typification	The internal orientation typifies stable markets where demand is homogenous. Orientation can be on consumer markets or business-to-business markets. Direct communication with individual customers is rare

The role of the Internet will remain limited. Mostly, the Internet will be used to help achieve cost reduction targets, as sale prices largely follow the market. The Internet is used to inform (potential) clients and facilitate business processes (intranet applications). The latter enables the organization to communicate more efficiently and flexibly with its distribution network and suppliers.

Target group orientation

The target group-oriented organization focuses on winning a market position among a specific, denoted target group. Specific products and services are developed for the target group. 'Nike', for instance, is a company whose organizational structure revolves around target group-oriented marketing. Its footwear and other products are manufactured to appeal to a certain group. Once this target group is reached, regular distribution channels are used. Marketing will rely on target group-directed media, e.g. adverts and promotions on selected television channels (MTV/ Eurosport) and in magazines for specific target groups.

The target group-oriented organization focuses on winning a market position among a specific, denoted target group

These organizations are strongly focused on empathizing with the target group. This is reflected in the marketing instruments used: promotions via target group-oriented media, a pricing policy that responds to target group expectations, and a distribution system that connects to the perception and desired image that exist in the target group.

In view of the orientation towards a specific target group, direct communication is an effective instrument for approaching the envisaged market segment. This form of communication is highly individual, yet without addressing the specific wishes of single individuals. Because of the fact that the potential buyer belongs to a certain target group, he/she will be confronted with the same advertisements, and communicate with other product users. Generally speaking, different target groups will have different consumer characteristics and criteria. The target group can be quantified and qualified, enabling people to be registered by name, address and relevant specifics and to approach them on that basis (telephone, mail). In many cases, a supplier that has adopted this style of marketing orientation will aspire to be a market leader. Different target groups often have different buying patterns and other features. As a result, market demand is very heterogeneous, creating the need for a target group classification that enables suppliers to address specific groups. Essentially, a target group is a cluster of potential buyers with the same needs and expressing a homogenous demand. Therefore, more direct communication between buyer and supplier is necessary to be able to respond accurately to target group demand. Generally, these markets will be more susceptible to dynamic factors such as trends, newcomers, and changing target group needs. The market stability which internally focused organizations depend on is clearly less in this category, and this is reflected in the way the marketing instruments are used. (See Table 2.5.)

Table 2.5 *Application of marketing instruments with target group orientation*

Marketing instruments	Application
Product	Different product features and product designs focused at certain target groups. Regular modifications/redesigns to respond to new trends and different target group behaviour (e.g. use of mobile phones)
Price	The target group largely determines pricing. The extent to which a certain product is 'hot' will bear on price, and so will target group expectations. In most cases there is no direct relationship between cost price and market price
Place	The distribution policy is largely determined by the target group. The chosen distribution strategy must connect to the envisaged target group: exclusive or intensive, direct or via a distribution channel. Target group behaviour and empathy determine the sales outlet policy
Promotion	Promotions are designed to appeal to the target group. Often, the 'tone of voice' is not product oriented but instead is tuned to the expectations and behaviour of the target group. Target group behaviour is marked by a desire to belong to a crowd and to join in with whatever goes. A mix of mass media instruments, target-oriented media and – sometimes – direct media is used to intensify the relationship between the supplier (products) and the group
General	Target group orientation means that products are specifically designed for a certain group of users or potential buyers. The target group in itself is a homogenous group, but it will differ from other groups. As a result, product demand tends to be heterogeneous. Often this is coupled to dynamic markets and a high level of changeability with respect to demand (trend-sensitive)

Customer-focused orientation

Customer-focused marketing orientations centre on the needs of the individual consumer. The supplier wants to establish a direct relationship with the individual customer to encourage producer/buyer bonding. This relationship can lead to a preference for certain products or distribution places. Therefore, it is essential that there is direct communication between the organization and the customer.

Customer-oriented marketing is at its most effective in the last phase of the distribution chain. For example, where the last link in the sales process is the retailer, then the retail outlet will be customer oriented. Where this is not the case, the organization must gain a competitive edge in other ways, for instance by competing on price or location. If the organization has no direct customer contacts, it must have a distribution strategy that corresponds to its objectives in relation to customer orientation. This would be a multi-channel strategy (direct sales, in conjunction with a distribution strategy) or a customer relations policy that combines sales via distribution networks with service desk information and support. A similar strategy is used, for instance, by Hewlett-Packard, whose products and services are sold through a distribution channel (OEM or 'retail trade'). For product support, however, the customers can contact the Hewlett-Packard service number. Likewise, the registration of warrantee certificates takes place centrally in the Hewlett-Packard organization. In this way, direct product support and customer communication are linked to the sales network of the distribution channel. In the market approach, the physical flow is disconnected from the information flow.

The Internet has been an important agent in stimulating this type of strategy. The organization's Internet Web site is used to provide information and for communicating with the customer on specific products and services (including transaction registration). In this way, the customer's identity is known, and the supplier is thus able to respond more effectively to individual customer needs. Interaction is the oil that lubricates this form of customer orientation. On the other hand, Tracy and Wiersema[6] propose that customer orientation ideally will be based on several elements, namely customer intimacy, operational excellence and product leadership. It is held that the best customer relationships are built by creating the right symbiosis between those three elements (see Figure 2.1).

Combining 'best product by customer perception' with the right price and an effective customer bonding policy yields a high level of customer orientation. In addition to the internal aspects of production and business operations, the external aspect – customer bonding – is equally important. (See Table 2.6.)

Network-focused orientation

Finally, a fourth orientation can be distinguished: the network orientation. This hinges on a much closer relationship between buyers and sellers and other relevant parties than would appear at first sight.

Figure 2.1 *Elements of customer orientation*

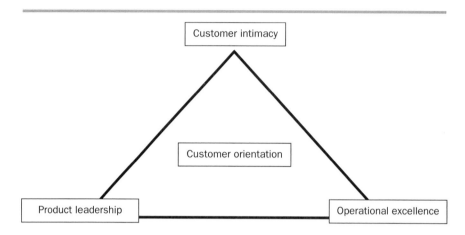

Source: Tracy and Wiersema (1994) *Discipline of Market Leaders*, Addison-Wesley

Table 2.6 *Application of marketing instruments with customer-focused orientation*

Marketing instruments	Application
Product	Designed to meet market requirements, often by tailoring service elements to specific groups or individual customers. The combination of physical product, service and perception determines the level of customization
Price	Largely dependent on the specific wishes of customers or customer groups. The price of the product reflects current market conditions and individual needs of customers and customer groups
Place	Again, dependent on the preferences of individual customers and customer groups. Target group needs are met as much as possible. This often requires a diversified distribution strategy
Promotion	In addition to general promotion, promotion focuses on individual customers. Often, there is a customer database including address data, purchase details and individual customers' preferences

It means that independent parties work together to offer customers a complete package. Each concentrating on their own competencies, the organizations are focused on achieving the most efficient and effective cooperation, enhancing both customer value and the value of the individual organizations. The network orientation is firmly secured in the fabric of the supplying parties. Because customer relationships are intensive, there are close bonds between customers mutually as well as between customers and sales staff. The strategy is to achieve straight-out win-win situations by matching specialist, total solutions with customers' individual requirements. This type of network organization appeals to the customers' collective, associated

The strategy is to achieve straight-out win-win situations by matching specialist, total solutions with customers' individual requirements

needs. This means, for example, that instead of selling a property insurance policy only, the supplying party anticipates a customer's total needs. For instance, in relation to a customer's home or property, a supplier may offer a total package of services, including insurance, security, garden maintenance and minor home maintenance. This can be done by tailoring the product and/or service to the customer's individual needs, presenting a total offer, enabled by different, independent suppliers.

The community concept seen on the Internet (groups of buyers that share the same interests or behaviour) has many of the aspects that are found in the network orientation. The customer feels connected to a certain label or community. This orientation also implies the possibility of mutual dependence and risk sharing between suppliers mutually and between suppliers and customers. (See Table 2.7.)

The desired orientation

The marketing orientation of the organization will determine how the organization uses available marketing instruments, how it deals with customers, and how it should be structured so as to achieve optimal results. Even though the current opinion may favour customer and network-oriented organizations, there are no firm rules to support this view. More likely, the optimal orientation is the one that creates optimal harmony between organization form, control systems and market orientation. It is in this combination that, ultimately, the potential lies for achieving maximum results. To be able to attain this balance, the organization must have a real understanding of its possibilities as an

Table 2.7   *Application of marketing instruments with network orientation*

Marketing instruments	Application
Product	Largely determined by the specific wishes and criteria of individual customers
Price	Determined in mutual consultation, often on the basis of risk sharing or risk participation (and revenue sharing). The partnership principle is part of the business concept and often incorporated in the other business processes
Place	Individually determined. Often, there is direct contact between the parties. The factor 'place' is no longer an issue
Promotion	On an individual basis, mostly through personal contact or an existing relations network
General	The network orientation assumes a high level of heterogeneousness in customer demand (individual wishes), mostly due to highly dynamic markets. Fast-changing and often far-reaching market changes inspire close cooperation between parties as a condition of survival. Participation in each other's business models and possibly risk sharing are consequential to the situation and the close relationships between parties concerned

organization, of the selection process that is to lead to the orientation that suits it the best, and, finally, of the potential role and influence of the Internet in the process.

The shift from an internally-focused, or inward-looking, orientation, focusing on production and transaction to a customer – or outward-looking – orientation is outlined in Figure 2.2. The results of the transition are reflected in increased levels of interactivity between buyer and seller, more personal communication, and greater ability to respond to more personal, individual needs. Taking this development a step further, the network orientation emerges, focusing on individual needs and requirements, on the basis of mutual interest participation. For a network orientation to be successful, it requires a high level of specialization and companies prepared to work together. Research shows that the choice of orientation is determined by several factors:

● the power of the internal organization;

Figure 2.2   *Marketing orientations*

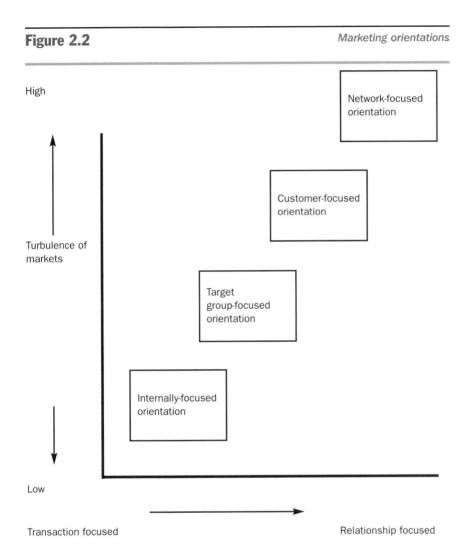

Source: Molenaar, C.N.A. (1997) *New Marketing*, Kluwer Publications, Deventer, p. 67
The marketing orientations show the correlation between the use of information technology and marketing focus; transaction focused versus relationship focused

- the dynamics of the market (turbulency);
- consistency of demand;
- scope for product individualization;
- added value of interaction and personal contacts.

Summary

An organization's marketing orientation to a large extent sets the framework for its commercial policy. Basically, a marketing orientation reflects the organization's constraints. Organizational structure, culture, decision-making processes, and the nature and possibilities of the infrastructures and technical instruments (e.g. ICT) determine the limit conditions. Together, these factors set the framework for the marketing orientation and the use of marketing instruments. Organizations that are internally oriented operate via distribution channels and are primarily sales focused: the transaction is the objective. It is in the product that they want to set themselves apart.

A target group oriented company wants to appeal to and empathize with a certain target group. The transaction is not the sole objective; interacting with the target group is just as important. In a customer-oriented organization, account management will be more intensive. Customer values are considered important, and the principle of providing 'lifetime value' is highly esteemed. The relationship is more important than once-only transactions. In a network orientation, the attention centres not only on the relationship with the customer. The organization has a keen eye for mutual interests, and the partners frequently participate in each other's business processes ('just in time management'). The importance of ICT increases where the customer becomes more and more the focal point, and the relationship more and more the engine of the commercial process. Consequently, the way organizations use the Internet will differ a great deal, depending on their marketing orientation. The Internet can be used to support and enhance that orientation; on the other hand, the direct customer contacts that are generated by Internet communication can lie at the basis of a change of orientation.

Which orientation works best for an organization largely depends on factors such as the desire to change, the dynamism of the market, consistency of demand, and the anticipated impact of technology. A network orientation or a customer-focused orientation is not necessarily always best. What matters is that a conscious choice is made with regard to the marketing orientation, and that an optimal balance is created within the organization's business processes and structures. This balance, obtained by harmonizing the processes and structures on the basis of the chosen orientation, ultimately decides the organization's success, its resilience and its responsiveness. The process of making these choices must be carefully thought through, and the possibilities offered by the Internet should be part of that analysis.

Notes

4 Molenaar, C.N.A., '*Onderzoek onder 1100 marketeers in Nederland naar de invloed van informatietechnologie op marketing*' (Research conducted among 1,000 marketeers in the Netherlands to establish the influence of information technology on marketing). Conducted in 1994, this survey provided the basis for a dissertation on the use of information technology in marketing, entitled 'New Marketing'.

5 Molenaar, C.N.A. (1997) *New Marketing, Applications of Information Technology in Marketing*, Kluwer Business Information, p. 67.

6 Tracy, M. and Wiersema, F. (1994) *Discipline of Market Leaders*, Addison-Wesley.

3

■■■■■■■■■■■■■■■

What the Internet can and can't do

If the interest of the customer prevailed over self-interest, profit figures would not be such a source of pride.

The Internet is a medium that is rapidly changing our lives, both at home and at work. It enables us to contact anyone, anywhere in the world, at any time of the day. It also enables us to use the facilities of suppliers anywhere in the world, and to provide information, in every possible manner, to any place and anyone in the world. As such, the Internet has developed to become a new infrastructure for information provision and communication between individuals, companies and government institutions.

It is precisely this infrastructure function of the Internet that lies at the basis of many changes that are unfolding around us every day. Eliminating restrictions of time, knowledge and connections, the Internet provides the basis for new relationships between individuals, organizations and governments.

Changes

With the benefit of hindsight, it makes sense to suggest that the existing organizational structures of businesses, government institutions and nations were long overdue for a change. After all, these structures were established in an era when sophisticated communication technologies such as the Internet were unthinkable. Many of the boundaries between nations were established in the 18th and 19th centuries, and based – the Balkans aside – on former power structures and frontiers that could be physically protected from intruders. Over the centuries, many of these power structures have changed dramatically, both in political and military terms. What were defensible frontiers in the past no longer provide protection today. Geographic divides, such as the Strait of Gibraltar, the Alps[7] and the seas, are no longer the important natural defence lines they once were. The balance of power within nations themselves has changed dramatically. Monarchies have had to relinquish many of their earlier powers, peoples have been emancipated, and democratic rule is established in most countries. Seen from a larger perspective, it is perhaps understandable why, under the pressure of these developments, the logic and value of many of our old-world structures and institutes are increasingly under siege.

The above developments are being stimulated and augmented by the Internet. The philosophy behind our import duty systems, for example, is rapidly being eroded by the new policy of free traffic of persons and goods (EU), the ability of individuals to purchase goods anywhere in the world via the Internet, and the public availability of information from a large array of highly advanced sources. Differences between tax regimes encourage people to seek financial advantage elsewhere. There is a veritable brain drain of specialists who are offered better working conditions abroad. Pensioners are drawn to more favourable tax climates, and asylum seekers are attracted by the promise of prosperity and safety in other countries. Large flows of people are moving from one place to another, inspired by different needs, hopes and expectations. The options governments have to exercise influence on these developments are limited.

The impact of the Internet, more specifically, is associated with the new freedom of information. Today's immigrants are able to maintain close relations with their home country, not only by being able to communicate personally with relatives and friends but also by being able to receive up-to-date news directly from on-line Internet news services. Share prices and investment value can be monitored on-line, and relevant sources can be consulted at any time. All these facilities are independent of place, enabling people to move about while being able to access all the local information they require. In essence, a virtual world is being created, in which the physical location is separated from the virtual location. It is this segregation that lies at the basis of the potential of the Internet, and that should guide organizations in developing their production and marketing strategies in years to come.

> **The impact of the Internet, more specifically, is associated with the new freedom of information**

Functions of the Internet

The Internet can play many different roles. Some people will use it only to send and receive e-mail, whereas others may depend on it to supply them with up-to-date information on financial developments, such as share prices. Often, the Internet will be used for buying, ordering or using goods and/or services on-line. In each case people are using new technological applications, facilitated by the Internet. The Internet creates possibilities for commerce and communication by enabling new forms of contact between suppliers and users. The supplier prepares information and offers new commercial products, but it is the consumer who decides whether – and when – he wants to use those products.

Whether or not there is a demand for a certain product or service can be measured on the basis of the number of site visits (hits) and sales effected. This immediate interaction between supplier and receiver is a characteristic feature of the Internet, and it has inspired many changes in industry. The supplier can communicate directly with (potential) consumers, and in that way receives first-hand information on what buyers are looking for. Former restrictions such as time, place, supply and language are no longer important. Given these developments, many companies are now having to decide what to offer on the Internet, why they should offer it, and how the Internet will affect their business processes.

The functions of the Internet cover four main areas of application:

● information function;
● communication function;
● transaction function;
● infrastructure function.

Note that the above grouping in four does not imply that we are dealing with four functions that are entirely separate. The opposite is true: each of the four functions influences the others, and in many cases all converge. This makes it difficult to isolate developments that are taking place in any specific function, and it also confuses people's perception of the possibilities of the Internet. For this reason, there is no clear understanding yet of the far-reaching consequences of the Internet and the changes it has brought about. It is all the more important, therefore, that we take a rational approach to defining the various functions of the Internet and its opportunities for industry.

Information function

'Knowing it all at the click of a mouse.' Life can be as simple as that. 'There's no reason to be ignorant any more.' Statements along these lines are indicative of the information function of the Internet, fulfilling an important need in enabling people to search and use information on any subject. It is this need that organizations must respond to. The Internet has given organizations an instrument that enables them to provide information cheaply, simply and timely. The Internet, furthermore, is a medium that makes life easier for consumers more than it accommodates suppliers. The classic or traditional media, e.g. newspapers, television commercials, etc., are supply-driven. The supplier determines what information is to be supplied and how. In addition, the information can be targeted directly by using a medium such as printed advertising. Again, the information supplier decides what information is supplied, and in what manner. Much time and attention is invested to ensure that the message is conveyed in a certain manner. The receiver's part is passive – he can only accept the information, and draw his own conclusions, by no means an easy task, even for the educated consumer. The supplier controls the information provision, and it is thus the supply that rules the demand. The supplier can check the effectiveness of the advertising message – the information provision – on the basis of market share or sales figures. In any event, it is the supplier that determines which information is supplied, and when it is supplied.

The Internet has changed the traditional supply-driven information structure (information pushing) by enabling the consumer to determine how, when and in what manner they wish to receive the required information. The consumer can gather the required information via a medium that is controlled by the supplier, e.g. an advertisement or homepage on the Internet. In that case, the consumer knows that the information provided is subjective. However, the Internet also provides other channels for obtaining the required information. For example, the consumer can consult the Web sites of information providers such as Nielsen or Forrester, use search engines to find other relevant information sources, or join newsgroups and chat rooms. Whichever channel they choose, the information received is no longer supplier controlled. Instead, it is the result of a conscious search, initiated by the consumer, for objective information, so as to enable objective choices to be made. The information supplier no longer controls or directs the process. As the supplier, you are dependent on other sources of information. Thus, the challenge on the supplier's part is to find new ways of exercising control over the process. For this, you have the following options:

- *Developing your own Web site.* In addition to supplying standard product information, you can provide other information and include links to relevant sources.

- *Setting up newsgroups or participating actively in newsgroups and chat rooms.* The supplier need not disclose that they are the initiator of the site. Participation in e-communities enables the supplier to keep a close finger on market developments and monitor consumer trends. The information released via such channels can be influenced by participating actively in chat room communities, which enables the supplier to contribute positive news where sessions may take a negative turn.

An appealing site can help attract and retain regular visitors

Drawing customers

Creating an attractive site that assures a high level of stickiness can be effective in order to exercise influence on the information provision process. An appealing site can help attract and retain regular visitors. By including relevant links, the site owner can point the way to other sources of information, thus providing a valuable additional service. Proposing other links also allows the information provider to exercise a certain (limited) control over the information, by making sure that only those links that provide positive information are included. If a site already contains links on the same topic, visitors will be inclined not to search any further. To achieve this, however, the following conditions are important:

- the site must be attractive and sufficiently interesting for others to want to be linked to it;

- the Web site owner must be perceived as a reliable source of information, both by visitors and by partners (other links);

- the site must be magnetic enough to attract visitors in the first place. At this point, market leaders and companies that sell strong brands are in a better position than local parties or unknown, smaller suppliers.

Web site information will relate in the first instance to the goods and/or services supplied, as well as reflecting visitors' expectations. If you visit the Omo site, for example, you expect to find information on Omo products, advice or washing instructions, and possibly retail outlets. You would not, for example, expect to read about Unilever. Unilever could, nevertheless, be mentioned on the site to enhance brand status. Most visitors will not quickly establish a link between Omo products and their manufacturer, Unilever. Rather, the visitor would be looking for product information and instructions for use. They might possibly look for logical combinations, or perhaps require advice on stain removal or washing instructions. For this site to offer, say, travel arrangements would not make sense.

Besides general product information, other information may be provided on behalf of specific groups. A corporate Web site may provide information on share prices, the organization, and the chief executive officer (CEO).

In brief, the supplier's information provision will focus on:

- products and services;
- the corporation or organization;
- related information, e.g. suppliers, sales outlets and service advice.

Communication function

The communication function of the Internet enables communication to take place between organizations and consumers, between individuals (private and professional), and general communication. Essentially, each of these communication forms is possible because the Internet enables direct communication between and with any parties. The Internet is essentially a facilitative technology, enabling communication via the following routes:

- e-mail;
- responding to Web site information;
- chat rooms;
- newsgroups;
- newsletters.

Each of these is facilitated by the Internet. Which form of communication is used will be determined, to an extent, by the communication function(s) offered by the organization. This may be via an e-mail address for responding to specific information or special offers, or an on-line chat service to enable visitors to communicate with the management or with anyone else, possibly a celebrity. The various forms of Internet communication are the result of consumers' wishes to exchange views on a specific product or organization. An example is the site of the Aldi fan club in Germany. This Internet community was set up by people who had a desire to share their appreciation of the Aldi chain stores with others by communicating about Aldi in newsgroups and chat rooms (Klaus Fischer's Web site). It seems that the Aldi concern had no direct involvement in the fan club. Nevertheless, the company stands to benefit from the initiative in terms of image building. Naturally, organizations might take such initiatives themselves, and possibly even lend direction to them, provided that this is not conspicuous.

The above is an example of how organizations can be confronted with customer contacts that transcend their own sphere of influence. Of course, this happens in the real world as well. People meet socially and share certain experiences. However, because the Internet has far greater reach, the impact of such contacts is potentially far greater too, both positively and negatively. To exercise some degree of influence in this process, organizations may initiate and guide activities in this area. Possibly the simplest way to do this is via chat rooms and other such communication groups. Amazon.com aims to stimulate customers' reactions by asking them to give their opinions about books or other products. Shopping sites such as www.download.com enable consumers to communicate their opinion on certain products. The information is then used to convince consumers that they are buying a good product (reducing customer insecurity). The options are numerous, as are the possibilities for lending positive direction. Whichever route is chosen, the Internet provides suppliers with an excellent, cost-effective medium for gathering first-hand information on their products and organization, comparable to the results of traditional market surveys.

The options which the Internet offers for direct and interactive communication set the framework for the communication form and the relationship between sender and receiver. Communication can take place in any of the following ways:

- between an organization and its customers;
- via direct communication;

- via message traffic.

Between organizations and their customers

This type of communication can be conducted by e-mail (reply button), enabling customers to ask questions or voice complaints. Customers may be invited to subscribe to newsletters or may receive updates on specific developments. With this form of communication, the sender guides the process. The innovative element is that it is the receiver who actually requests communication. This is essentially different from mass communication (the receiver is confronted with the supplier's communication, like it or not) and even from direct mail (often unsolicited, always sent when it suits the organization).

Direct contact

This form of communication takes place at the receiver's request. The individuals involved can chat with other individuals or a select company, either via a special chat column or by using a 'call me back' or 'call me now' function on the Web site. The information requester controls the communication process, at a time and in a way that is convenient for them. The so-called chat rooms, where people can participate in open chat groups, enable a similar form of communication. Here, too, the information receiver decides how and when to participate in the information exchange, and when to end it.

Message traffic

The third option is where the communication takes place off-line. This form of communication differs in that there is a delay between the moment of sending and the moment of receiving the message. This occurs, for instance, with e-mail and voice mail. The voice mail message is spoken in at a time that suits the sender and heard when it is convenient to the receiver. This type of communication is suitable for both private and business uses, provided that the relationship between the sender and the receiver is clearly defined. Due to its intrusive character, voice mail is not a suitable medium for commercial messages. Because there is a high risk of

Due to its intrusive character, voice mail is not a suitable medium for commercial messages

annoying the receiver, the chance of achieving any commercial success is limited. E-mail, too, is a form of delayed communication, but a far less intrusive one. Again, there is a delay in communication between the moment of sending and the moment of receiving. However, in this case there is no intrusion but instead a 'renewed experience' of the communication moment. Being less intrusive than voice mail, e-mail communication can be a suitable medium for certain commercial purposes.

With e-mail, a one-to-one message is sent to a certain individual or an e-mail address. The e-mail function enables the user to send messages directly to individual people or organizations. In addition, the user may subscribe to newsgroups or newsletters. The user takes the initiative to communicate with others on a specific subject. With this form of communication, the function of the information is more important than the interactive process.

Specific features

Internet communication has a number of features that are specifically associated with this form of communication, i.e.:

- communication is time-independent;
- communication is direct;
- author and sender are the same person;
- communication is objective and uniform.

Communication is time-independent

The Internet is a low-threshold communication medium, enabling different forms of contact. It is not necessary to decide beforehand with whom one wants to communicate. Logging on to the net is sufficient. The Internet has, not entirely surprisingly, the same functionalities as the telephone. It enables people to communicate whenever it is convenient – that is, when it is convenient for one party to send a message, and for the other to read it. This makes it a unique communication medium, since most other forms of communication require at least one party to respond to a communication at a time that may not suit them. A reply phone call is made when it suits the receiver of the original message, and direct mail is sent at a time when it is convenient to the sender. In theory, one can, of course, postpone reading a letter received by post, but this is not usually what happens. A letter received by post is more compelling than an e-mail message; posted letters are usually read as soon as the addressee receives them. Organizations in fact rely on this habit in timing their direct mail actions, ensuring that the communication is sent – or at least likely to be received – at the end of the week. An e-mail message is more likely to be left waiting in the recipient's in-box.

Communication is direct

E-mail communications are generally more informal than fax messages or letters. A letter is usually written with attention to detail: correct salutation, the right wording to convey the message, presentable layout, no typing errors, appropriate style, etc. A letter says a great deal about its sender, not just in terms of its contents but also in terms of presentation, including the type of envelope used. E-mail communication seems to have dispensed with much of this protocol. The language used is often informal, salutations – if any are used at all – are always brief, and the message quite direct. There is no padding, no social chat, no ice breaking: the message is tight and to the point. Because the value of e-mail is not in the form but in its practical convenience as a communication tool, messages are often brief and concise. Moreover, very little attention is paid to the traditional rules of form and style. Typing errors, flawed grammar, stylistic errors, it all happens, and nobody is concerned about it.

Direct contact, topicality and the content of the message are what counts with e-mail. The reply button is a practical function for avoiding having to enter address details when responding to a message. This function not only saves time but also eliminates the chance of error. Another advantage is that it returns the original message with the response message, which can be especially useful where there has been a considerable delay between sending and replying.

E-mail users may forward any number of e-mail messages in any one day, often using the cc function, and often impulsively. As a result, they may not remember every message they have sent, or the precise contents. The reply button eliminates that problem. The automatic save function for incoming e-mail addresses is another practical function that ensures that addresses are always kept at hand. The chance of a typing error is eliminated, and forgetting e-mail addresses is not a problem any more.

The functions described above, and the advantage of e-mail communication in comparison with traditional correspondence, has resulted in intensive use of e-mail. This has improved the quality of communication, since e-mail messages are generally experienced as a more personal and direct form of communication. The moment of reading is experienced as a moment of personal contact, perhaps of recognition, joy or sadness. Whatever the occasion, the communication is a personal moment for the receiver, and this is seen as one of the important benefits of e-mail.

Author and sender are the same person

Business letters are usually not prepared and written by the same person. In most cases, they are prepared and typed by others, while the 'author' merely signs their name. This separation of duties is standard procedure in business communications. In private correspondence, a handwritten letter – however difficult to read – is still regarded as a personal form of communication. The receiver knows that the person who sent the letter also wrote it. A handwritten letter is always a personal message from one individual to another. With a printed letter, this personal character is largely lost, since it could have been typed by anyone.

With a business letter, the author may have nothing to do with the person who is responsible for its contents. If the author does happen to be personally responsible for the information in the letter, they will sign it by hand. A personal signature is always written in real ink. For the same reason, mail-order companies often print a signature at the bottom of standard cover letters in blue ink, to imitate the effect of a personal signature. What this means to say is that the author is *personally* responsible for the information provided, and that they wanted to communicate *personally* with the addressee.

E-mail dispenses with all these formalities. An e-mail message is directed immediately to the individual concerned, and addressed to their personal e-mail box. The sender knows that the addressee will open and read the message personally. With the reply button, the response is just as personal and effective, and leaves no doubt that a particular message has been answered. So doing, the e-mail function has created a new infrastructure for direct personal communication, whereby there is no need for the 'substitute signature' protocol. At the same time, it is important that the personal character of e-mail is used wisely. It must never be abused, as in it lies the great strength of e-mail. This explains why most e-mail users resent receiving commercial e-mail and unsolicited e-mail (spamming). Spamming trespasses on the personal and direct character of the medium. The fact that the communication is personal explains why e-mail users are more tolerant of linguistic imperfections such as typing errors, poor stylistics or grammatical mistakes. What matters most with e-mail is the personal communication, not the form.

Spamming trespasses on the personal and direct character of the medium

Communication is objective and uniform

Communication is often disrupted by emotions, poor listening skills, or personal interpretation. The 'noise' this creates accounts for much miscommunication between individuals and even between companies. Most of us routinely assume that a message says only what it says, without realizing that it might have had some colour added by the messenger, or that it may be subject to the receiver's personal interpretation. A communication may have been coloured knowingly to 'take out the sting', or for political reasons. Or else to enhance the role of the individuals concerned, or, conversely, to play down their part. The receiver will place the message within the framework of his own perception and understanding. This means that the receiver must be able to record, organize and process the message in their mind.

The word 'fire', for example, might evoke different associations in a fire fighter than it would, say, in the minds of an insurance broker, the occupant of a dwelling, or the property owner. In each case the message 'fire' will be processed and interpreted in accordance with the potential personal impact of the message on its recipient. Cultural background could play a role too. How can we be sure, for instance, that the message 'fire' would be interpreted in the same way in the Netherlands as it would in, say, America, China or India? Such thoughts may seem far-fetched, yet for those who use the Internet on a global scale they matter.

The uniformity of the communication is essential for objective judgement and decision making, as it is this basis for conclusions and decisions that could have important implications for an organization, for the individuals in that organization, and possibly for its customers. Traditionally, organizations have had formal communication lines and informal ones. The proverbial corridors have always been considered to be a more reliable source of information than the official channels. The latter tend to be more affected by the 'noise' that comes with personal interpretation, often for political reasons. The information transferred in the corridors is passed on in a much simpler way, and is less charged by personal emotion. Often, the message is simply passed on from one person to another without any comment. Personal notes are usually provided separately, and in more flowery tones. The informal style of communication makes it easier for the recipient to extract the objective contents from any subjective elements added by the messenger, and thus enables a more objective judgement.

If a company uses e-mail for internal information provision (communication), it is important that subjective and objective elements are kept separate. The Internet appears to impart that separation almost by nature. Messages can be passed on by simply using the 'forward' function, possibly adding an e-mail message or a brief personal comment. The latter is probably not even necessary, since the receiver reads a strictly objective message, which is entirely theirs to interpret, with or without a subjective e-mail comment.

This is the philosophy underlying the 'cc' function. The original message is sent to the addressee, and copies are sent to any number of others using the 'cc' button. Everyone else receives the same message as the addressee, without any noise, subjective comments or personal interpretation. Therefore, the information is more objective, and thus provides a better basis for decisions to be made.

The importance of e-mail as a communication medium was underscored by a survey conducted by Pew Internet & American Life Project in June 2000. The results of the survey confirmed that the Internet has not led to the social isolation feared by many. The survey revealed that Internet users generally felt that e-mail communication had improved their relationships, and that they had more frequent contact with friends and acquaintances than before (see Table 3.1). The improvement was felt by women in particular.

Table 3.1 *Effect of e-mail use*

Effect of e-mail use	Percentage surveyed
Better ties with the family	55%
Better contact with friends	66%
More frequent contact with friends	60%

Source: Pew Internet & American Life Project, June 2000

Transaction function

Many people tend to associate the Internet with e-commerce. In fact, what they are talking about is the transaction function of the Internet. This transaction function enables goods and services to be purchased using the Internet as the transaction medium. A unique feature of this function is the electronic distribution facility. The sales process no longer requires a physical infrastructure, e.g. telephone or direct mail, nor does it require the physical presence of the goods or the traditional sales entourage of a retail network, sales person or representative. The electronic distribution channel enables sales to be registered directly, and facilitates the buying process. A new form of communication is created, enabling a new form of direct registration. Essentially, the electronic channel, i.e. the Internet, is used as an infrastructure, and the specific possibilities of the Internet are used, as much as possible, in the sales process. However, because our attention tends to focus on the function described above, we are at risk of creating a false picture of the possibilities of the Internet and the changes it has brought. The functions described earlier already made this clear, but the transaction function of the Internet has also given rise to misconceptions.

The transaction function is perceived as a commercial process similar to those seen in the traditional, real world. The most characteristic aspect of these processes is that the supplier tries to persuade potential customers with commercials (usually product focused), advertisements (usually transaction focused) and direct mail, or other relationship-focused media. The potential customer in the real world is seduced by a spectrum of sales promotions, e.g. billboards, special offers, shop displays and product presentations. The whole process serves to persuade the customer to visit a certain retail outlet, where, once trapped, he must then be lured into buying the product. Essentially, each of these steps forms part of a process that begins by drawing the consumer's attention, raising their interest, motivating them, and, finally, stimulating them to buy (the AIDA rule). Advertising is aimed at creating traffic (people must come to the shop), generating product recognition (top of mind position), and encouraging a transaction (sales promotion). Many companies have attempted to follow the same route in generating Internet sales, only to find that the traditional strategies simply do not work on the World Wide Web.

Traditional strategies simply do not work on the World Wide Web

Attracting potential customers to your Web site is the first obstacle. Guiding them and retaining them as visitors is the second. The final obstacle is persuading visitors to buy your product. Taking a closer look at each of the steps, a number of problems surface that are typically associated with the Internet.

Persuading people to visit your site

Persuading people to visit your site means competing with millions of other sites. How are your potential visitors to know which supplier offers them the best deal? Internet businesses have tried to take this hurdle by using traditional advertising campaigns, but this has proven to be an expensive affair, as well as posing a number of restrictions in terms of reaching the markets companies want to do business with. The global character of the Internet, and the large number of suppliers that are active in similar fields on the Internet, are factors that do not appear to harmonize with the traditional approach to drawing customers, and persuading them to visit an Internet site. The costly advertising efforts of many companies that are active on the Internet have painfully demonstrated the deficiency of this approach. Amazon.com, one of the most successful Internet companies, has invested hundreds of millions of dollars in Internet marketing. An Internet fashion store, called boo.com, was bankrupted because of its inability to attract sufficient visitors and trade, despite huge marketing budgets. Many other Internet companies are bound to experience the pitfalls of trying to attract enough visitors to generate trade on the Internet.

In addition to using the traditional media, the Internet offers more specific possibilities for attracting visitors:

- via search engines, whereby it is important to secure a place somewhere at the top of a 'hit list', since some 70% of visits guided by search engines are made to the Web sites of the first ten suppliers listed in a selection (first page), while 15% of visits are made to suppliers listed on the second page, and the remaining 15% to other suppliers;

- via click-throughs, e.g. banners and icons. For this, an advertisement is placed on Web pages that are visited frequently, e.g. search engines, ISPs and busy sites belonging to other suppliers (portals and communities);

- via other more popular suppliers. This is the philosophy behind affiliate marketing – hitching on the backs of other suppliers of more established repute, and offering complementary products that do not evoke negative associations with the customer. An example of this is Amazon.com. If the visitor uses a search engine to scan the Web on a specific term, Amazon.com will at the same time present a selection of book titles. This is a good example of how search engine data that correspond with visitors' interests can be used for commercial purposes. The (potential) consumer initiates the information produced by the search engine, and the owner of the site receives a commission from Amazon for actual sales booked. This form of affiliate marketing is enabled by the possibilities of the Internet in linking demand and supply. Not surprisingly, it was Amazon.com – the forerunner of Internet commerce – which first introduced the concept.

Points to watch when buying goods on the Internet

Consequential to their ability to sell physical products or services on the Internet, many suppliers have discovered the physical problems associated with Internet sales. After all, selling is one thing, but packaging and dispatching orders is quite another. Timely gathering and dispatching of Internet orders is a challenge. The annual delivery problems of Internet suppliers around Christmas time have demonstrated, time after time, that many suppliers have yet to come to grips with some serious bottlenecks. And even if the basic logistics are under control, there are yet other problems to be solved: who will ship the goods, when, and how fast should this be done? Many Dutch Internet customers have been punished for their frugality by choosing sea freight delivery. Articles, bought in seconds, have taken months to be delivered to their buyers. Cheap transport is often slow transport.

Finally, there are several other, less spectacular but equally important problems to be solved. Who takes delivery of the goods? Many people enjoy Internet shopping because of its convenience. Often, however, the customer will not be at home to accept the goods. So, how are they to collect them? If this has to be done from a distribution centre, the overriding advantage of the Internet, in comparison to regular shopping, instantly evaporates. Another problem, noted by many financial institutions, is the question of payment. How reliable are the facilities for payment offered by Internet businesses? How do suppliers collect their money, and how can buyers be sure that the right amount is debited from their account? These are all issues that are frequently raised in discussions on Internet commerce. To deal adequately with them, organizations must take a fresh look at their marketing and communication processes. Possibly, they may need to adjust their internal organizational structures to the specific requirements of Internet commerce, as well as stimulating customer bonding and working consistently on gaining and retaining customer trust.

Despite the problems and changes outlined, the transaction function of the Internet is set to become increasingly important, for a number of reasons:

- The convenience of Internet shopping will eventually beat the teething problems described above. Customers who really want to shop on the Internet will be prepared to pay for it, and suppliers will learn to deal with the problems described.

- The convenience of shopping with suppliers located all over the world will outweigh loyalty to local shops. As shopping trends become global, buying from foreign suppliers will be an entrenched element in consumer behaviour. This is already happening with Amazon.com's book sales.

- Suppliers will be increasingly aware that selling on the Internet, with the traditional know-how and resources, is a non-starter, and that shopping on the Internet is a consumer-initiated business, combining information gathering, communication and sales in a single process. Finalizing the transaction, there and then, reflects the needs of consumers in a fast-moving world.

- Not all sales concern physical products. The sale of services and 'virtual' products is on the increase, notably because the limitations of the Internet do not play a role there. Non-physical sales include downloads such as documents, letters, news and software. Because there are no physical impediments, 'the moment of buying is the moment of delivery', in the same way that sales are conducted in the real world. Acceptance of this way of buying supports acceptance of the concept of Internet shopping generally, which in turn will accelerate the adoption of other Internet possibilities.

Organizations and suppliers will, of course, cite many other reasons why the Internet is an excellent medium for selling goods and services. However, it is clear that the strength of the Internet lies in its function as a buying medium. The Internet provides a low-threshold shopping medium that people can use privately, either in the workplace or at home. The Internet is particularly effective in facilitating the buying process, in any way that is convenient to the customer. At the end of the day, it is the buyer who will decide the future of the Internet as a transaction medium.

> **The Internet is particularly effective in facilitating the buying process, in any way that is convenient to the customer**

Infrastructure function

The fourth Internet function is infrastructure. During the 1980s and early 1990s computer networks became an increasingly popular technology for providing an infrastructure for internal and external electronic communication in companies. The technology of connecting different computer systems enabled data (files) to be sent to different computers. This meant that organizations no longer had to use the same networks, software and computer systems to be connected. Cisco (www.cisco.com) played a pioneering role in developing computer network technology. Its beginnings read like a fairy tale. Two professionals in love,[8] Sandra Lerner of Stanford University Business School and Leonard Bosack of the computer science department of Stanford University, wanted to send each other notes at work but couldn't because their computer systems were different. Low spirits prevailed until Leonard Bosack patched together a box (router) that made it possible to convert outgoing messages to match the protocol of the receiving computer. The success of Bosack's homemade technology quickly outgrew the capacity of his workplace. Stanford University, however, was not interested in co-financing any such new developments, and thus a new organization was born (Cisco is an abbreviation of San Francisco). Using their bedroom, garage and living room for a workshop, the couple built an organization that in 2000 had the largest market capitalization in the world. And although they are no longer associated with the company or with each other, the couple's brainchild has forever changed the world of computer technology.

Initially, computer networks were mainly designed for internal use in the organization (LAN). Later, however, it also became possible to connect an organization's LAN to computers outside the organization (WAN). In the last tier, a technology was created that enabled different systems to be connected, as long as the data transport matched very specific rules and protocols. The process of creating uniformity and order in the protocols for electronic data interchange was well under way by the late 1980s. Then came the Internet.

The Internet emerged as a universal platform for data transfer, based on the use of a standard protocol (FTP, file transfer protocol). Acceptance of the Internet as the new standard rapidly gained ground when the World Wide Web was introduced, enabling individual servers to act as network hosts. This hosting service enabled individual computer users to access the Internet directly, lowering the data transfer threshold. The flight which the Internet has taken since is common knowledge. Many suppliers saw opportunities, and created facilities for providing Internet access, data transport and new services and commercial activities. The data network became a user network, and we are today close to witnessing the introduction of a multi-device platform, enabling access to all services currently provided through the various media: computer, mobile phone or personal digital assistant (PDA). As such, the Internet has become the new infrastructure for a range of applications, services and facilities.

Due to this infrastructure function, the future Internet user will be unaware of whether the data are transmitted by telephone, cable, point-to-point connection or via the Internet itself. Likewise, as speech, data and image transmission converge, a different medium can be selected in each case. The Internet as an infrastructure is not specifically interesting to end users. The technical experts will simply choose the infrastructure that best suits the specific requirements and criteria of the situation. The use of the Internet for a broad spectrum of applications will lead to complete integration of the Internet in our private and professional lives. Just as the cable net and the telephone system are no longer an issue, the Internet will be an established infrastructure technology, several years from now. Users will choose their hosting service or ISP in the same way that they now choose a cable service provider, an energy supplier, or a telecoms operator. By that time, the Internet infrastructure will be completely detached from the applications and services it enables, yet this is a development that is not unique to the Internet.

Acceptance problems and potential conflicts

The problems associated with the use of the Internet as a distribution medium can be grouped as follows:

- insecurity regarding payment: *security conflict*;
- unfamiliarity with logistics: *transaction handling conflict*;
- lack of clarity in legislation: *legal conflict*;
- lack of clarity concerning customer relationships: *buying conflict*.

Security conflict

Conflicts that belong in this group are frequently seen as an impediment to the further development of the Internet. This is why initiatives are undertaken in every related area to solve or minimize this type of conflict. Examples include the so-called 'secured servers', which use access codes, passwords and other forms of protection to enable customers to be approached more directly and more safely. Offering a credit card payment facility also stimulates acceptance of the transaction medium. Because credit card payments must be verified, there is additional security, and the payment must also be guaranteed by the credit card company on behalf of the seller. Therefore, it is in the supplier's interest that the transaction is as safe and secure as possible, as well as in the credit company's interest. Furthermore, there are developments under way to increase security by so-called 'trusted third party' agreements, using signature checks to give the suppliers more security. There are also developments in the area of 'digital money', a system whereby a third party, e.g. a bank or other party, administers a guaranteed bank balance that is available via the digital media. Suppliers will accept payments effected with digital money on account of the fact that the third party provides the necessary security. Essentially, this is an advanced, very specific form of credit card payment, whereby recognition and identification do not occur by showing a credit card and signing a form. Instead, other forms of verification and security are used, such as a digital signature or a pin-code, combined with a password. The Internet market is in need of buyers who are happy to pay with digital money, and sellers who will accept it.

In anticipation of further general developments ir ˙ ˙
suppliers are making use of specific instruments to incre
This can be, for instance, by protecting and reserving certa

**The Internet market
is in need of buyers
who are happy to pay
with digital money,
and sellers who will
accept it**

Web site for authorized users only, in addition to publicly accessible pages. This is enabled by a protocol that verifies the personal data entered by the user, combining the user's home address data with credit card data, or issuing the user with a password. Suppliers who choose to authorize users directly will use home address data in conjunction with credit card information. Using credit card details, the supplier can establish the identity of the visitor, and finalize the financial transaction. Most suppliers selling products and services on the Internet use this system.

Using a combination of a passcode and a password, it is possible to lend access to a certain site, or to enable a transaction using postal communication, thus eliminating the insecurity factor. The visitor requesting access to a certain Web site receives the procedure and password by post, several days later. This at once provides the supplier with security as to the identity of the person requesting access. For the customer, it is reassuring to receive physical information in the form of a password or code, printed on old-fashioned paper. In the Netherlands, the Chamber of Commerce operates on that basis. Businesses can request to receive a copy of the trade register if they have been assigned a password. Once they have received their password, they can access the computer at the Chamber of Commerce and print out the required page themselves. Payment is effected by direct debit from their bank account. ABN-Amro is an organization that uses a system based on an off-line generated access code to enable customers to access its on-line investor Web site. The user receives a pin-code based calculator which enables them to access the site and to trade on-line. Despite all these provisions, there is no conclusive evidence yet that it is the payment factor that most stands in the way of acceptance of the Internet as a transaction medium.

Transaction handling conflict

Another potential area of conflict concerns the delivery of the products (logistics). Placing an order on-line is only part of the process. The goods must then be sorted, packaged and shipped. Each of these steps requires an efficient handling process and close cooperation with buyers. If the supplier chooses to handle the logistic process, he must keep sufficient products in stock (Internet buyers place orders quickly and expect quick delivery), and ensure that they are properly packed and shipped. All this results in extra costs, which are not always necessary with traditional forms of distribution, where the customer simply selects a product from the shelf and takes it home.

Alternatively, the supplier can outsource the physical handling of the order to a (logistical) specialist. This is a company that takes care of the necessary sorting and packaging of orders as part of its core business. This is often a more efficient approach than entrusting the logistical part of a transaction to an organization that handles that type of work merely as a sideline. Alternatively, it may be possible to have the goods delivered straight from the factory. However, this requires a delivery agreement with the manufacturer(s). Whether an organization chooses to handle or outsource delivery will reflect its marketing orientation. The specific problems associated with Internet sales require organizations to reconsider their role in the process, and the options for outsourcing certain tasks to partners. Of course, apart from the selection and packaging of goods, the order must still be delivered to the customer's address.

Obviously, there are specialists such as TNT and DHL that can do this, but the goods must be physically handed over to the customer. The USP (unique selling point) of Internet commerce is that goods can be ordered on-line any time, anywhere. However, delivering those goods at a particular time to, say, a shift worker, a two wage-earner household or a single household can be a problem. Thus, a facility must be available for orders to be parked at central delivery points with extended opening hours. Alternatively, the dwelling of the future must be designed to accommodate consumer deliveries. If goods are delivered to an address in an apartment building with a doorkeeper, they could be left in the custody of the doorkeeper. If there is no doorkeeper, extra mailboxes for delivery might be installed. Alternatively, cooperation with existing suppliers that already have extended opening hours, such as petrol stations or supermarket chains, could solve the problem. In Japan, for instance, there is a supermarket chain, 7-eleven, where customers can deliver and collect orders at any time. Another trend that seems to be on the increase is that the customer who places the order is asked to advise where and when they wish to have the goods delivered (at home, work, another address, a particular day or time of day). As the number of working couples and single households is steadily growing, there seems to be less logic in delivering orders to people's doorsteps as a matter of routine. Suppliers and logistical organizations should be well aware of this.

Legal conflict

There is a potential conflict in regard to legal matters associated with Internet commerce. Is the transaction subject to the laws of the customer's country or the supplier's? Where could either turn for legal protection and how can claims be ruled out? The legal structures in the sender's country or state as well as those in the receiver's are more and more being recognized as the ruling criteria. Thus, the receiver of a delivery could take legal action against a supplier on the basis of the laws prevailing in the receiver's country or state. As a result, suppliers must be aware of the implications of every applicable law in all countries where deliveries are made, and must be prepared for possible legal procedures. This aspect could have a negative bearing on international trade via the Internet, and possibly collide with the founding principles of free trade.

Buying conflict

This conflict has two elements:

- the customer is not sure where to buy;
- the customer is not sure why he should buy on the Internet.

The first element is a typical Internet problem. There are countless Web sites and suppliers, but who are they, and how do you find them? How this information is made known to the customer largely determines the supplier's success. The most logical routes to achieve this are:

- the traditional (mass) media, advertising a hyperlink within the message;
- target group-focused media, making customers and prospects aware of the site;
- links with other sites (hyperlinks on relevant sites);
- adverts on other sites (banners);
- ensuring that your organization gets a place on the first page of search engine listings, and that your site is shown as one of the 'hits' found;
- notifications in newsletters.

From there, it is up to the site owner to make sure the customer's attention is retained and to persuade first-time prospects to revisit their site.

People who are not sure why they should buy on the Internet are a different class

People who are not sure why they should buy on the Internet are a different class. There are no general guidelines or principles for persuading this group. Most customers have specific buying behaviour, either reflecting the needs of a certain group or individual requirements. To reach them, ingrained habits have to be changed in order for these people to be prepared to buy on the Internet. Such a change could be achieved only if the supplier is willing to meet their demand, and if Internet buying can satisfy that demand. There is a complex of factors that the supplier may choose to respond to. There is no doubt that people who buy on the Internet have specific, often individual reasons. To date, Internet suppliers have been unable to match the appeal of the traditional shopping structures. Apparently, the traditional retail industry offers advantages that are not so easily replaced:

- local presence and identifiability;
- physical presence of products and services;
- personal contact;
- instant delivery.

In order to compete with the above, Internet suppliers can and should focus on the following aspects:

- 24-hour shopping;
- better knowledge of the customer;
- price advantage;
- better sales support;
- sales direction;
- payment facility.

Note, however, that the race between Internet commerce and traditional retailing has only just begun, and, moreover, that this race is likely to develop very differently from one country to the next, and in the various industrial sectors.

Summary The Internet has four principal functions. The present discussion centres largely on the role of the Internet as a medium for commercial transactions (e-commerce). This function is probably the most spectacular from the consumer's point of view. It has important effects on how business is done, and in which way organizations are structured commercially. It is, however, only one of the functions of the Internet. The ability to send data and messages to computer users, anywhere in the world, no matter what computer they use, has galvanized the acceptance of the Internet's communication function. Similarly, organizations have been quick to catch on to the Internet as a medium for providing information relatively cheaply, and users quickly discovered the ease with which information can be gathered via the Internet, securing the future of the Internet as an information medium.

Combining the information and communication functions in relation to the transaction function has enabled a large degree of interactivity between users, organizations and customers. This interactivity snowballed a series of changes. Interactivity became the basis for customer contacts, information provision and communication. The Internet's potential for interactivity, over and above globalization and approachability, has, especially, been responsible for the huge impact on organizations and consumers that we see every day. The challenge for organizations today is to respond effectively to those developments, to interpret the consequences of the new interactivity accurately, and to implement the measures that will enable them to deal effectively with the consequences and opportunities of the Internet.

Notes

7 Ohmae, K. (1999) *The Invisible Continent,* Harper Business.

8 Bunnell, D. (2000) *Making the Cisco Connection, the Real Story behind the Real Internet Superpower*, John Wiley & Sons.

4

Getting the best out of the Internet

If everyone were the same, knowledge of the customer would be unnecessary.

The use of the Internet in commercial processes is leading organizations to re-evaluate their working procedures and structures. For the marketing function this entails an assessment of the consequences of the use of the Internet within each specific marketing orientation, since its use will need to facilitate the opportunities available for interaction and for customer contacts.

Organizations will need to reconsider their approach towards customers, and the consequences for marketing and the organization. In many cases it will probably not be feasible to implement changes throughout the entire organization; organizations will instead opt to use those Internet applications that can be implemented and managed by the organization. In fact, this involves reviewing opportunities available within the organization, and the implementation of only those functions that are compatible with the organization's marketing policy and chosen structure. Initially this may not seem to lead to many modifications and changes. Nonetheless, it will rapidly become apparent that the introduction of the Internet in effect constitutes a decision to implement a gradual process of change. Consequently the short-term impact on marketing and the organization will appear minimal. However, this does not imply that changes can be avoided, only that they can be postponed. Market trends will subsequently determine whether these changes are worthwhile. Irrespective of which system an organization chooses, it will be necessary to tailor the system to the market. Market dynamics will determine which choices are made and when they will need to be implemented.

A marketing model

The core issue confronting marketing is how to achieve sales and which products to sell. Everything depends on presenting the product to the right target group in the right way. Of the marketing tools already mentioned, two are used to determine the ins and outs (product and place) and two are used to shape the desired communication (price and product). This classification can be used to create a model (Figure 4.1) that can be used to determine strategy and to visualize changes. The model can also be used to link the specified functions of the Internet to price and distribution marketing tools.

In this model the product is located on the vertical axis. As mentioned previously, the product can be defined as encompassing physical, service (virtual) and perception elements. This represents the extent to which a product is tailored to the individual requirements of the customer, ranging from a standard product at the one extreme to a customized product at the other. The horizontal axis depicts the distribution form (the place), i.e. the extent to which a distribution channel is used – with, at the extremes, direct delivery and delivery by distributors. This results in a model with quadrants as shown in Figure 4.1.

The bottom left-hand quadrant represents the characteristic domain of traditional marketing, i.e. more or less standard products that are marketed in stores (the distribution channel). Advertising is effected by means of mass communication, and the products and services usually have a fixed price (which is specified in advance). All customers pay the same amount for these products and services, irrespective of their value to the individual. Organizations that supply their goods via a distribution channel will normally be internally oriented in character, since customer approach is determined only in the last link of the supply chain, i.e. in the store by the sales staff.

> **Advertising is effected by means of mass communication, and the products and services usually have a fixed price**

The top left-hand quadrant also uses traditional marketing techniques. Organizations in this quadrant have products or services for a specific target group (with a number of product and service variants), use a selective form of distribution, such as specialist stores, and relate their prices to the target group. However, in this quadrant

Figure 4.1   *Marketing model based on the product and distribution variants*

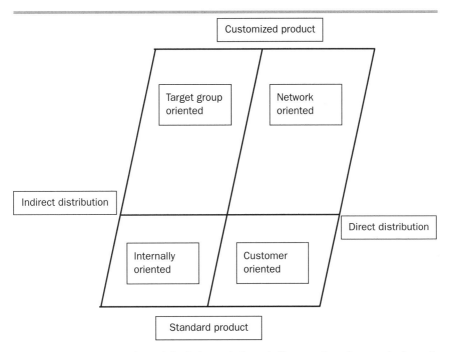

Marketing model based on product and distribution marketing tools. These two dimensions can also be used to determine the orientation of an organization.

the customer is offered a greater range of products and often has a different perception of the product. Service is becoming an increasingly important factor in this market approach. Organizations that provide products and services for a specific target group and choose their marketing tools on this basis are usually target group oriented in character.

In the bottom right-hand quadrant there is a different distribution form. The organization no longer delivers its products and services (solely) via distributors, but also directly to customers. For example, direct writers in the insurance world offer customers standard products that can be bought over the phone (and, nowadays, on the Internet). It should be noted that the products are standard products. These allow organizations to communicate in an unambiguous manner, often using mass communication. The only difference in this quadrant is that a different distribution channel is employed, i.e. direct contact. If organizations wish to take advantage of direct contact with customers (either by telephone, reply coupon, or the Internet) they can respond to the individual needs of the buyer by asking target questions or carrying out advanced analyses and submitting a 'customized offer' based on the information gathered. A customer-oriented approach is essential in achieving the desired level of contact with the customer.

The last quadrant is the top right-hand one. Organizations operating in this quadrant offer a wide variety of products based on consumer requirements. In fact, these organizations are perceived to offer customized products and services. Direct sales are the logical consequence of the need for direct contact with the customer. Businesses operating in this quadrant are usually network oriented. However, certain differences emerge when the model is analyzed further in terms of marketing and the use of the Internet. The differences are entirely dependent on which type of distribution is chosen and the extent to which a product has been customized or can be perceived as having been customized. These differences can serve as a basis for linking an orientation to the manner in which the Internet can best be used for that orientation. (See Table 4.1.)

Changes in the nature of the product

Technological developments are making it increasingly easy to manufacture many product variants. The use of product modules and optional components will result in a gradual decrease in the number of standard products and, in turn, an increase in the number of product modules and pseudo-customized products. This is represented by an upward shift in the model – a shift that has immediate consequences for the strategy adopted. How should customization be communicated? Interaction is essential to (pseudo) customization. In car sales, already there is interaction, for example in the showroom between the customer and the salesman. The customer specifies the vehicle according to their wishes. Once this procedure has been completed, the car is ordered and, in due course, delivered to the customer. As a consequence products are increasingly becoming individualized. The standard product is no longer the sole logical product – products are becoming available in all shapes and sizes, and companies are increasingly manufacturing to order.

These developments also have consequences for the use of marketing tools. Is the price still determined on the basis of the characteristics of the product and the cost price, or on the basis of its value to the customer? The need for interaction increases in proportion to the

Table 4.1	*The applicability of the marketing model*
Target group oriented Target group orientation	*Customer concept* Network orientation
Target group-oriented prices Different product variants Target group communications (direct marketing) The Internet as an information medium and a communications medium (*key medium*: store, often supplemented with a teleservice)	Based on direct interaction, therefore offering opportunities for customization. Many different forms of communication are used, especially direct communication. The method chosen depends on the objective of the communication. The use of the Internet is focused strongly on transactions *Key medium*: the Internet, teleservice assistance
Fixed prices Mass communication Standard products The Internet as an information medium (*key medium*: store, distribution channel)	Fixed prices Mass communication and direct marketing (customers/prospects) Standard products The Internet as an information medium, and as a communications medium Limited transaction function *Key medium*: telephone, Internet support
Mass communications Internal orientation	*Direct interaction* Customer orientation

degree of product diversification; however, the need for direct contact with the customer will also increase. Consequently organizations will start communicating more directly with their customers (see Figure 4.2). As a result of the developments outlined above, direct marketing will become increasingly valuable and the use of mass communication will decline. Many changes are related to product range, the manner in which customers make their purchases (the distribution concept), and the role the Internet plays in the buying and selling process.

Changes in product concept

The opportunities offered by today's technology are resulting in an increased degree of diversity in the products offered for sale; however, the customer's perception of the product is also changing. Customers increasingly perceive service to be an integral part of a product concept.

Figure 4.2   *Relationship between the function of the Internet and marketing*

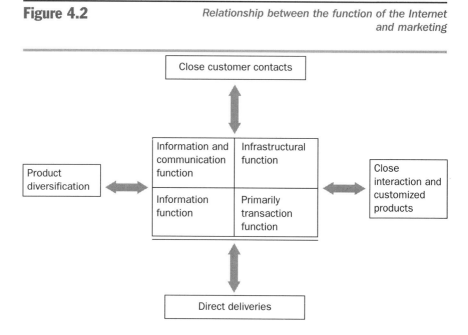

Standard products are characterized by the fact that the customer recognizes them and can buy them without major assistance. In fact, the interaction required for this process consists solely of motivating the customer to buy the product. Customized products or the provision of a large amount of service in connection with a product, however, requires a certain degree of interaction. A company will have to determine the nature of the customer's wishes, the intended use of the product, and the relevant product modules. This requires the provision of advice, and interaction.

However, advice and interaction are not required solely for customized products. Some products are sold simply following advice and interaction. Books are an example of this group of products. The traditional joke 'I already have a book' is based on the fact that books are not alike. There are differences in author, layout, content, as well as other differences such as in the genre. The ability to assess which book is required will require interaction between the product, the buyer and the consultant. The Internet is restricted in the degree of interaction that can be established between the product and the buyer, and consequently this interaction will need to be achieved by other means – by the provision of information, for instance, or the supply of references and reviews, and by creating trust by guaranteeing that the book can be returned should it prove to be a disappointment. Consequently it may be concluded that the buying process on the Internet exhibits characteristics and underlying principles that are different from those in the outside world.

> **The buying process on the Internet exhibits characteristics and underlying principles that are different from those in the outside world**

Buying on the Internet requires a new dimension, i.e. the need or possibility to interact. A potential buyer can, for example, begin by familiarizing themselves with a certain product on the Internet. This orientation could involve a search for product references, requests for users' experiences, or a specification of the product the buyer wishes to purchase. Armed with the answers, the customer will then be able to go to a store to buy the product. In fact, the Internet is providing support for the buying process, while the actual purchase is still made in the store. This support will result in marked changes: customers will plan their purchases more carefully, will be more motivated, and will spend less time in the store. Consequently it will result in a shift from emotional (impulse) buying to rational (planned) buying. The Internet will greatly promote this change in buying patterns.

The supplier drives the selling process; the message is focused on the market (the target group). The market includes potential customers, or *suspects*. Suspects who are seemingly interested (according to information received, or expectations) in the products on offer are termed *leads*: leads are thought to be interested. Leads who are actually known to be interested in the product are termed *prospects*: prospects have indicated that they are in fact interested in purchasing the product. Only once a purchase has been made does the person become a customer. Consequently the status of customer is restricted to a given point in time. A person who buys the product becomes a customer, and then a user of the product, and frequently, once again, a lead or a prospect for other products, or for a repeat purchase. (See Figure 4.3.)

A rational and sales-oriented site

The buying process is demand driven. The potential customers are aware of a given need, and are under the impression that they know

Figure 4.3 The buying process versus the selling process

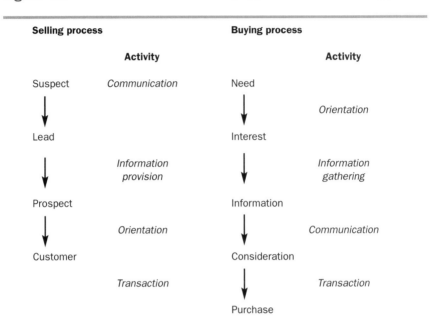

what they want. They exhibit interest in a product or a group of products, look for information, then give consideration to the purchase. Only once they have become certain that they wish to buy the product will they proceed to the purchase. The buying and selling processes differ with respect to the party driving the process (the buyer or the seller), and the party taking the initiative (is the initiative taken by the buyer or by the seller?). The objective of the buying and selling process is also different: a seller will wish to sell (complete a transaction), while a buyer will wish to fulfil their needs. This difference in the underlying principle results in a different approach to the market and the customer. In a selling process the salesman will focus deliberately on product-based sales arguments, whereas the customer's reasons for buying will be based on needs. Consequently the customer will endeavour to translate these sales arguments into reasons for buying a product. The seller will find it difficult to counter the customer's reasons for buying a product, since they are usually highly individual and, consequently, unknown. Even the actual customer is not always capable of expressing the reasons for buying (objectively) since there may also be secondary (hidden) reasons a customer may not even be aware of. Examples of these secondary reasons can be associated with status, a wish to belong, or an impulse decision. This is why the seller finds it easier to resort to the use of product-based reasons in enticing the customer to purchase the product.

This difference is of essential importance to the use of the Internet. A selling process is supported by information about the product, reasons for buying the product, correct positioning of the product, and the facilitation of the transaction. Selling-oriented sites are strongly supply driven, product oriented, and focused on transaction; in other words, they offer products and services.

A buying-oriented site accommodates the customers' individual wishes and their individual (buying) behaviour. These sites will incorporate more questions to customers, and they will offer a variety of methods to navigate through the site. The provision of information is an essential task of these sites. The site will also accommodate customers' individual wishes. Buying support can include individual newsletters and the use of

A buying-oriented site accommodates the customers' individual wishes and their individual (buying) behaviour

comprehensive selection features. The Internet's ability to support individual behaviour on the one hand and provide the possibilities for customers to search for and take the initiative to search for the information they require on the other renders the Internet, by definition, a medium providing support to the buying process. A survey carried out by Pew Internet & American Life in June 2000 revealed that 74% of those with access to the Internet had used this medium to obtain information about products and services, and that 48% had actually purchased a product on-line (primarily books, CDs, toys and clothing). As in a buying process, the initiative to make use of the Internet lies with the customer, thereby imparting it with a focus and a driver different from those of a selling process. Organizations do not sell products or services on the Internet; the customer purchases them – the process is a buying process, not a selling process. This in turn means that the support provided by the Internet must be based on customers, analyses of customer behaviour, and a suitable response to this behaviour. It should assist the customers in their search for the products and services they require. (See Figure 4.4.)

Treese and Steward[9] combined the conditions for using the Internet and the manner in which a buying process is determined according to

Figure 4.4   *The integration of the selling and buying processes in a market place*

the differences between buying and selling on the Internet. They concluded that a distinction can be made between four phases, and that these four phases constitute the four basic functionalities that should be offered by a good Web site:

● attract;

● interact;

● act;

● react.

The attract function will need to respond to the basic needs within the buying process. It will also be necessary to incorporate elements that render a visit to the Web site more fun. Once visitors arrive at the site it will need to provide opportunities for interaction. This can be achieved by offering search possibilities, and by offering facilities to go to specific parts of the site subsequent to the provision of some extra information (the e-mail address, or clothing sizes). The behavioural information gathered from these site visits must be used when responding to the visitor. The site should provide direct support to the buying process with the provision of facilities for ordering, paying and completing the transaction (the 'act' functions). The last function, the 'react' function, is focused on attracting the customer back to the site and providing support to customers. Customer service, for example, is considered to be part of this function. The Web site must support these stages in the buying process.

Conditions for a good Web site

The aforementioned functionality, in combination with the fact that the customer will personally need to decide to visit a site, largely determines the requirements for a good Web site. The need to support the buying process exerts an influence on the range of products offered, the provision of information, and the design of the Web site. The product range will focus on the individual components a buyer may choose (in the manner used by Dell.com), or the provision of information that will help the customer make an appropriate choice (as practised by Amazon.com). The design of the Web site will need to meet three important criteria:

- a logical navigation method;
- a suitable 'look and feel';
- an appropriate apportionment of the emotional, rational and 'stickiness' elements of the site.

A logical navigation method

The method use to navigate around the site must be clear to the customer, and it must focus on the needs that led them to visit the site. These needs are highly individual. A chance visitor to the site will not wish to examine the site in great depth, and should not be compelled to carry out lengthy searches through its contents. The visitor will immediately want to know what to do. For this reason preference is given to a navigation method based on tabs. A visitor searching for highly specific information will certainly be willing to scroll through a number of possible links or tabs. Visitors will want to scroll only if they are certain that the site will provide them with the information they require. Such visitors are, in general, rational buyers. As we will explain later, rational buyers are more frequent among women than among men. Women are more inclined to make a conscious decision to visit a specific site, and do not find it irritating to scroll through a menu bar in order to gain immediate access to the appropriate information or the appropriate products. Men exhibit more erratic, less rational and less structured behaviour; consequently they prefer to be able to see immediately what is offered for sale (men surf more than women).

A suitable look and feel

The feeling a visitor gains from a site must be compatible with the products on offer. Lastminute.com's look and feel comprises the offer of economical products and a sunny combination of colours. This is compatible with the proposition offered by the company. This look and feel largely determines the buyer's emotional relationship with the site. The choice of colours, the layout, text, photos and the functionality contribute towards the required look and feel.

Emotional and rational elements

A last aspect that plays a role on the site is the choice between reason and emotion. It is essential to support both choices, since it concerns the support of two different types of buying behaviour: chance purchases and planned purchases. Visitors making a targeted search should be supported by a rational navigation structure, and surfing visitors should be supported by a navigation structure that accommodates their emotions. This means that the layout of the site will exhibit four features:

- a navigation structure (tabs and/or links);

- a rational section that provides immediate access to the appropriate section of the site supported, where relevant, by search facilities;

- an emotional/social section with brief reports, a photo or supplementary information;

- a stickiness section that must impart the site with the appropriate look and feel, and which must contribute towards the visitor's inclination to return to the site. This can be achieved, for example, by means of games, special offers, brief information or new products.

Product policy

The changes resulting from interaction and the manner in which organizations endeavour to achieve customer loyalty become apparent when there is a shift from standard products to customized products or intermediate product modules. The underlying product components (perception and service) will increase in importance in proportion to the extent to which the product adopts the nature of a customized product. It should be remembered that the visitor is unable to take the product away, and must place more trust in the supplier (perception). The visitor is also unable to see or try out the product; consequently they will need to have confidence in the after-sales service and in the organization's status as a bona fide supplier.

The elements of perception and service will play an important part in the decision to buy. This means that product features – being determined by personal preferences – will determine a supplier's strategic choice to a lesser degree than other elements such as service and perception, which will become increasingly important. Consequently the organization should focus on relationship excellence rather than on product excellence.

> **The organization should focus on relationship excellence rather than on product excellence**

A crucial aspect of customization is that the customer has a suitable perception of the relationship prior to the purchase, and that they enjoy a good relationship subsequent to the purchase. The relationship between the supplier and the customer will be much more intense than in the event of a standard product, since the latter involves only a bond with the product. In opting for customization the organization will endeavour to greatly increase the role of service elements; this can be achieved by modifying the product concept to encompass a total package of services and physical products. The model displays the changes resulting from the decision to offer more customized products (an increase in services).

Conversely, an organization that endeavours to market a standard product will need to ensure that the customer senses a loyalty towards the product, and will need to distinguish itself from the competition by means of its product. In this situation the organization will endeavour to achieve a competitive advantage by means of product excellence. Customer loyalty to the product will then be stronger than is generally the case with branded products. With customized products the loyalty will be to the distributor. The Internet provides the possibility to interact, which will result in more pressure on interaction as far as the supply of (perceived) customized products is concerned. This development, initiated by the suppliers – and in combination with the technological opportunities available – will result in an increase in the number of customized products. However, it will also result in the Internet acquiring an important marketing role and the fact that, probably as a consequence of this role, customer loyalty will be based on the relationship rather than on the product. (See Figure 4.5.)

Figure 4.5

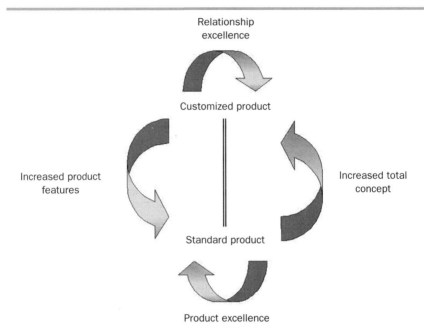

Relationship
excellence

Customized product

Increased product
features

Increased total
concept

Standard product

Product excellence

The transformation of a standard product into a customized product also results in a shift in focus from product excellence to relationship excellence

The product concept and affiliates

The reasons why customers decide to buy can be used as the basis for deploying the Internet to support the buying process. An organization that offers products for sale assumes that the customer perceives this service as a means of satisfying their needs. Customers will certainly begin by searching for the information they need to make a decision. They will then continue by opting for a type of product or specific product and, finally, they will choose a supplier. Customers will not only want to have confidence in the product or type of product an organization supplies but also in the organization itself. Suppliers have a number of options to choose from:

1. Product range.
2. Associated range.
3. Concept.

1. If an organization opts for selling a product range it means that the organization will offer products or services only. This is the traditional marketing method. The customer decides which combination of products to buy and where to buy them. A variant of this approach is the department-store concept, which is also seen on the Internet (one supplier and a large number of products). One seller may perhaps offer products from a number of suppliers, i.e. the traditional concept. An example is smartdress.com, which sells designer clothes. Suppliers could also collaborate in offering their products and services, i.e. a market concept. The various portals (such as Yahoo! or download.com) are examples of this market concept. The customer weighs up the pros and cons, and makes a deliberate choice to purchase a product. The market constitutes nothing more than a 'serving hatch' for individual sellers.

2. Another option is to look for associations. This option relates products and services via network constructions. A visitor expressing an interest in a given product or service can immediately be referred to affiliated companies or associated products. This development leads to customers being steered more towards specific products and suppliers on the basis of the interest they express, or the empathy they exhibit. This can be seen, for example, in affiliate marketing: a customer who expresses an interest in a specific product is immediately provided with a suggestion for other products. Altavista's search engine is an example of this approach. Visitors who search for information providers in the Netherlands are also offered books about the Netherlands (from Amazon), or the opportunity to book a holiday to the Netherlands. The visitor can then click on the offer to go directly to the supplier's Web site, and is immediately presented with the appropriate product range. Search engines make extensive use of network links between suppliers based on the interest expressed by the visitor.

A visit to a site is a sign of interest in itself. Visitors to a specific site may receive suggestions for other products and services. A visitor to an investment site, for instance, may be presented with banners and pictograms from suppliers of related products and services: buying or selling shares, a book about investments, or an offer of insurance. And, finally, it is also possible to use the information in the visitor's profile to offer a logical range of products. This profile can be drawn up from the visitor's behaviour, or from specific questions put to the visitor, for example on the registration of passwords. An investment site that attracts largely wealthy and well-educated men can incorporate suggestions for exclusive (designer) clothing, for luxury vehicles or

> A successful site will make visitors feel at home and make them want to return and make use of the affiliates

sports cars. In this case target group profile information is used to offer a specific product. The extent to which the organization is able to accommodate the associated needs of the visitors (product related, behaviour related or profile related) will largely determine the stickiness of the site. A successful site will make visitors feel at home and make them want to return and make use of the affiliates.

3. The final option associated with buying behaviour is the product concept. This involves suppliers collaborating to offer a total range of products and to launch such a concept on the market. Customers have only one contact, and pay one price for all services. The Internet then becomes the virtual platform where supply meets demand.

Changes in distribution

Changes in distribution may consist of changes in the way products or services are sold (either directly or via a distribution channel), but also in the way they are bought. There is also a difference in focus, i.e. either on the product (transaction oriented) or on the needs of the customer. In the latter case, a supplier will endeavour to achieve customer loyalty based on behaviour or association.

Product focus can be based on the marketing model (see Figure 4.1), in which a distinction is made between direct distribution in the right-hand quadrant, and indirect distribution in the left-hand quadrant. As mentioned, the real world offers the advantage of a distribution channel which, for the suppliers, should result in product loyalty. If there is direct contact between the buyer and the seller, product loyalty will be less important than loyalty based on personal relationships. In the distribution channel this is the relationship with the store or the account manager. The sole opportunity available to the producer is to distinguish himself by means of the characteristics of the product, and to endeavour to achieve a preference for the product. A customer who does not buy products via a distribution channel will immediately feel a sense of loyalty towards the producer or his supplier, in which case the degree of customer loyalty based on producer preferences will be the dominant factor.

This is also true for the real world. The degree of loyalty a buyer feels towards a physical product is a different type of loyalty than that felt towards personal factors (such as the store's image). Consequently the distribution axis also has a bearing on the way customer loyalty is achieved. Direct sales will be characterized by personal loyalty based on knowledge of the customer; however, when sales are effected using a distribution channel, the supplier will have to strive to create loyalty based on product perception.

The model also depicts the changes that may occur when focus shifts towards direct sales. A movement along the distribution axis, i.e. a shift towards direct sales (to the right) or a shift towards the use of a distribution channel represents these changes (to the left) in the marketing model (Figure 4.1).

The decision as to whether to sell products and services directly or via a distribution channel is an essential one for the supplier and, in fact, also for the buyer. An organization can decide to use a direct channel so that it can offer its customers a better price (reduced costs) or because it needs specific information from the customer in order to offer customized products or services. Organizations will aim to offer lower (selling) prices for standard products that do not require a lot of sales support. An example of this type of organization is an insurance company that sells annuities and, for example, indemnity insurance directly to its customers. These purchases can be completed without difficulty; the buyer does not need much advice or support, and a brief discussion will be sufficient to conclude a sale. The information obtained from the customer can be used for all kinds of direct marketing communication (cross sales).

However, an organization that produces customized products or services (or supplies a customized product) will also wish to have direct contact with the customer so as to use the information obtained from the customer or the interaction to produce and supply the product. Companies supplying computers use this approach. Interaction with the customer enables the latter to select all the modules required for a personal computer, as well as the software to be installed. In effect, this process results in a customized computer. Dell is an example of a supplier that sells customized computers based on interaction. Interaction originally consisted of a call centre, which accepted orders by telephone. Nowadays 90% of the company's turnover is obtained from Internet sales, where the customer chooses the computer hardware to be used to construct the computer, and the required software.

Consequently, the direct relationship with the customer results in savings in costs, and the information obtained from the customer can be used for direct communication or cross sales. If a distribution channel is used, customer support and the provision of service are delegated to the distribution channel, thereby enabling the organization to concentrate on the manufacture or supply of standard or standardized products or services. When a distribution channel is used, the supplier will focus on product features and on product excellence, so as to distinguish the product from those of the competition. The distribution channel provides for the delivery of goods to the customer, and imparts an added value to the purchase by means of the provision of services, advice, and an appropriate presentation of the product. Consequently, the customer can either choose to buy via the distribution channel – in this way they are assured of personal advice and a relationship based on trust with a store offering a wide range of products and services – or they can opt for direct delivery. While this involves greater risk (the customer cannot see, feel or taste the goods, or take them home), it also creates greater opportunities for providing customized products. The integration of these developments in the model is shown in Table 4.2.

Table 4.2   *Relationship between distribution and customer loyalty*

	Loyalty based on product features	Customized product based on interaction and a relationship	
Distribution channel	The channel offers substantial added value. Suppliers concentrate on product excellence	Supply based on interaction. Strong focus on the development of personal relationships	Direct deliveries
Standard products			

An important aspect of the traditional marketing approach was that the time of purchase coincided with the time of delivery. The Internet differs in this aspect in that the time of purchase does not coincide with the time of delivery. The resulting time span between the time of purchase and the time of delivery is the specific playing field of Internet strategy: how can this time span be used? The supplier must motivate the customer to wait. Should they motivate the customer by providing a price discount, or with specific products that are not otherwise

Figure 4.6   *Changes in distribution policy*

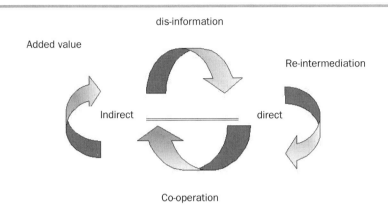

available, such as special foreign products (Dutch liquorice for foreigners), diet products or special wines? Or should the customer be motivated to wait for a customized product, which always involves a wait? Choosing a method to motivate customers is an important decision for suppliers intending to use the Internet for deliveries. Why should customers be satisfied with poorer service than they are accustomed to from normal distribution channels? (See Figure 4.6.)

Choosing a method to motivate customers is an important decision for suppliers intending to use the Internet for deliveries

To recapitulate, customers can buy on the Internet but they cannot see the actual product or take it home. All they see is a show model. At this point it speaks for itself to go to a distribution channel that accommodates interaction and maintains personal relationships – I know you, nice to see you again, would you like to have a look at some books we think will be of interest to you (www.Amazon.com)? Or would you like some suggestions for your share portfolio (www.quicken.com)? We can keep track of all the shares in your portfolio for you, so all you need to do is click to see how much profit (!) you've made.

Important values

Existing distribution channels derive their value from the presence of physical goods and services that customers are able to see, pay for and take away. They can also obtain 'live' advice on their use. Moreover, personal contact often plays an important role in the provision of services. An organization can create trust by giving proper personal advice, and the customers can form an image of the company or of the salesman or woman, which ultimately determines their confidence in the organization. On the Internet the organization will need to compete on the basis of other values such as low price, speed of delivery, 24-hour service or the provision of information.

During the past few years existing distribution channels have indeed made attempts to establish similar personal relationships with their customers. The many loyalty systems, such as those offered by UK supermarkets, are evidence of suppliers' endeavours to achieve customer loyalty. However, the multitude of programmes of this nature – as well as the fact that customers participate in more than one programme – reveals that the degree of customer loyalty that can be achieved by these means is in fact restricted. Customers regard these kinds of saving programmes more as a form of disguised discount than as a reward for their custom. Consequently, suppliers rarely incorporate more than a reward for the transaction in the programme; they are not (yet) able to accommodate highly individual wishes or to amend the marketing concept to accommodate the wishes of a small group of customers. Suppliers should concentrate on their strengths rather than their weaknesses. They should concentrate on the strengths of the concept rather than the opportunities offered by the Internet. The use of the Internet certainly fits into the concept as far as existing distribution channels are concerned; this will primarily involve the (limited) provision of information and communication. New distributors will focus largely on the transaction function. The really big challenge facing them will be to combine Internet deliveries and physical deliveries or, in other words, what is often referred to as the combination of 'click and mortar' ('brick and mortar' is often used to describe existing forms of distribution).

The Internet as a selection channel

As discussed earlier, the Internet can fulfil a number of functions in the buying process, namely an information function and a communication function; moreover, it can also function as a distribution channel. Suppliers can respond to customers depending on the way they use the Internet. This results in the advent of a new type of supplier who can

Figure 4.7   *Independer.nl helps customers select the best insurance*

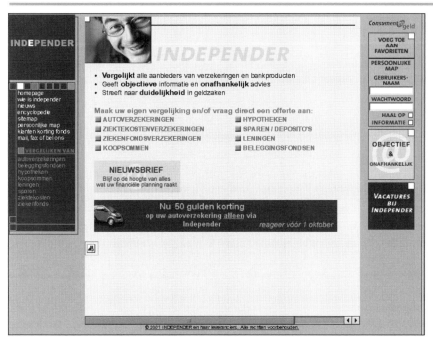

The site has introduced a new type of intermediary which does not merely render the range of products and services more transparent but also combines this service with advice and personal selection

act as intermediary by rendering the range of products or services transparent, or by linking suppliers. Consequently, customers will modify their behaviour; they will no longer go directly to a store but begin by visiting such a combination site before they go to a store of their choice. A supplier such as independer.nl provides access to the Dutch insurance market. Customers can indicate their demands and preferences before being connected directly to the site of the insurance company concerned. Thus independer.nl has become a new intermediary.

A 'portal' is another form of intermediary. In fact, a portal is a new type of shopping centre that accommodates a number of suppliers, where customers are shown the way to similar suppliers, or suppliers selected according to subject. A portal achieves customer loyalty by the provision of news items, and by offering a convenient manner of finding suppliers, products, and services. Portals also offer a number of extra

By attracting visitors, portals can assume the new role of intermediary

facilities such as a search system. Internet service providers are pleased to fulfil this role, since this encourages Internet users to employ the providers' pages as their homepage. Providers of search engines such as Yahoo! and Altavista have become portals since this offers more ways of ensuring that customers will return, of gaining customer loyalty by means of a default homepage setting, and also of gaining supplier loyalty. This results in a large number of visitors, which is important for attracting advertisers (banners and icons) and for calculating commission for referrals. (See Table 4.3.) A British study revealed that customers attach importance to these portals. By attracting visitors, portals can assume the new role of intermediary – in fact, they are more like information brokers and gateways to the Web sites of many suppliers. This saves time for the customer, both with reference to (restless) searching and surfing.

Table 4.3   *Most frequently visited Web sites*

Portals	80%
ISPs	63%
Services	57%
Businesses	52%
Fun/entertainment	40%
Buying/retail trade	39%
Search engines	28%
Financial news	28%
Information	25%
Software	24%

Source: MMXI, Europe, May 2000. Regular visits are indicative of the percentage reach

Virtual communities

In addition to product focus, which must result in sales, suppliers can also focus on customer needs. These needs can serve as the basis for the development of new concepts in which the Internet plays a facilitating role. This focus on (individual) customer needs also requires a shift in commercial focus, i.e. from selling to buying. The Internet is the medium that can facilitate such a shift: suppliers can more easily record visitors' behaviour and by visiting a site customers also reveal their behavioural characteristics. This provides better opportunities for achieving customer loyalty in a different and more individual manner. This loyalty can be achieved by means of a proactive response to the behaviour and interests exhibited by customers.

A portal is characterized by the different ways in which suppliers present their products and services; a community is characterized by the customer's loyalty in response to the stickiness factor. A stickiness factor can be a characteristic that determines the behaviour or interests of a visitor. This characteristic can be used to search for like-minded people with whom the visitor can communicate, and to search for information, products and services. The result is the creation of a 'virtual' community of kindred spirits. Examples are communities for men and women (where the stickiness factor is sex), for football or golf fans (where the stickiness factor is the hobby – see Figure 4.8), or for investors (where the stickiness factor is wealth or investments). The stickiness factor is important to the visitor and determines the type of visitor.

Suppliers can respond by actively or passively affiliating themselves with a community – they can either facilitate the development of a new community or can offer their services to an existing community. The supplier is in fact target group oriented and uses the logical meeting place of the target group, and, in its absence, provides a logical meeting place with the objective of achieving stickiness and an association with the intended target group.

The requirements to be met by a successful community include the following. It must:[10]

● be possible to achieve an adequate critical mass;

● offer a strong stickiness factor;

● provide direct interaction with its users (the use of feedback to modify the concept);

● provide for regular communication;

● be capable of facilitating direct contact between its members (such as chat rooms);

● use tools and activities suitable for the community;

● respond, where possible, to all the motives of the participants;

● create a community around the behaviour and interests exhibited by the target group.

Figure 4.8   *Golf.com, a community for golf fans, with news, information, products, chat services, all focused on golf fans*

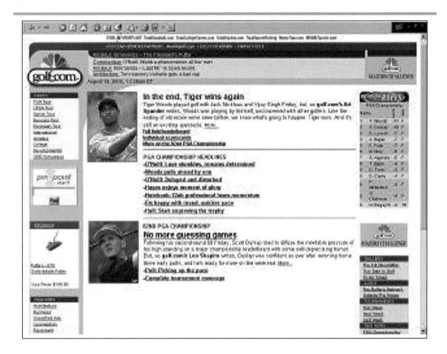

In addition to these general principles the community will need to enhance stickiness in other areas. It can, for example, acquire authority by assigning a prominent role to experts, i.e. specialists, and by the provision of publications and opinions. The community should also adopt a proactive role in communicating with its participants by employing all the familiar one-to-one media such as letters, newsletters, e-mails and on-line presentations.

In other words, the community should respond to the specific needs of the target group. This can be achieved only if a supplier knows precisely what someone's motives are for participating in the community, what binds them, and what their identity is. Consequently, a good database system, with profiling facilities, constitutes the basis for a community of this kind.

The procurement function

In addition to the changes brought about by the Internet with reference to the way products and services are sold, the Internet may also bring about changes in the way organizations buy products. The procurement function may use the Internet for:

● on-line orders;
● direct links to suppliers;
● joint procurement, in collaboration with other organizations.

The Internet may also bring about changes in the way organizations buy products

On-line ordering

Companies can also purchase products and services on-line. In fact, there are no significant differences with the consumer market, either for the buyer or for the seller. The characteristics are the same: the buyer plays a dominant role in the process, the relationship is less close, the relationship can be established each time a purchase is made, and the terms and conditions can be different for each purchase.

Direct links

A direct link between an organization and a supplier requires precise coordination with reference to the way in which a purchase is effected, the internal processes, and harmonization of the delivery and the terms of delivery. Organizations will need to reach agreement about the people authorized to purchase products or services, the standard terms and conditions that will be applicable, and other relevant conditions governing the transaction. Changes are brought about by organizations entering into permanent relationships, which allows them to reach agreements about authorization, and about the specifications of a product or service. Through collaboration, companies hope to cooperate more closely to achieve faster deliveries, use on-line ordering to make order processing more efficient, and create a lasting relationship, which will lead to better terms and conditions and price agreements.

However, the nature of this direct procurement function will depend on the products and services bought. The procurement of products and services that do not pertain to the organization's primary processes (product related) will need to meet less stringent criteria than those directly involved with the primary processes. Consequently, a supplier of office equipment will attach great importance to a direct link with its business relations, but will still take the same time to deliver the goods.

However, a supplier of components operating on the basis of a 'just-in-time' strategy will need to enter into strict agreements about delivery times. These agreements are vital to the organization.

A supplier participating in or assuming part of an organization's processes enters into a very close relationship in which the supplier adopts the responsibility for specific functions from the organization. This function can, for example, involve maintaining an inventory, but it can also encompass the logistics function (see Figure 4.9). A supplier could assume responsibility for managing the level of stock in a store or manufacturing company, and at the same time decide when to supply items. This close collaboration is a characteristic of a network organization – it will result in an intense bonding between parties and a permanent relationship with the customer, and it will also result in unambiguous and standardized agreements.

Joint procurement

When arranging a direct link, an organization in effect selects the party with which it wishes to enter into a close relationship. However, organizations can also opt to combine their procurement power. In effect, this results in a form of procurement comparable with that in the consumer market (see priceline.com). The major difference between the consumer market and the business-to-business market is that organizations inform each other of their intention to join forces in their procurement activities. This results in their combined purchasing power, and the collaboration enables them to adopt a stronger position in their negotiations with suppliers.

A similar collaboration has been in existence for many years in the advertising world for the purchase of advertising space from the media (advertising space and television time). For example, at a European level supermarket chains such as Ahold, Tesco, Casino and K-mart have combined their purchasing power in the WWRE. A similar kind of initiative has been taken for computer and aircraft components. These are all instances of collaborative arrangements that provide for procurement as a part of the primary process. This will result in the levelling of purchasing terms and conditions and suppliers will have to compete more fiercely for customers. This will bring about changes, based on purchasing power, in the competitive relationships between collaborating parties and non-collaborating parties. Moreover, this will also affect the competitive relationships between collaborating parties,

Figure 4.9   *The link between buyer and seller systems*

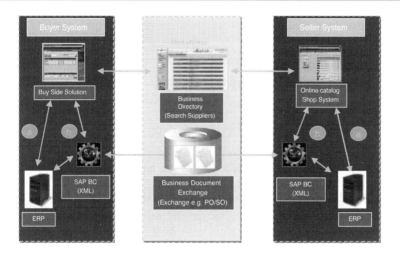

Source: Mysap.com. The middle section is the market place, which brings together buying and selling

because they have the same purchasing terms and conditions and will therefore, more than ever before, need to concentrate on establishing customer loyalty and attracting new customers.

Summary

The technological developments of the past few years have resulted in major changes in the products offered for sale. They have led to a greater variety of products, more product features, more products composed of modules and even customized products. Customers are becoming increasingly aware of the opportunities available to buy products and services that are, above all, compatible with their individual and personal specific needs. This is possible only when customers make their wishes known, which in turn requires close interaction between suppliers and buyers. This interaction can be achieved in the distribution channel, or by means of direct media such as the telephone or the Internet. Suppliers are thus faced with a choice: either they can support the distribution channel using the new facilities and endeavour to enter into close relationships with the various links in the chain, or, conversely, they can enter into close relationships with buyers by means of direct delivery.

The role of the Internet can be inferred from the various functions that the Internet can fulfil – namely an information and communication function, in addition to a transaction and infrastructure function. The choice made by suppliers will largely determine the manner in which they maintain their relationship with the market and their customers. Many traditional marketing tools will be modified to accommodate the new opportunities offered by technology, changes in distribution, and customers' new and more demanding requirements.

The use of the Internet in contacts between companies will lead to changes in their competitiveness. Organizations will be able to collaborate more closely; moreover, they will be able to share or assume each other's functions. This will result in improved efficiency. Organizations' combined purchasing power will bring about changes in the balance of power. Parties will change the preconditions for competition, and companies will more than ever before need to compete for customers on the basis of customer loyalty and service.

Notes

9 Treese, G.W. and Steward, Lawrence V. (1998) *Designing Systems for Internet Commerce,* Addison Wesley, chapter 4, p. 41 ff.

10 Williams, R. and Cothrel, J. 'Four Smart Ways to run On-line Communities,' *Sloan Management Review*, vol. 41, no. 4, pp. 81–91.

5

■ ■ ■ ■ ■ ■ ■ ■ ■ ■ ■ ■ ■ ■ ■ ■ ▶ ▄

E-customer focus

How may I help you?

Customer focus is regarded as a means of achieving customer loyalty towards an organization. Customer focus requires a thorough knowledge of the customer, and of the target groups. It should not be confused with the term 'customer orientation' used in the previous chapter, which involves the ability to respond immediately to the individual needs of the customer and to use knowledge of the customer to offer products and services that may be of interest to them. Customer focus refers to the ability to meet customers' expectations, which can also be achieved by other orientations. Customer focus may also consist of supplying a good product at the right price, providing the appropriate information, or providing a proper service.

In principle, a distinction can be made between two forms of customer focus, namely direct customer contact and non-direct customer contact. Direct customer contact involves interaction with the customer at the time of sale, i.e. the presence of a contact element that results in a transaction. Non-direct customer contact involves the right product at the right price, the right location choice, and the right opening times – which, in fact, are the basic conditions to be satisfied for the achievement of customer focus.

This chapter reviews the operational aspects of customer focus, including the role and function of the database, the telephone/service desk and the Internet. Together these elements are referred to as customer relationship management. In view of the important role the Internet plays in CRM, attention will also be given to the relationship with the Internet in the maintenance of customer contacts.

The role of the database

In the first instance the commercial use of the Internet was focused on the sale of standard products using a new form of distribution. Amazon.com is the most successful example of this approach. All at

The marketing activities for targeting prospects were based on the combination of information in a customer database and data purchased from third parties

once books could be ordered on-line and delivered to customers' homes. This development is in fact comparable with the advent of the new role of the telephone as a distribution medium at the beginning of the 1990s. New telecommunications facilities enabled organizations to use the telephone in a manner that had hitherto been impossible. Voice-response systems, personal numbering, intelligent routers and auto-dial systems are examples of new facilities that came to be of great value to the commercial use of telecommunications systems. Customers could be contacted quickly by call centres, which automatically rang the number in the database. A personal telephone operator (referred to as an agent) conducted a commercial interview with the person contacted. The marketing activities for targeting prospects were based on the combination of information in a customer database and data purchased from third parties. The techniques that made this form of market approach feasible consisted of:

- deriving data from in-house databases containing sales information and using anticipated data based on profiles or socio-demographic information;

- purchasing information from third parties;

- linking up and analyzing the above data to assess the probability of people being interested in a purchase.

The market was initially approached by traditional direct mail and subsequently, from the beginning of the 1990s, by telephone: telemarketing had made its appearance. The techniques of importance to telemarketing are:

- outbound facilities for calling prospective buyers or customers. In addition to the information contained in the database the organization could make use of auto-dialling facilities, scripting and other techniques available to a modern call centre;

- inbound facilities for customers calling the organization. Call centre agents could answer customers' questions immediately as this technique enabled relevant customer information to be displayed directly on their screens. The systems often incorporated a direct link with the caller's telephone number, thereby obviating the need to enter a customer number.

The technique enabled staff to rapidly connect the caller to the appropriate person in the organization, or to route the call to the relevant person inside or outside the organization. It also enabled the organization to provide preferential treatment to specific customers (priority routing). The management of the department was able to keep track of productivity by virtue of recording and analyzing all staff actions, providing them with precise information about the nature of the questions raised and the agent who was able to conclude calls in the shortest time. The downtime of each agent and the speed with which they were able to deal with a call were other indicators of agents' productivity. The management was also able to determine how many people were on hold, and how long they were kept on hold. All this information enabled the management to keep track of and manage the level of service provided by the service desk.

The specific problems involved in processing these telephone calls resulted in the development of specialized companies and staff engaged in conducting outbound telemarketing. These were usually traditional telemarketing bureaus, which used telephone scripts, i.e. the pre-determined dialogue of a commercial telephone conversation in the form of an automatic and dynamic script. These bureaus were also called in for inbound services involving large volumes of calls that required little specific knowledge of the product. It was possible to integrate the knowledge available in the system to enable agents to answer questions by means of, for example, a keyword. The use of these techniques allowed people with little experience or specific training to answer questions and to approach prospects.

The role of the service desk

Sometimes specific knowledge was required, or the organization considered customer contacts to be too important to outsource them. Organizations responded to these situations by setting up an in-house telemarketing department. This department usually took the form of a customer-service department, or a service desk. These de ˙ resulted in the maintenance of customer contacts that had been maintained through highly regulated channels su distribution channel, the account manager or the marketing depart-ment. Organizations started preparing for new contacts and intensify-ing relationships with existing customers. Customers were now offered:

- support prior to, during and subsequent to the purchase;
- the possibility to make direct purchases;
- the advantages of the supplier taking an active approach to the market.

Support prior to, during and subsequent to the purchase was usually made available by organizations that marketed their products by means of a distribution channel, and were aware of an evident need for advice. General Electric was one of the first organizations to provide widespread support. As early as 1989, the telephone was used to provide purchasing advice, as well as advice on repairs and maintenance subsequent to the sale. Up-to-date records of guarantee cards were maintained in a database, which served as the basis for targeted communications and analyses of the market. The retail trade concluded the actual sales. One of the benefits of this approach for the retail trade was that customers were better informed and more motivated when they entered the store – they had already thoroughly familiarized themselves with the available products, and knew precisely what they needed. This resulted in a 50% reduction of sales transaction time, which in turn increased the productivity of the sales staff.

The use of the Internet is having the same effect. Customers are now better informed, which results in a reduction of sales transaction time in the store – in fact, customers have already made up their minds before entering the store. In the Netherlands in 1993, Philips established a centre comparable to that of General Electric. As from 1998, all teleservice activities have been concentrated in a European centre in Eindhoven, the Netherlands, where customers throughout Europe can obtain product information in their own language. Once again the database is vital to knowing the customer and analyzing trends. Organizations that employ telephone services in this manner are usually internally oriented or target group oriented. However, the knowledge they acquire about their customers and their products' sales processes will result in a shift towards a more customer-focused approach. When this occurs, organizations will have to decide whether to continue using the telephone solely for service purposes or to offer facilities for buying (some of the) products by telephone.

These options are comparable to the current options for using the Internet.

Other parties, such as mail-order firms and direct writers, came to recognize the importance of the telephone to the sales process when customers increasingly began to use the telephone to obtain information or order products. Customers will speak to agents in situations in which specific advice is required, which is almost always the case with insurance. However, when calls simply involve recording a transaction – for instance when the customer has already made a choice from an advertisement or a catalogue – it will suffice to record the transaction in a voice-response system. As such, the telephone can be used to provide information on the one hand and to record information on the other. The efficiency of the medium and the fact that it enables quick and immediate access to customers and organizations has led to its rapid acceptance.

In brief, the telephone is used to actively approach the market. It is an extremely direct and effective technique – and as such, must be approached with the necessary caution. Some people become irritated by the mere fact of being approached, by the great number of commercial calls, and by the aggressive sales techniques that are often employed. Yet this technique can be effective provided that it is used in an appropriate manner. Some hints to avoid irritation include:

Many of the underlying principles applicable to the use of the telephone in commercial processes are also applicable to the Internet

- always ask whether the call is convenient;
- give an explicit explanation of the reason for the telephone call;
- make sure that the call is to the benefit of the person who has been called;
- make sure that the person being called can identify the organization. It is easier – and usually preferable – to call existing customers rather than making cold calls.

Many of the underlying principles applicable to the use of the telephone in commercial processes are also applicable to the Internet. It is, therefore, better to let customers choose which channel they prefer, i.e. the telephone or the Internet. The marketing policies of organizations will only change to a limited extent as a result of the new opportunities offered by the telephone. In the first instance, organizations will focus more on the direct approach of customers, and on the direct maintenance of customer contacts. At the same time, organizations will endeavour to increase their knowledge of customers by employing database information systems. Finally, they will try to achieve customer loyalty by means of customer cards, as well as increasingly tailoring their services to the individual needs of their customers.

One-to-one marketing

Organizational changes were limited. The service desk was perceived as a separate department, often also as a cost item, and was accountable to the sales department (occasionally the marketing department).

The consequences of direct customer contacts for marketing were reviewed in Don Peppers and Martha Rogers'[11] book on one-to-one marketing. Organizations that acquire knowledge about individual customers are able to accommodate customers' individual needs. Peppers and Rogers designate this technique 'one-to-one marketing'. This has two distinctive characteristics:

- It devotes more attention to existing customers. After all, the information in an organization's database means that an organization knows more about its customers than its non-customers. The extra attention will also benefit customer loyalty, which means that customers will buy more from the organization. In this way, organizations are able to communicate directly and individually with their customers, and respond proactively to their customers' buying behaviour.

- It provides for a customized range of products or services. Perceived customization leads to increased customer loyalty and more interactions. A thorough knowledge of and an ability to anticipate customers' needs means that organizations can offer customers the products they need and also make them aware of other products they may be interested in buying.

eppers and Rogers advocate that organizations should not stomers for their products. Instead their relationship with ge of existing customers should be such that organizations and services that accommodate their customers' present and future needs.[12] They propose a plan comprised of four phases to achieve this situation.

1. Know your customer (identify)

Make sure you know your customers, i.e. that you know who they are and what they need. This is often a problem for the existing retail trade, since purchases are usually made in relative anonymity. The introduction of customer cards is intended to ensure that customers manifest themselves (hand raising), and it allows sales to be recorded. Other ways of acquiring knowledge about customers are keeping track of credit-card information (supplemented with the address, on request), offering customers a (free) newsletter, or offering them the opportunity to be kept informed about specific special offers or other developments.

Recording customer data is simpler for sales effected via (electronic) media, as customers need to provide their address for the delivery of the goods or services they have purchased. Purchasing information and address data are then recorded as part of the core process: this is applicable to direct sales by telephone, reply coupons and the Internet.

2. Not all customers are alike (differentiate)

Customers have different needs and different purchasing wishes, patterns and circumstances, but it is often feasible to group them as similar customers. In this way organizations can endeavour to create an approach that may be perceived as a personal approach, albeit only by one group. Groups need to be compiled on the basis of factors characteristic of their behaviour. In the absence of individual customer data marketing, managers often group customers according to objective data, thereby assuming that objective data may be representative of certain uniform behaviour. This results in customers being grouped according to age, sex, income, race, origin or education. However, in the past few years it has become apparent that this type of clustering is not precise enough for the identification of truly distinctive buying behaviour.

The information in a database can be used to search for additional factors that are indicative of specific buying behaviour. In effect, individual characteristics are then used to compile (aggregate) identical clusters. These individual characteristics include, for example, the aforementioned objective characteristics, but also purchasing patterns, purchase frequency, the amount spent per purchase, per week and per

month, the time of purchase, and other factors, such as the distance the customer lives from the store. Records of sales made by telephone can also be aggregated to obtain similar clusters based on individual characteristics. The Internet, finally, provides for an extremely simple compilation of these clusters by virtue of the automatic registration of all visitors to a particular site, and their purchases. The use of techniques such as cookies (small pieces of software placed on a visitor's computer) and the unique number assigned to and carried everywhere by each Internet user provides for the immediate recognition of visitors to a site. This is an advanced way of clustering behavioural information.

The behaviour-driven clusters constitute groups of customers who exhibit similar behaviour in certain circumstances. This helps organizations respond to future and similar buying behaviour. It enables them to influence the behaviour of the groups in such a way that the behaviour of specific individuals is projected on the entire group. This is termed 'collaborative filtering'. Should a member of a defined uniform group book a holiday to Greece, for example, then this implies that other members in the group are probably also extremely interested in a holiday, and quite possibly to a sunny country. Companies such as Amazon.com use this technique to make suggestions about products to existing customers.

3. Direct contact (communicate)

Direct contact can be used to achieve interaction between an organization that claims to know its customers and a customer who wishes to enter into a relationship with the organization. This form of communication will need to be personal – and make use of the available information – if it is to be effective. Personal information and suggestions are essential to effective direct contact.

4. Customize

The last phase in Peppers and Rogers' plan is customization. This focuses on individual needs and may consist of two dimensions, namely a product dimension and a marketing-tool dimension:

- The product dimension refers to the supply of customized products derived from basic products. These may be physical products, although this is often difficult to achieve in practice (a modular construction is an alternative). Customization may also encompass product-related services such as, for example, extra after-sales service, an extended guarantee, or deliveries to the customer's home. It may also be customer-perceived customization, i.e. a perception of customization. This perception arises by virtue of the customer's ability to specify their wishes, a situation which is applicable to restaurants or car showrooms.

- Customization can also be employed with other marketing tools, for example, a price that is determined on the basis of the relationship with the customer (extra discounts in the event of a larger number of purchases) or which is based on the customer's personal wishes. Customers ordering shirts from the Bonivo.be shirt manufacturer in Belgium, for example, can specify their shirt from a number of modular options. The surcharge they pay relates to the preferred time of delivery – they can arrange for next day, next week or next month delivery, and will pay a surcharge commensurate with the reduction in delivery time.

Sales promotions can be based on buying behaviour and anticipated future needs. Customers receive highly personalized letters containing information about special offers and discounts. However, there are other forms of communication, such as e-mail, voice mail and information kiosks in stores. Personal offers supplied by organizations such as supermarkets help ensure that customers feel that they are both recognized and appreciated, which in turn greatly facilitates the relationship between the store and the customer. Finally, of course, a customer can choose from various types of distribution. They can purchase on the Internet, by telephone, in a store, or in another manner. Customers are free to choose – but, irrespective of their choice, they are always recognized and offered assistance. Organizations can use universal databases for all channels or integral customer databases to effectively support any part of the buying process. This also contributes towards the customer's perception of customization mentioned above.

Organizations can use universal databases for all channels or integral customer databases to effectively support any part of the buying process

The four phases defined by Peppers and Rogers constitute the basis for one-to-one marketing, albeit largely initiated by direct marketing principles. They are focused on the direct relationship between a supplier and its customers, and on direct personal communications supported by the information in a database. Two other elements are of vital importance to achieve the change to this one-to-one approach:

- the integration function;
- the retention function.

The integration function

Many organizations encounter problems during the implementation of one-to-one strategies as a result of the limitations in their existing (information) systems, which are largely designed to accommodate the core operational processes involved in logistics and finances. The traditional elements involved in the marketing function are recording information, selling and the provision of means for direct communication. Each channel usually possesses its own database system, based on the requirements imposed by the relevant channel. This is particularly expedient in banking. If a customer were to compare their bank balance via different channels, such as a bank statement, a cashpoint, the Internet and a telephone call, each channel would be likely to specify a different balance. Often there is a total absence of links between the various channels. This problem often results from the various ways of recording customer information, i.e. depending on whether the customer is an account holder, an individual or a family, with different security protocols and timing (a bank statement takes longer to deliver than an Internet message).

The retention function

The retention function is important as an organization will want its customers to return. In fact, there must always be a pro-active policy to ensure customer retention. This can be achieved by encouraging customers to return by providing special offers or discounts, loyalty programmes, savings schemes and offers of unique services or products. Customer loyalty is a core concept of one-to-one marketing. Organizations, rather than endeavouring to complete a transaction, should concentrate on establishing a relationship. Consequently their efforts are focused on profit at a relationship level rather than at a transaction level.

Figure 5.1   *The one-to-one marketing phases*

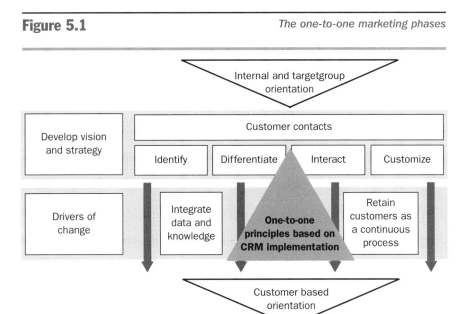

This can result in entrepreneurs searching not merely for new customers but also for new products and services that are suited to their customers. This enables them to prolong customer loyalty, and to further the relationship. Peppers and Rogers' one-to-one marketing phases have become topical precisely because of their use of databases as these enable organizations to record, analyze and use customer data in communication. In the first instance, the value of one-to-one marketing lay in the opportunities it presented for direct contact with the customer. In the second instance, interaction, which enabled the organization to respond to what customers were saying, added to this value. In the third and final instance, one-to-one marketing enabled organizations to supply customized products and services.

Customer relationship management

The one-to-one marketing strategy is also part of customer relationship management. CRM is a collection of individual functions and facilities used in combination to enable a more direct approach to the customer and to improve the management of customer relationships. The objective of CRM is to know a customer well enough to accommodate their wishes, to pro-actively approach them on the basis of their anticipated needs, and to provide them with active support during the buying process. This requires knowledge of the customer (the database) and the customer's past behaviour, as well as an ability to analyze the customer's profile in order to assign a customer value and predict a customer's buying behaviour. It is also necessary to communicate pro-actively with the customer, and to provide passive support if required – by telephone, Internet or in person.

Customer relationship management is the overall strategy whereby organization, marketing and information and communication techno-logy are structured in such a way as to optimize individual contact and the individual relationships with customers. This essentially involves three operating sectors:

● information and communication technology (ICT);

● marketing;

● organization.

Information and communication technology

Information supply should be based on the customer entity. All fixed and variable customer data should be available when required. This information can be used to provide optimum support to the customer during the buying process. Customer information should be available at the moment of contact, i.e. the moment of contact is the moment of information. An interaction module should be able to support and manage the dialogue with the customer. To this end a call centre will use a scripting module, while the Internet will employ an advanced navigation model. Call centres and the Internet will in fact use information that is already available on the customer, previous analyses of this information, and information from the dialogue (the contact). The information system must classify information according to customer entity (fixed customer data), customer entity and product (sales data) and customer contact (communication data). It will also carry out analyses in order to cluster customers. These clusters may be determined on the basis of anticipated customer value, target group characteristics, or anticipated actions. Customer contact is determined by rules for communication and by the campaign manager.

These rules and the automated campaign manager determine the moment of communication and the communication itself on the basis of past behaviour or patterns in buying behaviour. Certain specific triggers can also give rise to communication. Examples of triggers include a change of address, birthdays, changes in patterns, or contact moments. An important factor in information supply is the immediate availability of relevant customer data and historical buying behaviour at the moment of contact. It is also important to record every customer contact. This results in the continuous acquisition of customer information. By comparing this information with that of other customers, organizations will be able to anticipate their buying behaviour, which will in turn result in increased customer loyalty and positive buying behaviour.

An important factor in information supply is the immediate availability of relevant customer data and historical buying behaviour at the moment of contact

The essential difference between a CRM system and other information systems is the objective of the system. The data is not stored for administrative purposes, or to keep records of what takes place; data is maintained in order to analyze patterns, and to determine the further actions that could be taken. The information system must be available to and serve the front office (the telephone, the Internet and the account manager).

Marketing

The CRM philosophy is based on a marketing strategy that is focused on individual customer approach and requires direct contact with customers. With reference to marketing orientation, it means that CRM is particularly important to customer and network-oriented organizations. In target group-oriented organizations CRM will usually be restricted to supporting telephone communications or sellers (service-desk facilities). In actual fact this is not an application of CRM as described above, since the organization only uses certain functionality offered by the CRM software.

Customer approach based on the application of customer relationship management rests on the following elements:

- recording customer behaviour, and relating it to possible future behaviour;
- ensuring the objective management of sales;
- ensuring a direct and interactive approach;

- adjusting the marketing tools and activities to the individual contacts.

Recording customer behaviour

It is important not only to record the data but also to interpret it in the appropriate manner, and to use it when communicating with individual customers. In view of the ultimate objective – sales – it is essential that there is a direct link between a customer-focused strategy, direct communication and sales. Sales provide important information for analyses; analyses, in turn, provide more knowledge about the sales process, the behaviour of customer groups, and the future behaviour of individual customers.

Ensuring the objective management of sales

An important part of CRM is pipeline management, i.e. the management of the sales funnel. The traditional classification of customer contacts is applicable to pipeline management, namely:

- *Suspects* are potential customers who could belong to the target group.
- *Leads* are potential customers who are seemingly interested in making a purchase within the foreseeable future.
- *Prospects* are potential customers who have indicated a desire to make a purchase within the foreseeable future (they have shown an interest), and with whom the organization already has close contacts (*hot prospects*).
- *Customers* have already made a purchase.

In the last instance the delivery and the after-sales services are important areas for attention. The CRM approach does not conclude with the transaction or with the customer, as is the case in the sales process; in fact, this is where the CRM process actually begins. It is important to ensure that the provision of service, interaction and communication provides for a continued relationship with the customer (in order to obtain follow-up sales) and encourages the customer to purchase increasingly expensive goods and services (upgrading). Any phase in the sales process can be analyzed to obtain an indication of the number of customers in the pipeline, and of the probability of them making a purchase. This will not only enable organizations to improve their scheduling, which will result in quicker deliveries and better stock control and financial management, it will also enable organizations to improve their account management.

Ensuring a direct and interactive approach

Communications will also adopt a different form subsequent to the implementation of CRM. Traditional marketing approaches usually use mass-media communications, such as TV commercials, newspaper advertisements, and other facilities such as billboards. The direct marketing approach was usually based on direct communication using only very limited information, often no more than a name, an address or a telephone number. The organization wrote a letter or rang the contact. These forms of communication were usually intended to conclude a transaction, i.e. to sell.

CRM involves establishing a relationship, followed by the subsequent development of the relationship – an approach that requires much more specific communication. It requires more knowledge about the customer – not just historical information on behaviour, but also information on anticipated behaviour – since the ultimate objective is to establish a relationship. This can be achieved only when the right customer receives the right message at the right time. One possible way of achieving this, as discussed earlier, is the use of corresponding group behaviour (collaborative filtering techniques). The organization relates the anticipated behaviour of members of the group to that of others. Should many people who buy Bill Gates' book *A Road Ahead* also buy a CD of Beethoven's 9th symphony, then this will not lead to an analysis of the situation; however, the other members of this specific group will then receive information about a special offer. This is what is meant by corresponding buying behaviour – communication is based on knowledge of the group as well as on knowledge of individual customers.

Adjusting the marketing tools to the individual contacts

It is also possible to manage communications on the basis of a set of pre-defined rules, i.e. 'rules-based' communication. The rules are drawn up in advance, and as soon as a certain situation arises it is met by a pre-determined communication. The simplest example is a birthday card. Someone whose birthday falls on a specific date receives a card since the system has determined that a card will be sent (system date plus 2 = the date of the birthday). Consequently the card is prepared two days before the relevant person's birthday, mailed the day before the birthday, and the person involved receives a card or a letter of congratulations on the correct date. Many more rules are feasible. These rules can be based on events, on times or on behaviour.

Organization

A company that opts for a customer-focused strategy will need to modify its organization (see Figure 5.2). The marketing orientations have already been used to demonstrate that there is an integral relationship between the marketing orientation and the structure of the organization. An organization which opts for a CRM strategy will at least need to ensure that customer contacts are dealt with in the best possible way. This not only means that it is necessary to have the right information to deal with contacts but also that it is necessary to have the authority to do so. Customer contacts form the basis of a customer-focused strategy, which in turn means that the person who maintains the contact will also need to be authorized to collect information, to interpret the information, and to use this interpretation to make decisions in connection with the contact. Customers will be irritated when they realize that they are being assisted by a person who does not possess the necessary authority (so they don't think I'm important enough) and find themselves continually being put on hold for consultations. However, worse situations are conceivable, when customers are continually put through to someone else in the organization, or have to wait until they are called back. These are all signs that the organization does not attach enough importance to customer contacts to empower its people with the necessary authority.

Customer contacts form the basis of a customer-focused strategy

An organization that implements a CRM strategy will need to delegate greater responsibility to its front office, its account managers or its customer relationship managers. These employees must also be explicitly involved in decision making. Consequently, the changes brought about in the organization by the introduction of a CRM strategy will also apply to the organization of customer contacts.

Figure 5.2   *The traditional organizational structure*[13]

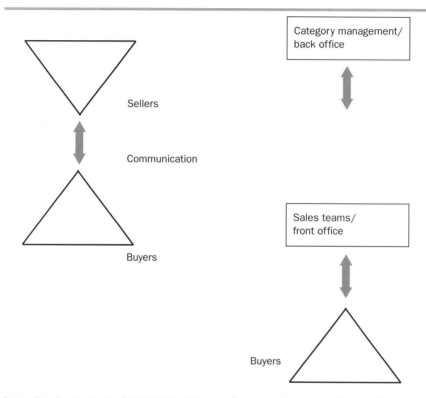

Source: Based on Westland, J.C. (1999) *Global Electronic Commerce*, Massachusetts Institute of Technology, p. 181

Adjustments to marketing tools and activities

Marketing tools and activities will also need to be based on an organization's customers. This means that the organization will have to offer its customers a choice of purchasing methods (multi-channel), and that it will need to anticipate when a customer is likely to purchase and make special offers that may be of interest to them. These special offers are not generic (for the market) but specific to a given customer. Organizations may also relate pricing to customer value. A good customer will receive more service or pay a different price for specific goods than other customers. The airlines' loyalty programmes are an example of this approach. The gold-card holders – at KLM the 'royal wing' customers – are given a preferred upgrade if the class they normally book is full. This means that they are placed in a more expensive class without needing to pay extra for the upgrade. This is a limited form of price discrimination for the benefit of valuable customers. Adjusting marketing tools to individual customers is an adjustment of product concept (more service), individual pricing, direct communication and, finally, also provides customers with the opportunity to make purchases in a different manner or at a different time. Special evening opening hours offered by some stores (such as Marks and Spencer and Bloomsbury) to customer card holders is, to some extent, an example of the modification of opening times for favoured clients. (See Table 5.1.)

Table 5.1   *CRM model based on customer contacts*

Customer					
Interaction module, such as call centre and the Internet	Service-desk telephone				Communication 'rules' and campaign manager
	Permanent customer data	Purchasing data	Analytical data and profiles	Communi-cation data	
	Analysis engine				
Supply					

The model is based on a number of groups:

- customer data;
- analyses and clustering;
- interaction with customers;
- communication with customers.

Customer data

Customer and customer-related data are stored at the heart of the model. These consist of fixed customer data, such as the customer's name, address and date of birth, or fixed company data. Records are also kept of the purchases they make – what, how many and when. Obviously this information will differ from customer to customer, but it will also vary from organization to organization. A supermarket will keep much more extensive records than, for example, a supplier of office furniture will. However, the principle involved is always the same: precise information is required about *what* the customer has bought. This information is then used to get a better insight into customer value and potential customer value, which is determined by means of analyses. The information can, for example, be used to construct what is termed a customer pyramid, in which customers are ranked according to the turnover they generate. The 80/20 rule will often be applicable, i.e. that 20% of the customers generate 80% of the turnover.

Key issues for the organization are to make sure that valuable customers are retained and motivated to continue buying and that other customers are encouraged to generate more turnover. This can be achieved by using a pro-active policy towards these customers, for example by motivating them with discounts and special offers; however, it is also possible to approach customers more frequently with commercial messages, such as letters.

Analyses and clustering

The analyses of importance to customer relationship management can be classified in terms of a few techniques that are very often used for this purpose:

- *The customer-value analysis* – classification according to turnover and profit.

- *RFM, regency, frequency and monetary value* – this involves an analysis of the number of different products purchased (regency), how often purchases are made (frequency) and the value of the sales made to the customer (monetary value). Depending on the selected strategy, customer approach can be designed to encourage customers to purchase more items in one sale, or to purchase a wider range of products. Many mail-order companies and supermarkets apply this principle by continuously making special offers for products that are not yet purchased from the organization. Organizations will also try to create traffic by making extra-special offers, in the expectation that there will always be customers who will buy them. This is usually impulse buying. Finally, an

> An organization will endeavour to encourage its customers to make more expensive purchases, and in larger quantities

organization will endeavour to encourage its customers to make more expensive purchases, and in larger quantities. Prior to the adoption of any strategy it will be necessary to review its feasibility and the actions that will be required. To this end the organization will compare the valuable and the less-valuable customers within a cluster. The choice of strategy used will depend on the conversion costs, i.e. the costs incurred in persuading customers to buy more.

● *The customer pyramid* – this methodology is based on the philosophy that an organization should try to increase existing customer loyalty and retain existing customers, as it is much more difficult to acquire new customers than it is to retain existing ones. This technique can be applied thanks to the knowledge of the customer, the information in the customer database and the information about customers' purchases. Obviously a database and direct communication are both indispensable to this approach.

Organizations will analyze information in order to classify customers into homogenous groups on the basis of identical characteristics. These groups can be clustered according to turnover, profit, the frequency of sales, the number of visits, and the quantities purchased. It is also possible to form objective clusters based on socio-demographic information, branch codes or age. In fact, the objective is to cluster customers in such a way that comparable customers (individuals and/or companies) are classified in the same cluster. Subsequently, all members of one such cluster are approached in the same way. Clusters are thus regarded as groups of customers or potential customers that are expected to exhibit homogenous buying behaviour or have homogenous needs. For this reason all members in the group are approached in the same manner, and with an identical message. Obviously, the clusters will contain customers of different value, i.e. those who make substantial purchases, and those who make smaller purchases.

In fact, the objective of clustering is to enable an organization to approach a group of customers in the same manner, and to communicate with them in the same way. This will certainly result in increased customer loyalty and, obviously, in increased turnover. Often the major customers within a cluster will determine the potential customer value of the cluster. This can be used to calculate how much turnover these customers are still expected to generate. A much-used term is 'share of wallet'. This involves assessing which share of customers' potential buying power will be used to buy products from a particular organization. This can be based on a percentage of the total buying power or on the relationship with the most valuable customer. The calculation of this potential can result in customers being approached either more intensively or less intensively, or in receiving either more or less service.

A variety of analytical techniques can be used for the measurement and assessment of customers. These may involve:

- socio-demographic analyses based on characteristics of a customer's home or neighbourhood linked to income and standard of living;
- company-specific characteristics such as industry code or the number of staff or positions within the company;
- new techniques that search for relationships between buying behaviour and fixed-objective criteria. Neural analytical techniques use this approach to group customers who, in objective terms, may have nothing in common but who, when assessed in subjective terms, nonetheless have certain characteristics in common that determine their homogenous behaviour.

Interaction with customers

Interaction with customers and buyers is usually achieved by the following three means:

- personal contacts;
- telephone (call centre);
- the use of specific media (the Internet or information kiosks).

Personal interaction is effected between a customer and a salesman or woman. The salesperson has at their disposal an information system that contains records or information about the customer, the customer card, and the special offers the customer has received. In fact, this system constitutes the basis for customer knowledge and customer contacts. This methodology was actually not developed until the mid 1980s, subsequent to the introduction of database systems focused specifically on increasing the efficiency of the sales processes.

Interaction by telephone is supported by a system that contains the same basic customer data. In addition, it has a dialogue module for telephone conversations (scripting) and an analytical module for the efficient handling of telephone traffic. The analytical module can incorporate facilities to measure how long people are kept on hold and the number of people in the queue. It can also facilitate the dynamic routing of calls to ensure that the right call or the right customer is passed on to the right person and to measure the efficiency of the agents processing the telephone calls.

Finally, it is possible to interact through a medium such as the Internet. Internet interaction also requires a database containing basic customer data. The database will, however, need to be supplemented by an interaction module that will support and measure visits to the site, as well as supporting the buying process.

There are different methods of recording customer data for the various forms of interaction. With personal contact the salesperson will need to enter the information in the system. The disadvantage of this method is that it will result in the inclusion of subjective information in the records, the possible incomplete or incorrect entry of information, or occasional omissions. These problems can be avoided in part with interaction by telephone, where information such as the date of the call, the length of the call, the subject of the call, and the agent's name is recorded automatically. With the Internet, all records, inclusive of every detail, are recorded automatically and objectively. It is even possible to make records of where visitors have come from, what they do on the site, and where they go. Tagging visitors and linking them to a general information system also allows companies to keep track of their behaviour on the Internet.

The support of interaction as described above occurs during conversation or contact; however, the rules are determined in advance. Two techniques play a dominant role. The first clearly defines what to communicate, how to interact and the possible course of contact – in effect, the specification of rules. These 'communication rules' are determined in advance, and laid down in a system. A call with a valuable customer, for instance, can follow a different course to a call with a less valuable customer. A call with a customer who has not yet responded to a quotation can differ from a call with a customer who regularly complains, or does not pay on time. In fact, the entire set of 'communication rules' governs the communication process for both the seller (albeit to a limited extent) and the buyer during the telephone conversation, and certainly during a visit to a site on the Internet.

The communication rules, the customer value and the anticipated customer value can also be used as a basis for pro-active communication with the customer. The organization will endeavour to supply the right message at the right time, a process that can be effected by the use of a 'campaign manager'. A campaign manager will employ historical behaviour, corresponding buying behaviour of people with the same profile, and external and internal triggers to form a picture of the customer so that he may assess which message to send when. Insurance companies, for example, can use the stage-in-life element to offer services to a customer: people aged 40, for example, give more thought to their pension than young people of around 20. Customers who have just had an addition to the family will be more aware of environmental issues and the future of their child.

A wide variety of triggers can give rise to a communication: birthdays, holidays, Christmas, an addition to the family, a new job, and a change of address. Different behaviour may also be a reason for seeking contact with a customer, for example if a customer has not made any purchases lately, or has started purchasing more, or has started purchasing different items. Analyzing the information and interpreting it in terms of communication rules and communication messages is a back-office task for the marketing department. The results can be used in a communication module to support the front office.

Communication with customers

In addition to the aforementioned direct interaction, it is possible to communicate with customers for reasons based on:

- events such as a birthday;
- time, such as the duration of a contract;
- behaviour: more contacts or, conversely, fewer contacts.

Events

An event is a specific occurrence or, in CRM terms, an occurrence that gives rise to a communication, such as a birthday, a change of address, a birth, a promotion or the completion of a course of study. The specific nature and type of communication to be used on these occasions can be determined in advance. An example is a birthday card – although this type of communication is generated by the system it does, nonetheless, result in increased customer loyalty.

> **An event is a specific occurrence or, in CRM terms, an occurrence that gives rise to a communication**

Time

Communications based on time may use specific dates. For example, if a customer's contract is due to expire, an organization should seek contact. Time intervals also play an important role. It is advisable to call customers a few days after they have received a quotation, or to send them a reminder if they have not yet settled a specific invoice. It is also possible to use the time interval between a customer's normal visits to a store or normal contacts with an account manager. If the usual interval of one week suddenly extends to several weeks, it may be indicative of a decrease in customer loyalty. Some type of communication, such as a letter, telephone call or e-mail, is then appropriate. Intervals can be used for the management of processes, such as a sales process, where the seller is prompted to contact customers or prospects, or to generate letters or telephone scripts, or to send e-mails. A proper analysis of customer behaviour (and corresponding behaviour) will enable the organization to assess, in good time, whether there is a risk of losing a customer, or whether contacts should be intensified.

Behaviour

Behaviour can also be a decisive factor in communication. Situations in which customers purchase less than normal, suddenly buy different items, or buy more than normal are all departures from the normal pattern and reasons for intensifying contact. Buying behaviour should be analyzed before determining the nature of the communication to be used. The RFM analysis discussed earlier is an excellent tool for the classification of customers and the determination of strategy at customer level. This strategy is then controlled on the basis of recorded customer behaviour and assisted by communication (based on standard rules). Ultimately, both behaviour and action will be analyzed and used to define new (communicative) actions.

Figure 5.3 shows that CRM is an integrality of information systems used for customer contacts as well as for the control of sales and the support of the various (distribution) channels and services. It is essential to link CRM with existing systems to ensure access to and availability of relevant data. The phases involved in one-to-one marketing can also be integrated in the model. The CRM systems offered by major international suppliers, such as Siebel, SAP, Vantive and Pivotal, form the heart of such systems. These systems consist of a front office for direct customer contact (the tele-service desk), a link to

Figure 5.3

Integrated CRM model

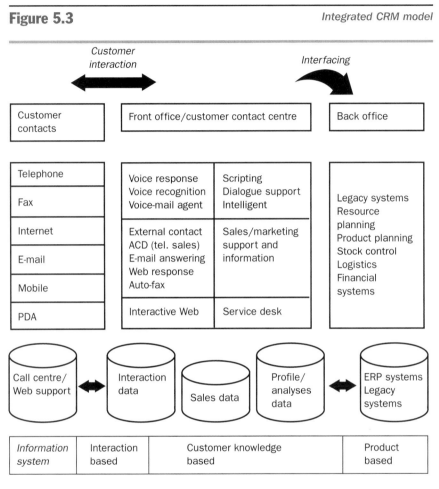

The integrated CRM model can control sales, be linked with existing (legacy) systems, and maintain customer contacts through various channels

the Internet, facilities for customer support and the management of customer contacts, an interface with existing systems and, finally, facilities for direct communications based on data.

The problems encountered during the implementation of such systems are due to the complexity of interfacing with existing systems. It is important to realize that a CRM system is constructed around the customer, while the existing data is based on orders, items or invoices. As such, it is not surprising that the suppliers of legacy systems have also started providing front-office systems. After all, in this way it is easier to realize the necessary interfaces. Examples of such suppliers are SAP and Oracle. Both initially concentrated on the development of database applications (Oracle) or on the installation of efficient information systems in organizations (ERP). A logical next step for organizations with such a basis was to optimize customer contacts with CRM. The above developments have allowed organizations to respond to the changing market (more customer oriented) and to the problem of linking CRM systems to existing systems.

Most system problems occur when organizations automate the front office with CRM software before linking the software with existing systems. These problems are not just caused by linking the various systems but also by data integrity and uniformity. The way data are stored can differ from one system to another. It will not be difficult to appreciate that the need for name and address records to be correct in every detail is more important for a CRM system than, for example, for vendor accounts. Even the name of the contact will differ in both systems, i.e. the names of the buyer and the bookkeeper respectively.

It is possible to distinguish two other key areas with reference to marketing approach, namely the multi-channel approach and communications

Based on this model it is possible to distinguish two other key areas with reference to marketing approach, namely the multi-channel approach and communications. In adopting the multi-channel approach a supplier offers his customers not one but a choice of channels. The customer could, for example, buy the supplier's items from a store, via the Internet, or by telephone. The customer is free to choose. However, as soon as the customer contacts the organization with a question or a complaint, the organization will need to have the necessary customer information to provide adequate support to the customer. This requires an integral software platform that can provide complete integrated customer information at the moment of contact. This is possible only if the customer can be designated a unique means of identification, such as a customer number, a unique combination of postal code and house number, or another form of identification. This unique key will enable organizations to recognize the customer, and to link all relevant data to the customer concerned. One of the challenges facing CRM is to make this possible and so provide customers with optimum service. It is,

Figure 5.4

Core competencies of CRM

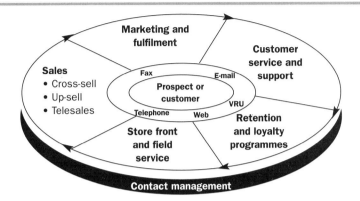

Source: Kalakota, Ravi and Robinson, Marcia (1999) *e-Business Roadmap for Success*, Addison-Wesley Longman

therefore, essential to be linked with existing systems (or to have access to data in existing systems).

Figure 5.4 shows the core competencies of CRM. Again, the customer occupies a central position and in the model applications are linked directly to an organization's interaction with the customer. Interaction itself is multi-channel and the customer can decide which method of interaction they prefer. This multi-channel facility is offered in an integral form to the customer in what may be regarded as a front office. The marketing approach is represented by the various functional areas such as loyalty, fulfilment and services. The entire concept is based on data, knowledge of the customer, and contact with the customer – i.e. the contact management system. Contact management plays a pivotal role in this model, and in CRM.

Summary

Customers need to be approached on an individual basis and organizations need to improve customer loyalty. These needs have heightened the interest in customer relationship management and one-to-one marketing. Both methodologies are based on direct customer approach, a range of products and services which accommodate customers' individual wishes, and both are founded on database information and direct communication. However, the following pre-conditions are essential to the application of these methodologies.

Buying behaviour must be repetitive. Customers who rarely make purchases will have little need to keep in contact with a supplier, as in the example of contact with an estate agent if a customer moves house only once every ten years, or contact with a kitchen supplier, or with a swimming-pool company. Repetitive buying behaviour results in the customer's perception of a relationship with the supplier, in which case personal contact will be appreciated.

The profit margin must be large enough. Personal communication and databases do not come cheap. Consequently, each transaction and each customer relationship should offer sufficient potential profit for the effective use of these methodologies. In a retail segment such as confectionery, for example, this will be more difficult to realize than in other segments such as clothing.

There must be a logical need for association. The customer must want contact. Sometimes customers will not want their behaviour to attract personal attention. It is not difficult to imagine that the customers of an Amsterdam sex club will not appreciate receiving a telephone call or a letter a week after their last visit encouraging them to call again.

However, CRM will offer many organizations a major opportunity to create a bond with their customers, and consequently foster customer loyalty. In a world of fierce competition and a jungle of suppliers and products, close customer relationships may well provide the competitive edge that companies are looking for.

The database will become crucial to customer approach and the Internet will emphasize this. But to realize this organizations will first have to review their sales processes, assess the buying process on the Internet and, finally, gain a clear insight into the changes caused by the Internet.

Notes

11 Peppers, D. and Rogers, M. (1993) *The One-to-One Future*, Piatkus Ltd, London.

12 Molenaar, C.N.A. (1993) *Het einde van de massamarketing*, Management Bibliotheek, Amsterdam; also published in an English-language edition under the title *Interactive Marketing*, Gower Publications.

13 Westland, J.C. and Clark, T.H.K. (1999) *Global Electronic Commerce*, The MIT Press, Cambridge, Massachusetts.

6

■■■■■■■■■■■■■■■

The digital market place

Let new opportunities inspire you: change is a condition for progress.

Initially, the Internet was used as a new outlet for selling standard products, e.g. books and Cds at Amazon.com. The consumer's role was confined to choosing the distribution channel. The supplier (Amazon) was looking to secure a share of the market by competing on price. Next, Amazon began providing background information on titles and assisting customers in finding specific titles by offering advanced search methods. Then, customers were approached on a more personal, pro-active basis, by bringing other relevant titles to their attention. This was enabled by sophisticated analysis systems based on customer profiles and buying behaviour, as discussed under customer relationship management in the previous chapter.

The first Internet buyers and their impact

Not all products by any means are suitable for Internet marketing. So far, the most successful products sold on the Internet are those that are often purchased on impulse, and that also require a certain amount of interaction. This explains the success of the Internet book store and CD sales. Both concern an 'emotional' product, and with both products there is a need for interaction and support. If these conditions are satisfied, the customer can be persuaded to 'give it a try'. In both cases, buyers will not be overly concerned that they may be disappointed with the quality of the product, since the purchase involves only a small risk. After all, how many CDs are played after the novelty has worn off in a few days? How many books are read from the first letter to the last? Therefore, the barrier of trust is not very high.

Initially, the traditional suppliers and outlets (booksellers, etc.) showed little faith in the new distribution medium. Hence, it was left to the 'start-ups' to experiment with new forms of selling, sales support and marketing. However, the traditional sales channels (brick and mortar) are being compelled to respond to important changes in the area of customer requirements and behaviour. Technological progress has enabled other forms of customer contact, and buying processes and behaviour can now be recorded automatically, creating an infrastructure for stimulating customer loyalty (e.g. newsletters and e-mail service). Furthermore, the established organizations can improve importantly on their efficiency by teaming up with others to increase their buying power. The development of the 'electronic market place' is a good example of this. In Chapter 2, we discussed possible changes with regard to distribution and product concepts. The development of Internet commerce creates new market relationships, leading to far-reaching, innovative changes in the traditional distribution and product concepts. This is because the Internet creates possibilities for customer bonding, whereby personalized customer information can be used for direct communication and intensive interaction.

The Internet creates possibilities for customer bonding, whereby personalized customer information can be used for direct communication and intensive interaction

The above developments are outlined here on the basis of the model of Kierzkowski (a senior consultant at New York firm McKinsey), expressing the influence of the Internet in a model that indicates the need for interactivity on one axis, and the potential for customer bonding on the other. These two angles of approach are uniquely associated with the Internet. The Internet can respond interactively to the buying process and respond to individual customers' needs. In addition, it can enhance customer loyalty. This direct relationship with the customer leads to a different market model, as discussed in relation to distribution and product concepts. The question is whether this will be applicable in all situations, and what the consequences are if this is not so. Will everything return to the way it was?

The Kierzkowski[14] model shows a number of products, services and sectors. The first movers, or innovators, who recognized the potential of the Internet are shown in the top-right quadrant. Books and CDs, financial services, real estate brokers, etc. are among the products and services found in the front ranks of e-commerce. Amazon.com, Cdnow, Fidelity, Charles Schwab, Quicken (intuit) belong to these 'first movers'.

Figure 6.1

The impact of interactivity on market relations

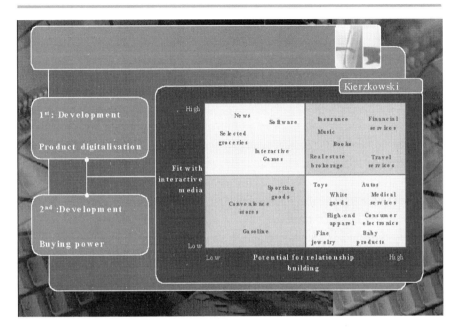

In the first instance, the use of the Internet for commercial purposes was primarily transaction focused. Companies wanted to sell, using the new technologies for electronic registration that were enabled by the Internet. Pizzas, books and CDs were some of the first products sold on the Internet. However, before a supplier could sell any such product, they had to ascertain what kind of books or music the customer enjoyed, and how they liked their pizza. Because most customers knew exactly what they wanted, not much interaction was required, apart from some basic instructions to guide the buying process. The Internet soon proved to be an excellent medium for these kinds of transactions. It could show a picture of the product, it could provide samples, and it enabled the item to be ordered immediately and payment details to be advised.

The various functions of the Internet were used as a matter of routine. First, this happened more or less by chance, as with many new developments. The supplier added some text or other information to the product, and enabled the customer to search a database. This already combined the Internet's information function with the transaction function. Further, the supplier soon found that he could use the data left behind by buyers or visitors as the base material for direct, interactive communication. Purchases could be recorded, and the information thus obtained could be used to encourage buyers to purchase other products. This, essentially, was the way Amazon.com operated. If you selected a book, you received instant tips for other books in the same genre or on the same subject. While the transaction function remained central to the process, it was consolidated with product information (i.e. satisfying the need for interaction) and followed through with other communications (customer bonding).

However, for as long as these transactions were designed merely to sell existing products using a new sales channel and a new routine, most consumers and traditional suppliers were unimpressed with the claimed potential of the Internet. The new medium and its potential applications were, in fact, appraised against the standards, conditions and commercial requirements of the real world. The Internet issue was seen as a sales question: how many of such and such were sold, at what price, at what cost, and what are the problems associated with a 'multi-channel' strategy? However, the innovative value of any new technology stands to be underrated unless one is prepared to appraise the innovation on its specific merits and potential, and provided that the use of the new technology relies on its innovative qualities. This also applies to the Internet. In recent years, many new concepts have been introduced that depend on the possibilities of the Internet, and which are not possible without it, or at least not in the same form. The effect and the effectiveness of these concepts rely on Internet technology, in combination with its unparalleled reach. In the Kierzkowski model (Figure 6.1), this is shown in the bottom-right quadrant. The new media focus on the typical Internet quality of enabling consumers to use those media when and how it suits them. This freedom of choice gives Internet shoppers more power than their counterparts in the real world, who have to comply with the conditions set by the supplier (opening times, product range, price, etc.).

This transition from 'push to pull' will have the effect of a channel reversal. In the real world, the sales process is directed by the supplier, following a specific supply chain management system. The products are pushed in the direction of the consumer. The consumer can choose from a specific product range. Essentially, it is a question of 'take it or leave it'. If, however, consumers are able to bundle their individual buying power, they can exert a certain negotiating pressure on the supplier.

Figure 6.2   *Priceline.com gives a boost to buyer power*

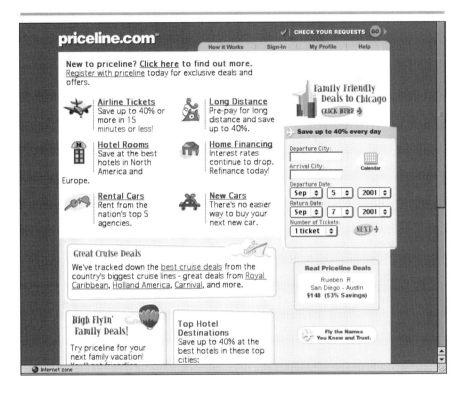

The Internet has given consumers an instrument that enables them to bundle their buying power on an unparalleled scale. In the real world, this can happen only on a relatively small scale, seeing that consumers have to be approached by the traditional, physical media, e.g. advertisements. The advantage of scale, in the real world, is confined by physical and logistic restrictions and limited media reach. To achieve a similar purpose, consumers can join so-called buying collectives, which will negotiate special price deals for their members. A buying collective might focus on a specific category of products, as occurs in the agricultural industry, or serve a specific professional group, e.g. public servants or corporate staff. The Internet has increased this reach dramatically, enabling organized groups and individual buyers to combine their buying power across industrial and even national frontiers. The Internet thus enables consumers to exert far greater buyer power than was ever possible in the real world. An example of this is Priceline.com, a site that negotiates special prices on behalf of potential buyers (see Figure 6.2). After slimming down Priceline.com was profitable in the second quarter of 2001.

In the same way, other groups will be set up by people sharing common interests, joining hands to negotiate special price deals. The 18th-century philosophy of the power of the collective is thus restored to full lustre, but this time to be applied on a global scale.

Minimum interaction, maximum customer bonding

Some products do not require intensive interaction; however, buyers may feel a strong sense of bonding. This may be from habit, preference for a certain brand, or by some form of emotional attachment. The buyer keeps coming back, and they express a desire to continue the relationship. The supplier responds to this need by consolidating the relationship, for instance with customer loyalty programmes. Moreover, such durable customer relationships enable suppliers to register and classify consumer demand relatively accurately. For instance, a customer who buys CDs regularly is not likely to purchase the same CD twice but will probably buy other CDs in the same genre. These are the types of products that people often attach to emotionally. If not, there would not be the same need for interactivity. Although the customer will appreciate some assistance, the product hardly needs any customization or differentiation. This group of products is shown in the bottom-right quadrant of Figure 6.1. These items are often bought impulsively, but there is a bond with the supplier. Often, the consumer will trust the product or the supplier. Many of the products in this group respond to emotion and personal involvement (toys, baby items), bought on impulse and not designed to last.

Durable customer relationships enable suppliers to register and classify consumer demand relatively accurately

This group could include products that are sold at a large discount, offering an immediate financial advantage. Of course, the products in this group can still be sold via the traditional process: looking, offering, buying and supplying. However, since distribution is an important factor, it may pay to consider alternative, new forms of distribution. For this, one must take a fresh look at the basic factors, e.g. why the customer buys a certain product, how to encourage customer bonding, and in what way a new distribution form could improve on the traditional channels. The bundling of buying power, for instance, is a development that can be facilitated by the Internet. The discounts negotiated with suppliers could be used to offer customers a better price. A further advantage is that items can be bought anywhere in the world, from whoever offers the lowest price.

The Internet, furthermore, plays host to target group sites that offer items on behalf of a specific group of potential buyers. Their objective is to secure customer loyalty by emotional attachment. In addition to selling certain items, they publish Internet newsletters and provide specific information.

An important event in people's lives is a new baby, and also one that creates the need for a host of information. Parents not only require medical information, but they will be keen to have information on products, and they may wish to share experiences with other mothers and fathers. After all, it is important to parents to know that they are providing what's best for their baby. baby.com is a supplier that responds to this target group, selling a range of items and investing in emotional attachment. The graphics ('look and feel' of the site) encourage emotional attachment (a picture showing a young mother breastfeeding her baby) with soft tones and shades, and the items shown are designed to evoke emotional associations. The site also has a column where visitors can ask questions about babies, pregnancy and motherhood, and there is a chat room for parents who want to communicate with other parents. baby.com offers a complete range of products and services, generating a high level of emotional attachment and providing for all the needs of new mothers.

Another development in the field of distribution is the link between suppliers and buyers. With the forms of distribution discussed earlier, the distribution function was still quite specific. However, by linking potential buyers and suppliers via the Internet, the distribution process can be facilitated without having to add value to the product or service. An example of this is the Internet auction. The first auction of this kind was held as early as 1995, using the traditional format and working method of auctions. Following the 'Dutch auction' formula, a starting price was set for the product, which was then gradually reduced until someone clicked 'mine' to buy. If no one had pressed 'mine' by the time the reserve price was reached (which was obviously an undisclosed figure), the item was withdrawn from the auction. However, you cannot

Figure 6.3   *www.baby.com not only sells a complete range for babies and expectant or new mothers but also provides a host of information, an on-line community and a chat room*

link buyers and sellers without a distribution link (such as a mail-order company). Therefore this function is performed by Web sites such as ebay.com (see Figure 6.4). If you want to sell or buy a product, you can list it with ebay. Visitors can bid on the item, and the highest bidder within a certain period of time is the new owner. ebay only facilitates the process.

Because the bidding is public (the highest bid at any given time, the number of bids made and the remaining time to bid are all tallied), a tension arises which many visitors and buyers experience as part of the fun. Visitors often return to see what's on sale, and Internet auctions have already become hugely successful. The fact that the buying and selling process is now an international affair is, of course, an important bonus, but the element of excitement plays an important role too. There is a playfulness about Internet auctions that many visitors find hard to resist. Meanwhile, other providers have set up similar auction formulas

Figure 6.4   *www.ebay.com is an auction site selling a large range of items, both new and used. You can offer items for sale, and there is a chat room*

in an attempt to increase 'site stickiness'. Portals such as Planet Internet and Yahoo! are examples of these.

Based on the correlation between interaction and customer loyalty, the conclusion appears to be that customer loyalty can be encouraged, even where the options for interaction are limited. If this is so, the supplier might provide more extensive information rather than merely offering a product for sale. This can be a community facility, a chat room or a FAQ column (frequently asked questions).

Another strategy that can work is changing the distribution concept. Options for this include buying combinations based on new technological options (such as priceline.com) or enabling a direct link between buyers and sellers, as with Internet auctions. The key with any approach lies in consolidating relationships and working on earning

The key with any approach lies in consolidating relationships and working on earning and maintaining the trust of buyers and sellers

and maintaining the trust of buyers and sellers, as well as keeping an open mind to new distribution concepts and possibilities.

Changes in the product concept

In addition to different distribution concepts, different product concepts can be used. This strategy can work in situations where there is not much opportunity for customer bonding but visitors nevertheless have a need for interaction. A news service is an example of this. Most readers probably take a special interest in specific news items, e.g. financial information. With stock exchange news, for example, readers would want to follow the general trend (common need), as well as being interested in more specific information on share prices that affect their own investment portfolio. Likewise, there would be a need for interaction with specific medical products, food items and software products. Another example of a change in product concept is the way wine is sold on the Internet. Based on personal preference and taste, the Internet way of selling wine allows people to choose the wine that best matches their preferences. The buyer's knowledge of the subject, together with their faith in the supplier, is the basis for the transaction. The Internet winery is a good example of a product that wants a certain interaction in order to match the supply with individual demand. Customers' knowledge of different brands (i.e. preference for particular chateaux) is apparently limited. Most buyers go by their preferred taste, colour and favoured region. Naturally, the latter also reflects taste. This formula for choosing and buying a product offers a wealth of opportunities for the supplier to combine customer knowledge and interactive processes. A registration form can be used to question visitors on their preferences, while purchase registration and individual product appraisal enables the supplier to respond at a more individual level. This, in brief, is the formula of www.wine.co.uk (see Figure 6.5).

Other products that are particularly suited to this style of interaction are the various news columns. Investment sites can provide personalized investment information, and news sites can offer customized newsletters. The personalization of the service is made possible by using the individual preferences communicated by the customer, enabling selections to be made from the news database which are then presented to the readers as 'personal' news. An example of this type of news service is www.mycnn.com. Based on their personal

Figure 6.5   *www.wine.co.uk sells wine on the basis of registered preferences and buyers' profiles*

interests, users compile their own news page, which they can access by entering a password. Alternatively, the user may wish to receive a personalized newsletter, containing selected news items only, based on pre-registered individual requirements. In all of this, interactivity is the key, as it enables users to select items from the available columns. Advertisers, too, may opt for their banners to appear only with the most appealing columns or only with certain personal newsletters. In essence, this service is an optimal form of 'targeted marketing'.

Other sites that lend themselves well to interaction are sports columns that not only include sports news but also have items on sports gear and training programmes, and special nutrition sites, e.g. vegetarian foods and other diets (www.vegetarian.com, www.exercise.com and www.diet.com (see Figure 6.6)).

The Internet is a more difficult medium when it comes to selling products that allow little or no room for customer bonding, and which do not require any interaction. A product like fuel fits into this group.

Figure 6.6 *www.diet.com responds to personal needs*

Although many people tend to visit the same service station (for convenience of location or service quality) and may prefer a certain fuel brand (image or loyalty programmes), it is difficult to stimulate product preference where the demand and the product are homogenous. Thus, the Internet could only play a role here if the concept itself was changed. This could be done, for instance, by introducing more product diversity, e.g. unleaded petrol, eco-friendly petrol, petrol for certain types of cars, or by changing the demand structure. Furthermore, quantum discounts can be negotiated by demand bundling, as at priceline.com. By registering purchase details, orders can be placed in advance, per unit of total tank volume. At the close of a period, a quantum discount is calculated, based on the total quantity purchased (as at United Consumers.com in the Netherlands).

The above approach challenges conventional distribution concepts, demanding not only more creativity but also a keen eye for the opportunities of the Internet, and an open mind to alternative forms of customer bonding and product sales. The Kierzkowski model provides a basis for a new approach to product and distribution concepts, based on customer bonding and interactive buying.

Product digitization

The shift in the model whereby there are fewer options for customer bonding clearly reflects a product-oriented approach. The required interaction with the purchase of a product is facilitated. This trend can be characterized as a 'digitization trend', whereby physical products are digitized to make them downloadable. This has the following important advantages:

- enabling product personalization in response to customer specifics;
- eliminating shipping costs and logistics problems;
- enabling various releases and time-bound licensing to be used.

Software is of course the prime example. By making software products downloadable, the potential buyer can sample the product, select software products on the basis of specific requirements, and download the product to their own computer. To ensure that a product meets the customer's expectations, a test version can either be supplied, or the product can be made available for a limited time, e.g. 30 days. Upon expiry of the trial period, the user must purchase a licence for the product if they wish to continue using it. For the software supplier this system has important advantages. It eliminates the need for a distribution channel, and it enables the supplier to maintain direct contact with his potential buyers and to increase his market reach. Communicating directly with end users enables the supplier to keep in touch with customer needs, with a view to future product releases, and to register customer preferences. As a result, different releases of software products can be developed to respond better to target group needs by incorporating more specific requirements and product elements. It also enables the supplier to stimulate demand by adding product features and improvements on a regular basis.

> **Communicating directly with end users enables the supplier to keep in touch with customer needs**

It speaks for itself that this form of digitization is much easier to realize with non-physical products than with physical ones. Physical products, typically, are restricted because they are always based to some extent on standard products, and because they must be shipped and delivered. The traditional product concepts and distribution channels, naturally, were developed to enable physical product trading. However, as the level of interaction continues to increase and product demand becomes more and more individual, the physical element of products can be reduced. This is possible by creating product components and modules, and by adding service elements. In principle, most products consist of three components – a physical component, a service component and a perception component. The service component in particular can be used to create an impression of personalization. In this way, the supply of the physical product can be separated from the provision of sales support through the digital media.

Essentially, a personalized service is provided with a standard physical product. The interaction is necessary to determine what product the customer wants and when it must be delivered. These factors also determine the price. Mail-order companies provide this kind of service. Landsend.com, for example, offers customers the option of tailoring a new-bought shirt to meet their individual requirements (see Figure 6.7). Single or double cuffs, two breast pockets or none, and collar type can all be chosen by the customer. The shirt can be delivered with or without a monogram, embroidered wherever the customer prefers it. The customer perceives the end result as a personalized product, while the supplier, in the process, is able to collect a host of information on customer needs and preferences.

Changes in buying behaviour

Several of the concrete changes introduced by the Internet were described on the basis of Kierzkowski's model. Broadly, these changes can be grouped into five directions:

- transparency for consumers;
- wholesale buying by new intermediaries;
- consumer buying power;
- direct link between buyers and sellers;
- product digitization.

In each case, the Internet has been instrumental in creating the conditions for the development. What matters is in how far customers are prepared to commit to a certain product, supplier or concept that could potentially change existing product and distribution concepts.

Figure 6.7

Landsend.com lets consumers create their own shirt by selecting and combining various components

Transparency for consumers

The first developments seen in relation to the new possibilities of the Internet are the advanced search engines. Search engines do not promote specific interests but create order and transparency in a massive supply of information. The 'old' search engines, such as Altavista.com and lycos.com, required the user to specify a subject, a company or a product so that the search engine could then scan the Web for 'hits'. Although this facility in itself does not signify a change, these providers have increasingly developed into Internet portals, such as Yahoo!, performing a search function as well as providing real information on sites found, and, especially, selling advertising space. However, the development of intelligent browsers and so-called bots is advancing quickly, now enabling users to add information and anticipating search behaviour on the basis of 'click' patterns. As a result, the Internet user is automatically guided to relevant sites, at the same time receiving tips on other sites of possible interest.

The supplier's challenge is to somehow control that process. Options include linking up with the portals through icons and banners, trying for placement at the top of search lists, and possibly participating in a bot or an intelligent browser. Another option for steering visitor patterns is ensuring that attractive information is provided on behalf of the target group. Defining the product or service in the clearest possible manner increases the chance of being re-routed. Therefore, it is important that the role of the search engines is fully appreciated, as increasingly these are the brokers that create transparency in the information supply.

Wholesale buying by new intermediaries

If demand is plentiful, it is possible for parties to negotiate special price discounts on behalf of end users. This is not the same as bundling buying power, in which case the demand for a certain delivery is bundled prior to negotiations with the supplier. Rather, certain goods are bought wholesale, to be resold later at a discount. This effectively creates a new distribution link, replacing the physical distribution channel link, e.g. a wholesaler or store that is part of the supply chain, with a distribution link that anticipates demand. Essentially, this is an example of the so-called 'demand chain', a development that is happening with products and services that cannot be physically stocked, such as hotel rooms, plane tickets or holiday accommodation. Wholesale buyers will reserve a number of rooms, seats or other time-bound accommodation, which enables them to negotiate special prices for services that are later resold at a discount.

expedia.com works like this (see Figure 6.8). The site enables consumers to reserve hotel accommodation and travel arrangements, with expedia.com serving as the broker. This is not, however, a case of shortening the supply chain or cutting out the middleman *(demediation)*, a development often associated with the virtual market place. The real change here lies in that fact that the demand – and the promotion of that demand – is no longer directed by the suppliers but by the demanding – or near-demanding – parties. A change, in other words, from 'push' to 'pull'.

Consumer buying power

With this development, individual customers bundle their needs for a certain product or service so as to be able to negotiate a better price with the producer/supplier. Bundling consumer demand can also be a

Figure 6.8   *Expedia.com buys in bulk to cater for future demand*

way for specific products to be developed and manufactured. Here, market reach is used to influence the relationship with the supplier or manufacturer. What this effectively creates is a new form of collective buying, based on individual needs. This differs essentially from the traditional buying collectives, which are founded on a universal demand.

> **Bundling consumer demand can also be a way for specific products to be developed and manufactured**

Potential market size is a precondition for this new concept. It is a concept that is particularly interesting because of the Internet's potential for bundling consumer demand on a worldwide scale. For individual markets, however, its use will probably be limited.

Direct link between buyers and sellers

The developments described above assume a new Internet function, i.e. that of a broker or intermediary. However, this intermediary can act merely as a facilitator, rather than actually performing specific buying or selling functions, as described. This is, in fact, the philosophy behind Internet auctions. The consequences of the development noted are as follows:

● relationship building on the basis of trust and membership;
● attractive deal due to price advantage;
● shift of power towards buying party;
● suppliers must approach target groups/target group agents.

Digitization of products

In order to supply personalized products and services and avoid logistics problems, more and more products and services will be digitized. Service products are the most suitable for this, but certain service elements of physical products can be digitized too, e.g. facilitating the buying process, providing information, and supplying user information/directions for use. The changes resulting from product digitization were demonstrated on the basis of the Kierzkowski model (Figure 6.1).

Summary The behaviour of Internet buyers still betrays strong bonds with the real world. Research has taught that the Internet is used mostly for finding information and shopping at established stores. Although there are new shopping concepts, e.g. auctions and last-minute options, there are no indications yet that consumers are turning to them en masse. It is clear that consumers need time to get used to new shopping formats, and that they have yet to deal with the fact that they are no longer totally dependent on the conditions of the supplier. However, it is expected that the opportunities of the Internet will bring about different consumer behaviour patterns, and that this will create a new balance of power between buyers and suppliers and in the supplying industry.

The changes brought by the Internet not only concern new ways of selling products and services. The Internet enables consumers to communicate with each other directly, and provides them with better, more, and more objective information. The future consumer will decide more consciously where they will buy (shop, telephone, Internet), how they will buy (home delivered or collect from shop) and in how much detail they wish to be informed. The Internet has enabled new concepts to be developed for certain products, i.e. total concepts for baby products, and has enabled the combination of digital services with physical products. By making products downloadable, the Internet creates opportunities for personalizing certain products and services, e.g. software, news and information services.

The Internet, typically, has stimulated the development of new distribution concepts, introducing a shift of power away from the supplier in favour of the consumer. Buying power bundling and consumer communities will enable buyers to negotiate discounts, and will lead to important changes in buying and selling behaviour.

Note

14 Kierzkowski, *McKinsey Management Review*, spring 1996.

7

■■■■■■■■■■■■■■■

Not everyone is equal on the Internet

Hiding behind semantics and jargon is concealing a lack of knowledge and understanding.

The ways in which people use the Internet are very different. For example, everyone has a preferred time for logging in, a preference for particular sites, and everyone spends a different amount of time on a particular site. In addition to this, affinity with technology, how people deal with a virtual environment and personal characteristics play a part. It is therefore not logical to simply assume that everyone uses the Internet in the same way. Consequently Internet suppliers set up their sites in such a way that they are geared to the needs and the behaviour of the target group.

Usually sites do not go beyond adding a language module in anticipation of visitors from different countries and creating a simple navigational structure to guide visitors to the right part of the site. However, to properly anticipate the behaviour of a visitor, you need to do more. Is it a once-only visitor or does the visitor come more often (record the visiting behaviour)? Where do the visitors come from (cultural influences)? What do they want (role of the Internet)? And finally, do visitors come to the site on purpose or by accident? In fact, suppliers should not wait passively for a visitor but respond pro-actively to the target group they wish to attract. For this purpose it is necessary to have a deep insight into the use of the Internet.

Recording

It is easy to surf from one site to another. Where do surfers go and where do they come from? This can easily be traced on the Internet. Analysis software can record where visitors have come from and where they go. Specific suppliers of analysis systems are capable of 'tagging' visitors (attaching a label) so that all aspects of their behaviour can be followed. As a result of 'tagging' nothing is actually secret on the Internet. It is possible to analyze exactly when someone does what, and what it is they do. It is important for a supplier to know about his visitor's surfing behaviour, as it will help him decide what information his visitors are interested in. However, while tagging may be nice for suppliers, it is highly doubtful whether visitors will appreciate it. Visitors may appreciate the fact that the information supplied matches their behavioural pattern, but they may find it unpleasant that everything is being recorded. These methodologies, however powerful, are an invasion of the privacy of the Internet surfer. The way in which the supplier handles this information determines the extent of the intrusion on one's privacy. Those who have a mail account at hotmail.com know from experience the effect of 'spamming' (unsolicited e-mail based on recorded surfing behaviour). Almost everyone finds this type of communication distasteful.

Another way of recording behaviour is to supply the visitor's computer with software by putting a small program on their computer

Another way of recording behaviour is to supply the visitor's computer with software by putting a small program on their computer. In this way a supplier is provided with relevant information every time the visitor logs on again. Such a program is called a 'cookie'. If the visitor is not aware of this, he could have hundreds of cookies on his computer. A cookie identifies someone as a previous visitor and allows certain attributes to be recorded. The advantage for a visitor is that they are recognized immediately and do not have to register with every visit. The disadvantage is the previously mentioned facility to analyze a visitor's behaviour and to change files on the visitor's computer without their consent. On a regular basis there are rumours about viruses being transferred to computers. A notorious one was the 'I love you' virus. The hard drive was erased as soon as the mail message in question was opened.

It is also possible to manipulate routing via the Internet. This is what happens when certain sites are displayed instead of the site the visitor intended to see, or when 'pop-up' menus are displayed at set times (every minute), or when it is impossible to leave a certain site because there is no exit option. This type of supplier is highly irritating to Internet users. Malafide companies can be found mainly on sex-related and gambling sites. Many suppliers, which are already dubious in the normal world, use the Internet in an aggressive way to bind visitors. In this way the Internet user can be irritated to the extent that a negative effect is achieved. Conversely, the technique of putting cookies on a visitor's computer has its advantages if it enables a visitor to navigate a site more quickly, if it supports buying behaviour by applying past knowledge to current behaviour and, for example, if it helps to remember passwords.

Another way of achieving the same objective, with reference to the supplier and the visitor, is to employ a registration procedure. If a visitor has to sign on every time they visit the site, the visitor's profile can be updated and used during the visit. The easiest way of doing this is by requesting a user name and password. The registration is then completed on the site and not on the visitor's computer. It is not until the visitor clearly indicates that they wish the password to be remembered that information is recorded on their computer. This is a better method of following a visitor than the method previously described. In the first case the supplier puts a cookie on the visitor's computer, often without the visitor's knowledge. In the second case the visitor determines whether or not the information is recorded.

Search behaviour

It is often thought that visitors surf the Internet at random, that they go from site to site on impulse (hyperlinks and banners) or on a whim. This behaviour is typical of those who are new to the Internet. Newcomers are easily led astray and they find it exciting to try out all kinds of possibilities and to visit all kinds of sites. Suddenly, a whole virtual world opens up to these beginners. More experienced users, however, have their preferences. They have an extensive list of frequently visited sites called 'favourites'. They are very judicious in the way they use the Internet. They do not simply go surfing in an unstructured way, allowing themselves to be manipulated. This contrast can be visualized in a model (see Figure 7.1) depicting the two dimensions of search behaviour:

- structured and unstructured;
- perceived security and insecurity.

If someone's search behaviour is structured, it means that they make a

Figure 7.1   *Dimensions of search behaviour*

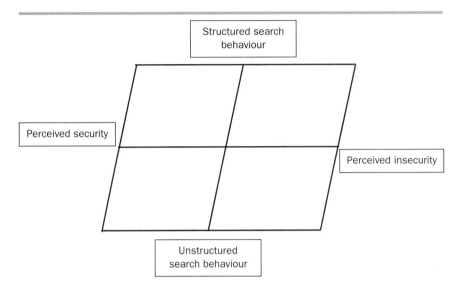

conscious decision to visit certain sites, whereas if someone's search behaviour is unstructured, it means that this person is led by suggestions or impulses. The other dimension that can be distinguished is security. When visitors go to a site, is it because they trust the supplier, or because the site looks familiar? The familiarity or, for example, the 'look and feel' of the site can provide a certain degree of 'perceived security'. It makes visitors trust the supplier. Trust is an important factor for doing business on the Internet. After all, you can only wait and see what happens to the data provided (including credit card data) and wait and see if the items ordered are also delivered. These two dimensions can be used to create a model on the basis of which it is possible to analyze the behaviour of Internet users.[15]

Unstructured surfers do not know beforehand where they will end up. They allow themselves to be strongly governed by impulses and suggestions. If they land on a certain site, they click banners and icons or react to hyperlinks. They often respond to the site impulsively, they are quick to judge, and the site must immediately invite them to click. The site must display all its possibilities almost as soon as they arrive. The sites that are visited on the basis of this kind of unstructured search behaviour must immediately convey a message and must have an image that meets the visitor's expectations. As unfamiliar sites are often happened upon by accident, they must convey the feeling of being scrupulous in their approach to visitors. This must be accompanied by a clear navigational structure: what possibilities are there, how do you proceed and how can you visit all facets of the site? This navigational structure can be displayed by means of tabs at the top of a site or by means of headings, often to the left of the site. Visitors can go directly to a certain section, let themselves be navigated and return directly to the home-page. Nothing is allowed to be unclear to the visitor. In addition, such a site must have the right 'look and feel'. Often light colours inspire more confidence than dark colours. After all, a black site will sooner convey a sense of foreboding. In the real world, black can be chic. That is, however, not the case on a computer screen.

If a supplier wants to approach the unexpected visitor, he must ensure that there is a logical connection between the site the visitor has come from and the site they will visit next

If a supplier wants to approach the unexpected visitor, he must ensure that there is a logical connection between the site the visitor has come from and the site they will visit next. It is often possible to recognize behavioural patterns, which can be based on:

- a certain interest;
- a certain need for news;
- a certain need for fun/entertainment;
- other.

The above-mentioned impulse-driven search behaviour must be founded on certain basic needs. People search on an area of interest and click from one site to another, often led by suggestions (banners, icons or mention in a newsletter). It is easy to build a network of related sites based on interests, all with something slightly different to offer. In principle, independent suppliers can refer visitors to each other in this way. This is a form of network marketing. Sometimes suppliers use this marketing method to keep visitors on their own sites by developing a multitude of sites that all refer to each other. For example, it is known that suppliers of sex-related sites have numerous sites with a different 'look and feel' that appeal to different interests. In this way visitors can surf from one site to another and still stay with the same supplier and the supplier can capture and follow the visitor.

Visitors interested in news can be routed in the same way. Often routing will not only be news oriented but also based on other activities. Suppliers of stock market data, for example, may leave the processing of purchase/sales orders to other parties and get their income from advertisements and by charging a commission for each transaction. The actual site will connect visitors to news, alert functions and portfolio management. If unequivocal agreements are made with the transaction party, parties may also agree not to enter into competition. In this way it is possible to use each other's information to make the site even more attractive for visitors.

If a visitor is on the Internet for fun, there are many ways of taking advantage of this. The easiest way is to offer a game that is related either directly or indirectly to the site. The site www.samenleven.nl, for example, allows visitors to do a partner test. They can compare their partner's character to that of the 'ideal partner'. There are also sites where visitors can play short games by, for example, guessing results. The site www.guezz.com allows visitors to gamble on the AEX index. Every day visitors can enter their forecast. The person closest to the actual closing index wins a prize. Depending on the number of visitors and their behaviour, suppliers can link commercial messages or banners, or provide hyperlinks. In the above case, the game is the carrier for stickiness and for the visit. In other cases, the game could form part of a site and only add a bit of 'fun', making the site more attractive.

There are many other reasons for going on to the Internet: to look for specific information, to conduct research, to compare competitors, to put a site onto the Internet, or just to have a bit of fun browsing booksellers or music sites or just to see where you end up. A supplier can approach visitors directly to steer their behaviour or prompt them to visit a certain site, for example by e-mail or by sending newsletters directly to their mailboxes.

Perceived security can be achieved by:

- a familiar name;
- a good and transparent site;
- a clear navigational structure;
- the right colour combination and site layout.

These are factors suppliers can influence themselves. Advertising campaigns can promote brands. However, they are extremely costly and it is very questionable whether the costs outweigh the effectiveness of such campaigns. It is far more effective to promote a brand name on the same medium rather than a different one. If a supplier uses a different medium, such as a billboard, to promote their product, the commercial message will not reach the consumer when they are on the Internet (the traditional media versus the Internet). Consumers are bombarded daily with a large number of commercial messages. The chance of such a message sticking is very remote. Internet companies put a lot of effort into advertising, which proves that it is difficult to achieve brand awareness using traditional media only. Although it is costly, it is more effective for a supplier to use a combination of different media to deliver a message. If a supplier only has a limited marketing budget, then the Internet is a good solution. A supplier can invest in banners, icons, affiliate marketing and search engines. In this way, natural behaviour logically leads to brand awareness. Add to this word-of-mouth communication, and advertising becomes a success. Two Swedish clothing companies both took a different approach to achieving brand awareness. Both companies were unsuccessful. www.boo.com (Figure 7.2)

Figure 7.2   *Despite considerable marketing effort, the clothing company www.boo.com was unsuccessful*

Figure 7.3   *In August 2000 dressmart.com decided to reduce its activities and concentrate on the home market in Sweden*

tried to achieve brand awareness by extensive advertising in the traditional media. Despite all the effort and an investment in excess of $100,000,000, sales were well below the break-even point, which meant that the owners were forced to close up shop.

On the other hand, www.dressmart.com (Figure 7.3) used the Internet as an advertising medium to attract attention. Using the method described above, it rapidly succeeded in creating brand awareness. However, this was not enough to capture a piece of the global market. In July 2000, it decided to reduce its global activities and concentrate on the home market in Sweden. This meant that all offices outside Sweden were closed down and marketing effort in other countries reduced to a minimum. It is still possible, however, for someone outside Sweden to log on to the site and order designer wear. This is typical of the Internet. Marketing reach remains global despite the fact that companies perhaps advertise only on the local or national market.

Both examples show that it is difficult to be active in many markets at once. The marketing costs involved in creating brand awareness in all these markets, especially when using traditional media, are unprecedented.

Domain names

A name that is short and catchy is easier to remember than a long one; a logical name is better than a fantasy one

A name also has to appeal to the public. A name that is short and catchy is easier to remember than a long one; a logical name is better than a fantasy one. Suppliers that are already established in the real world have an advantage over those that are not. Long-standing organizations can pride themselves on their credentials as well as on their reputation and name. Companies such as Gucci, Macy, Philips or Coca Cola are well known and have a regular clientele. These companies are usually also successful on the Internet. They do not have the problems that start-up companies have, they do not suffer from obscurity or a lack of credentials, and they have ample experience. At most, these organizations are burdened by their structure, culture and methodologies. To date, however, this burden has proven too much for the successful development of e-strategies.

Instead of well-known companies using the name they have in the real word, they can also use a logical name. Names such as diet.com, wine.com and food.com are not only easy to remember, but they also match the logical thought pattern of surfers looking for wine, food or special diet food.

A third alternative is a short name. A three-letter name is easier to remember than a long name. Unfortunately, however, all names, both at com/net/org level and at national level, have already been claimed. Brokers often deal in names. These names are, of course, still available, but in this way acquiring ownership is more expensive than simply registering domain names.

These days, companies choosing a name and wanting an Internet domain are increasingly faced with problems. Many names are no longer available. Logical names and short names are already being used or have already been claimed. Development is currently focused on using parts of a sentence rather than a name. For example, if the name dress.com is no longer available, companies may use mydress or smartdress. In this way it is still possible to make a logical connection. An alternative is to introduce a logical typing error. The 'AltaVista' search engine is known all over the world. It could, for example, be possible to start a search engine under the name of 'AltaVisa' (without the 't'). This is not only easy to remember, because it relates to an

Figure 7.4

*Privacy statement by www.smartmoney.com. This statement
also describes smartmoney's cookie policy*

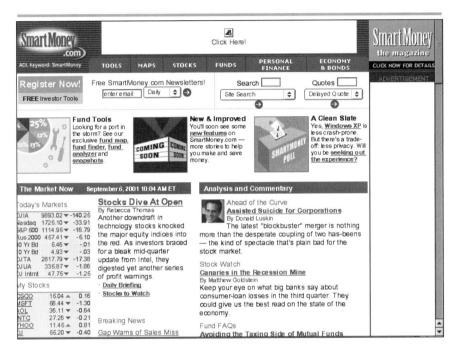

existing site, but in this way it is also possible to take advantage of the
logical typing errors visitors are bound to make. A domain name owner
must, therefore, also be prepared to claim names derived from logical
typing errors and route them to their own site. This is what happens
when people make a typing error in altavista.com. They are deliberately
re-routed together with the amazon.com logo. It is also possible to re-
route visitors directly without their knowledge.

Many sites are geared to protecting the privacy of their visitors.
Many US sites have included a privacy statement on their site, which
clearly states what the data are used for. In this way a bona fide
company can show that it respects the privacy of its visitors and at the
same time inspire trust for all its activities and services (see Figure 7.4).

Women on the Internet

Until recently, men outnumbered women on the Internet. But now
research has shown that since 2000 American women have taken the

lead and that it will not be long before the same is true for the more mature European markets (Scandinavia, the Netherlands and the UK). The male domain, as the Internet was called, is now much more a reflection of normal society. The question of whether women are more or less active on the Internet would be irrelevant if women showed the same behaviour as men. As male behaviour differs from female behaviour on the Internet, it is important for suppliers to know whether they have male or female visitors.

For example, men will have a better look around on the Internet before they buy anything. Men are likelier to spend more time looking for information and are more likely to have a quick look at the competitor. Women are more inclined to buy immediately from the site visited. This could mean that women orientate themselves using other media than the Internet before making a purchase and look on specific sites only for relevant information. Men are more likely to exit a certain site if it takes too long to find something and look elsewhere. Therefore, women's behaviour on the Internet is more deliberate than that of men. The items that are bought also differ on a number of points. Women have a tendency to want to see, touch and perhaps even smell items before buying them, such as items of clothing. Men go more for the look. This also influences their preferences for items on the Internet (see Table 7.1).

In both cases we can see a strong preference for books and CDs, which can be explained by the fact that such sites are usually mature sites (first movers) and that purchasing from these sites does not normally lead to problems. Furthermore, such sites supply extensive information. Based on the preference for these sites, research was conducted to find out whether these preferences also manifest themselves in the buying behaviour on the Internet. Here, too, there are differences between men and women (see Table 7.2).

Researchers have reached a number of conclusions on the basis of their findings:

- Men orientate themselves more than women on the Internet.

Research shows that men have a look at the supplier's competitor and also go to other sites for information before buying. Men are inclined to surf more than women prior to purchasing. Women are quicker to buy and perhaps more deliberate in their buying behaviour.

- Women are more aware of the security risks involved.

Table 7.1   *Favourite sites for men and women*

Favourite sites for men	%	Favourite sites for women	%
Amazon.com	55	Amazon.com	49
BarnesandNoble.com	31	BarnesandNoble.com	30
CDNow.com	30	CDNow.com	24
Buy.com	25	Etoys.com	21
Egghead.com	22	Drugstore.com	20
Office Max	16	JC Penney	18
Best Buy	15	Buy.com	17
Office Depot	14	Disney	17
Etoys.com	13	PlanetRX.com	17
Reel.com	13	BlueMountainArts.com	15

Source: Ernst & Young, April 2000

Table 7.2   *Favourite categories for men and women*

Favorite categories for men	%	Favourite categories for women	%
Computer	76	Books	64
CDs	60	CDs	60
Books	59	Computers	57
Electronics	44	Health and beauty	42
Videos	38	Toys	41
Air travel	34	Clothing (women's)	39
Menswear	29	Clothing (children's)	31
Toys	29	Electronics	26
Hotel reservations	26	Flowers	21
Sport items	19	Menswear	20
Health and beauty	19		

Source: Ernst & Young, April 2000

Women are more worried about security than men. What happens to information, will items be delivered in good condition and what happens to credit card information? This concern can be deduced from the fact that in 75% of cases the buying process is

> **Women are more worried about security than men**

interrupted before anything is bought. This means that people are aware of the fact that they are going through a buying process, looking for items, putting them into a 'shopping basket' and then decide not to buy. Presumably they realize the security risk involved just before the crucial moment of buying and decide not to buy after all. This behaviour is much stronger in women than in men.

- Women prefer to see and feel items.

This does not apply to books – after all, it is the information contained in them that is important. Appearance is not important. This does, however, play an important part as far as clothing is concerned. Research showed that, in spite of the quality of the site and mail order experience, women prefer to go to the store for this type of item.

- Men buy different things to women.

Table 7.2 shows the difference in buying behaviour between men and women. There are visible differences for electronics (men 44%, women 26%), men score higher on computers with 76% as opposed to 57% for women, and on sports items men and women respectively score 19% and 12%. Women on the other hand score higher on children's clothing (31% versus 18%), on health and beauty (42% versus 19%) and on toys (41% versus 29%).

- Women want more direct sales support.

Women have a greater preference for direct sales support. 'Click-to-talk-buttons', chat buttons and collaborative browsers are more popular with women than they are with men. Landsend.com, for instance, offers live support to visitors to its site (see Figure 7.5). Visitors can get direct assistance from a shopping consultant, or use a 'personal model' with the same measurements to see what the clothes look like. This site is specifically geared to the buying behaviour and preferences of women. Men prefer to search for information themselves, often by having a look on different sites. Women prefer to talk to a call centre agent who will help them with their purchase.

- Women buy at home, men buy at work.

Women more often buy from home than men do. Men often use the computer at work, whereas women have more of a tendency to keep work and private matters strictly separate. The peak in on-line sales on a Monday morning can therefore be explained by the fact that men use the computer at work to buy things for themselves and possibly also for their families. Behaviour shows that men and women also use the

Figure 7.5   *Landsend.com caters for women visitors*

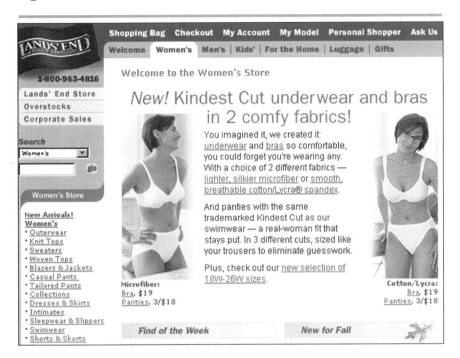

Internet at different times. Weekend buyers, just like evening buyers, are more often women.

Judging by research conducted by Ernst&Young and similar research by Forrester, Nielsen and eBrain, it would appear that men's behaviour is more impulsive and erratic on the Internet than that of women. Women are more deliberate and rational when using the Internet. This is paradoxical to their behaviour in the real world where women are more sensitive to the emotional and social aspects of buying. Whereas women go shopping together and happily spend an afternoon in town, it is not considered to be behaviour that is typical of men. If men go shopping together, it is usually for more technical items or toys, such as electronics and cars. Women buy clothes together; men buy computers and electronics together and perhaps even cars and sports items. Men display more rational behaviour towards other items, but usually they have an aversion to buying clothes. Not surprisingly, therefore, women often buy clothes for their partners.

This behaviour, which is so typical in the real world, is not so typical on the Internet. Men enjoy going onto the Internet. They enjoy surfing, visiting new sites and placing the occasional bet. Men's favourite sites and the items they buy on the Internet reveal that their behaviour is probably more erratic and playful than that of women. Women on the other hand make a conscious decision to go to and purchase from a particular site. If need be, women seek advice from agents (call-me button) and actually enjoy asking an agent or a friend (collaborative browsers) for advice. This is a very rational process. Although there is not much point trying to explain it, the reason for this behaviour can be found in the fact that technology is very appealing to men or that men have a greater affinity for new things than women. The fact that women worry more about the usefulness of a development (rational behaviour) or about the reliability of data may add to this. Perhaps women's behaviour towards new media is more mature than that of men.

The more people get used to a new medium, the more rational their behaviour becomes. This is because the medium and the way it is used slowly becomes part of their way of life and an integral part of their buying process. Surfing behaviour becomes less erratic. Instead, surfers visit only a limited number of sites (favourites). Although there will always be differences, in the long run male behaviour will more closely resemble female behaviour. Men become more rational in their approach to the Internet and are perhaps challenged again by new techniques or gadgets. Research conducted by MMXI Europe (May 2000) confirms this. The findings show that men are particularly interested in Web sites about hardware and software, investment, entertainment and travel information. According to this research women use the Internet more to save time (i.e. structured behaviour) and as a source of information for the family (such as Netdoctor.co.uk).

The intensity with which men and women use the Internet also differs (see Table 7.3). Men spend more time on the Internet than

Table 7.3   *The intensity with which men and women use the Internet*

Average use per month	United States	United Kingdom	Australia	Ireland
Men	9:54:57	5:52:51	8:01:41	5:18:42
Women	8:18:26	3:46:57	5:57:08	3:21:59

Figure 7.6   *Male and female search behaviour on the Internet*

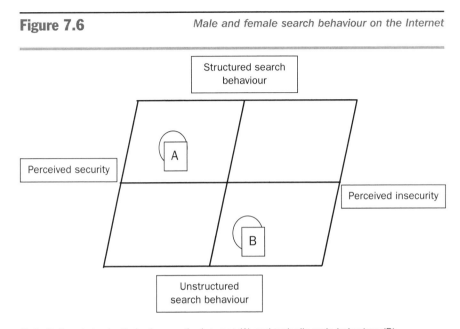

Typically female buying behaviour on the Internet (A) and typically male behaviour (B)

women do, which corresponds to the conclusion drawn earlier. This fact does not change, even if women are more dominant on the Internet, as in the US.

Figure 7.6 depicts typically male and typically female behaviour.

Other factors influencing the use of the Internet

Besides sex, other factors such as income, experience and education also play a part in the use of the Internet. American research conducted in January 2000 shows that people who are well educated use the Internet more than people who are not so well educated. There is no significant difference between men and women, but people under the age of 50 use the Internet more regularly. The Internet is used mainly at home or at the office. There are no longer any distinct differences between groups or users, which means that the Internet is gradually becoming a generally accepted medium. Eventually people owning a computer with an Internet connection will use it in such a way that it will harmonize with their natural behaviour.

It will become important for site owners to anticipate which functionality a site will require. In view of the above-mentioned

Site owners will have to decide on providing specific support if they want to cater for the different buying processes of men and women

research, functionality will be determined mainly by type of item and sex. Site owners will have to decide on providing specific support if they want to cater for the different buying processes of men and women. A generic site will no longer suffice. Either the site will have to support a different navigational structure, like the www.landsend.com site, or the 'look and feel' of the site will have to be adjusted to the visitors it is supposed to attract.

Internet suppliers will have to take the different user groups and their demands into consideration. For example, every site will have to have a privacy statement indicating the rules of the game that are being observed for the benefit of the visitor, how data are handled and which demands visitors may make on suppliers. Another good sign is when a site makes reference to acting in accordance with the rules and regulations of data protection legislation. The text on the site should contain the following three elements:

- a rational element;
- an emotional element;
- an attractive element.

Rational elements are for rational visitors who have either been to the site before or know exactly what they want. Rational elements allow visitors to quickly navigate through a site to where they want to be. A sales site, for example, will enable a visitor to go directly to the desired item via a search engine. Such a search engine can usually be found in the upper left-hand corner of the site. A user generally scans a screen from the upper left to the lower right-hand corner, but usually starts clicking in the upper right-hand corner. By entering an item or product group a visitor can go directly to the right part of the site or catalogue. A site can also use tabs for the functions it fulfils, such as:

- requesting information;
- placing orders;
- browsing;
- requesting newsletters.

A visitor can click on a tab to jump directly to the section required. If the site recognizes the visitor, either by a cookie or via the registration of a password, the visitor will first be routed to the part of the site that they are most likely to want to visit. This is based on historical behaviour. Amazon.com also has such functionality. First a visitor must enter a name. They are then shown a selection of relevant books based on historical buying behaviour and a profile analysis (collaborative filtering). Visitors are divided into groups. These groups typify the behaviour and, therefore, the wishes of potential buyers. Although the groups are classified on the basis of visiting and buying behaviour, they often also have other features in common, such as sex, age and education.

The emotional element of a site may consist of images and perhaps news items. In this way sites anticipate emotional behaviour or the need to associate (the need to belong). The attractive element will often involve a game or a special offer. The latter two determine the stickiness of a site, the wish to return and the wish to spend more time on a site. This stickiness will make visitors return more often, thus increasing the chance that they will buy something.

Cultural influences

It is often thought that the Internet is a universal way of communicating with many different countries and cultures. After all, it is the supplier who determines the method of communication. This is incorrect. Communication should also take into consideration the different cultural aspects of people and countries. A country code added to a domain name (e.g. nl, be, uk, es) clearly indicates where the supplier is from and must be taken into consideration when designing a site. If an address does not include a country code it is difficult to judge in which country a supplier is based. It is generally accepted that all addresses that have 'com' as a top-level domain name belong to US suppliers, even though there are several million suppliers with 'com' in their address in Korea (which has the greatest number of 'com' domain names after the US). In other words, it is impossible to find out where a supplier is established.

Nor is it possible to find out a supplier's market reach, i.e. whether it is only one country, Europe or the whole world. This complicates Internet communication because cultural differences have their influences on both the supplier and the receiver. This is clear in terms of the receiver, i.e. the way a receiver reacts to a message is known from the world of advertising. People's characters and preferences are known. When communicating on a universal scale it is necessary to take these differences into consideration.

Research conducted by the ErasmusUniversity[16] in Rotterdam showed that it is possible to form groups that display Internet-specific cultural similarities:

● American countries (Canada and US) and the UK;

● South European countries, including Spain, Italy and Portugal;

● North European countries, including the Netherlands.

When comparing these three categories we see that the Southern European countries use more colour, pictures and images on their sites. Nature's colourful character and the temperament of the people form an integral part of the 'look and feel' of the site. Northern European sites are smarter, more orderly and generally have better performance. Any playfulness and creativity havee been subjected to strict rules for layout and performance. The Northern European sites are structured in the same way as Northern European society and business.

People on a low income clearly use the Internet less frequently than people with a high income

There is no significant behavioural difference in different population groups that live together. US research by Jupiter Communications in June 2000 showed that no major differences between the various population groups in the US could be attributed to cultural factors. The most dominant and discriminating factors that determine the use of the Internet simply proved to be income and wealth. People on a low income clearly use the Internet less frequently than people with a high income. Low-income groups simply do not have the means. The fact that there are relatively more low-income groups among immigrants and the 'coloured' population means that these groups are falling behind on using the Internet. In other words, the reason is financial and not cultural. The cultural differences will be found mainly in population groups that behave differently as a group, because their cultural structures facilitate different behaviour (this applies, for example, to countries).

There are also noticeable differences between industries. Financial service providers use less colour and fewer pictures than, for example, bookshops or supermarkets. Typically, many financial service providers use white and blue on their sites. White conveys trust, transparency and virtue. Blue is often used in the logo or in the menu bar. A light colour, like white, is better for communication on a computer screen (as background colour) than a dark colour.

The following general conclusions were drawn on the basis of the Jupiter research:

- Internet penetration is lower in southern European countries. As a result the population has little knowledge of the possibilities of the Internet.
- Multi-lingualism can be found particularly on sites belonging to organizations based in countries that are also multi-lingual or in countries that have large ethnic groups (such as the Chinese language in Canada).
- The structure and design of northern European sites is 'smart'.
- German sites are relatively more textually oriented, which corresponds to the German method of communication (a preference for written communication).
- Dutch financial institutions often provide alternative ways of getting in touch (telephone, fax, e-mail or personally), which can be explained by the fact that Dutch people prefer to communicate 'face to face', especially on confidential matters such as finance.
- Southern European sites have more animation and images. One reason for this could be the informal way in which organizations in these countries communicate with their customers.

Differences due to the use of different devices

The third generation of the Internet supports the use of the Internet with other devices. It can also accommodate different infrastructures that are necessary to support specific devices and specific user requirements. People could, for example, use the television to link up with the Internet, in which case the cable would be the infrastructure and the television the device. The televiewer has specific requirements when watching television. Most of these are oriented towards entertainment. The standard broadcasting service offers a choice of channels. The programmes on offer change according to the time of day

Country	Organization	Leadership	Decision making	Meeting	Commnications	Others
Denmark	Transparent, hierarchy purely functional	Coach	Consultation with everyone affected, all go along with the decision	Frequent, agenda, start and end punctually, briefing, discussion or decison making	A lot of sideways communication, serial conversation (wait until it's your turn)	Highest proportion of women in workforce, humour in business – but not sarcastic, little social mix with colleagues outside work, not formal about names, really nice people
Sweden	Deeply systematic approach, a lot of informal interaction between levels	Coach, soft manage-ment	Slow, compromise does not have negative overtone		Serial conversation	Sharp dressers in Scandinavia, environmental issues in political agenda, proud of their countryside, punctual according to time, personal and business relationships are separated, good English speakers
Finland	Precise and systematic approach to organization	Technical orientated, small group of senior people (oligarchical)	Slow, often worst-case scenario	Important with meetings, forum for information sharing, problem solving and debate	Serial conversation	Important Swedish minority (tend to be more wealthy and own most larger private companies), not a Scandinavian country – but Nordic, big forest industry, no taboo on humour, slightly more formal about names than Danes, two official languages
Holland	Lean, practical, flexible	Egalitari-anism and openness, 'one-of-us'	Democratic after discussion	Regular, frequent, formal, decision making	'Buurten' about written communi-cation, open and transparent	Innovative, conservative, outward looking, entrepren-eurial maritime tradition, multi-lingual, rational, improvization
Germany	Oligarchical, strict vertical, functional	Strong, decisive, distant	After constant discussion, systematically pragmatic	Formal coordin-ation briefing, formal ratification of decisions, scheduled weeks in advance	Vertically to the boss, written	National pride, beat the system, elite corps, unrespon-sive to varying conditions, spasmodic, radical, distorted, manipulated, ignored rules, long-term view
Spain	Traditional style: Highly compart-mentalized, bureaucratic and clear authoritarian lines. Personal hierarchy Present trends: decentralization and functional specialization	Strong authority, courageous, critical, expected to know everything	Top down, quite independent in decision making	Communicate instructions, forums to express ideas, consensus: agreement chairperson-everyone, no strict agenda	One-to-one communication with the boss, closed doors, oral and face-to-face communication	Regionalism, lack of fore-casting/planning, don't work well in teams, family unit is important, vertical working relationships, informality in names and 'manners', human relationships are important, modesty and honour, procrastination and delay

Country	Organization	Leadership	Decision making	Meeting	Commnications	Others
Italy	President, managing director and department heads (other titles are meaningless). Conventional hierarchy for low levels. Middle to upper: hiearchies built on personal alliances	Autocratic father figure, charismatic and creative, implemen-tation and control	Decisions are taken by people not necessarily in the charge for that. Delegation to individuals who can be trusted	Unstructured and informal, difficult to impose an agenda, freedom for contributions, no decision making usually	Informal contacts, secretive formal presentations are not common	North-South, family ties, aversion to forecasting, rectitude and loyalty in personal relationships, inventiveness is prized, demonstrating education, few women in business, important good manners, formality in names, open, punctuality: 20 minutes late is accord
Portugal	Vertical personal hierarchy, strong control from the top	Essential directive, delegation to person one trusts		For briefing and discussion, no punctuality, freedom to make contributions, important private beforehand to reach an agreement	Informal	Rudimentary information systems and financial budgeting, sales and cashflow are key indicators, formality in names, quiet and understated people, business relationships are personal and informal
UK	Social class (top-down)	Legitimate	Group consensus	Scheduled, 10 min. delay, frequent	Top down approach, phone memo	Humour is expected at all level, socializing at the pub immediately after work
Canada	Functional (integration, casual)	Informal	Integration and shared responsibility	Frequent, informal/ social	Two-ways, open door policy	
US	Transparent, cope quickly with environ-ment change	Coach	Integration and shared responsibility	Primary communication tool, forum	Two-ways, open door policy	Business life extends into family and social life

and are geared as far as possible to viewers' anticipated requirements. During the day there are sports programmes and a few news broadcasts. At the end of the afternoon and early evening there are children's programmes. In the evening there are films and game shows, and finally talk shows and erotic movies.

This approach is clearly focused on target groups and is supply-driven. Each programme is supposed to attract a certain target group. Each group is subsequently targeted with communication messages. This traditional set-up may, however, be changed by the introduction of new technologies. One of these is ADSL (asymmetric digital subscriber line), which allows data to be compressed and digitally transmitted at speeds of up to 8MBs per second using standard telephone lines and connections. The advantages of this new technology are:

- simultaneous use of the Internet, speech and, for example, fax;
- the possibility to be permanently on-line, which means that it would no longer be necessary to log on to the Internet. There would be fixed rates and direct interaction;
- having video on demand, i.e. viewers can choose which film they want to see and when, and also watch television broadcasts at a later time. One of the advantages for suppliers is that they would know exactly who watched which film when, which would enable them to tailor commercials to target groups on the basis of the information gathered. The disadvantage for programme makers is that viewers could decide to watch the programmes at a later time without the advertisements, in which case the programme maker would be faced with the new problem of how to reach potential customers with mass communication. In such a case direct communication would be favoured.

In addition, it would be possible to offer interactive games and interactive services and facilitate home shopping on the basis of individual buying behaviour. In this way the possibilities and characteristics of television can be combined with the possibilities of the Internet.

WAP

WAP (wireless application protocol)[17] is an application based on mobile communication. The use of mobile phones has led to greater individualization of communication and the need for information and contact. This need is stimulating suppliers to offer other services based on mobile communication and stimulating consumers to want these services. In addition to the analogue network and the digital GSM network, it is also possible to use the UMTS infrastructure (Universal Mobile Telephone System), third-generation mobile telephony. UMTS can cope with high data transmission speeds, which enable intensive data, speech and image traffic. UMTS can be used to offer specific services that were previously only offered by the Internet or telephone or cable networks, such as the alert function for shares or bank balances, or even to request specific information or on-line games. To take advantage of these services a user must have a good screen and a modified telephone, a WAP telephone or a PDA.

A PDA is a palmtop computer, which is particularly popular with businessmen and women because of its calendar function, its contacts function and other supporting functions, such as memos. With a PDA it is possible to go on to the Internet and log on to the central calendar on the central database or to read or send e-mails. It is, of course, not necessary to log on to the central computer to send e-mails. These can be done directly by simply logging on to the Internet with the PDA. In this way a businessman is always assured of the right data and he can stay in direct contact with the office without having to use a full-sized computer. Developments in the field of central assistants for calendar and database functions allow central data to be used any time anywhere.

In addition to using specific Internet services with devices other than the personal computer, the mobile network offers specific possibilities. One of these is traceability. The GSM network can tell exactly where a person is. By linking the location function to a database it is possible to use local data to communicate with the owner of a WAP telephone. In this way the owner can be sent commercial messages by local stores or companies (not very pleasant for the receiver), or be kept informed about their route. It is also possible to build a certain pilot function into a WAP telephone that enables on-line navigation. The owner can then be led to a location of their choice, such as a station, a shopping centre, a disco or a bar. This link between location data and geographic location encompasses many possibilities for offering services. Examples of this are the alert functions for shares or the navigation function. Advanced applications are also possible. As a telephone number is unique to a user, it should also be possible with in-built security to use the telephone for making payments, for example, by linking up with a database by remote access using a password. In this way a hotel can know the location of its guests and guests would be able to reserve and pay for a hotel room remotely. Guests could use GPS (Global Positioning System) to choose the nearest hotel.

> In addition to using specific Internet services with devices other than the personal computer, the mobile network offers specific possibilities

I-Mode

The real challenge presented by the new generation of Internet and mobile telephony, besides mobility and GPS (knowing one's exact location using the Global Positioning System), is connecting speech, data and images. Today, we are on the threshold of this mobile development. Japan has made a head start on Europe with the i-Mode telephone and has created a separate data network for it (NTT Docomo) which facilitates the communication that is typical of the mobile phone. Specific services are being developed together with suppliers. I-Mode is like an advanced kind of SMS, a service provided for GMS telephones. The SMS service is particularly popular with young people, who form the large target group of i-Mode users. The applications are very strongly data and communication oriented (see Figure 7.7). People can play games, request and consult information and also receive images of limited quality. With 10 million users in the first year, i-Mode has been a resounding success in Japan. The applications and their use are, however, typically Japanese: a new picture daily, a different game every day and sending images and on-line messages to others. In addition to the cultural aspect, the moment of use also plays an important part. I-Mode has three peak times: early morning, lunchtime and in the evening on the way home after 11 o'clock. The Japanese use i-Mode mainly on public transport (what else can you do on public transport?). This helps to pass the time, since in the rush-hour madness it is virtually impossible to read a book or the paper. In situations like this, requesting information and communication by mobile phone is a welcome alternative to sleeping. In the mornings people can get news and stock market updates and on their way home they can e-mail that they are on their way.

I-Mode marketing initially focused on a target group of young people (aged 18 to 24), especially fashion-conscious young women. I-Mode was promoted as a fashion item and a gadget. Young people are compelled by the many different manifestations and the quick succession of stylish devices to keep on buying newer models to be part of the scene. Thanks to the special network, it is no longer necessary to log in. This bears a resemblance to ADSL, which is based on a data-oriented network and data-oriented technology. It offers advantages such as quick connection and on-line alert services, because users no longer need to log in every time. However, there is more to WAP than this. In view of the high initial costs of UMTS (the costs for the frequency alone already amount

Figure 7.7   *Use of i-Mode in Japan*

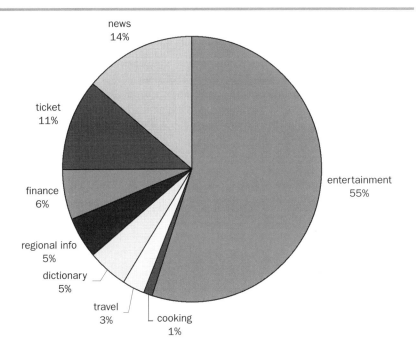

Source: NTT Docomo, Tokyo

to an investment of billions) it is unlikely that i-Mode or i-Mode technology will be used in Europe. It is, however, expected that it will be used in more Asian countries in the future. In Europe, WAP technology and the development of related services are becoming increasingly important.

In all cases it will be the user who determines what they want and when they want it

In all cases it will be the user who determines what they want and when they want it. There will be a specific need for every device and every moment of the day. Thanks to the new generation of Internet use it will be possible to fulfil all these wishes by offering standards and protocols for the various devices. Multi-device applications will develop and offer specific services so that every user can use them in their own way, with a personal computer, notebook, palmtop or telephone.

Summary Although the Internet allows us to communicate on a global scale, it is important to be aware of the fact that there are differences – in the behaviour of Internet visitors as a result of age, sex or culture. Suppliers who want to reach a large target group must structure their site in such a way that it provides for these differences in behaviour. This will often be difficult, in which case a supplier might be better to choose to create different sites for different target groups. The oldest suppliers like Yahoo! and Amazon do this for this very reason. They have sites for, among others, the US market, the UK market, the German market and the Japanese market. In this way they can adapt the subject and the 'look and feel' of the site to the behaviour of the visitors from these countries. This actually results in a diversification on the Internet, which is contradictory to the 'global' character of the medium. It also emphasizes the opinion that to use the facilities offered by the Internet effectively, the various communication methods and behaviour of the different groups must be taken into consideration.

On the basis of the observed behaviour, a distinction can be made between structured and unstructured search behaviour and between security and insecurity. On the basis of this behaviour it was stated that it is possible to distinguish between male and female behaviour. This conclusion must be taken into consideration when analyzing visitors and consequently designing the layout of the site. The real conclusion is that there is a global market, but that customers differ in culture and behaviour. In addition, differences can be discerned depending on which device is used. The development towards a multi-device platform will lead to people using a different device to meet their different needs at different times. Logically, therefore, different services will be developed for each device based on the users' needs, but also on the possibilities of the device or the network. The diversity in devices and preferences of users will result in a greater diversity in the use of the Internet. It is up to the suppliers to decide how to deal with it.

Notes 15 This model is based on the model by Dr P. Plasmeijer, as described in his thesis 'The influence of the Internet on prepurchase external search for financial services'. In the thesis, the axis for security is referred to as the axis of certainty, with the outer extreme being perceived as certainty, implying that visitors believe that they have at their disposal sufficient tools (media) to gather the required information. Uncertainty implies that customers feel that they need a lot of information so as to avoid making mistakes. In fact, both classifications correspond. The model used in the book is based on a limited number of information sources (notably only the Internet).

16 Research conducted by international business administration students on the cultural influences of the use of the Internet. This research was coordinated by Mr C. van Ham, Aegon Nederland (work placement supervisor) and Prof. Dr C.N.A. Molenaar (academic supervisor).

17 WAP is a wireless application protocol, a set of protocols that determine how Internet information should be made available for mobile devices. This takes into consideration the specific characteristics and limitations of mobile phones.

8

■■■■■■■■■■■■■■■

Strategic choices:
winning or losing

Waiting for the future is like musing on the past. Nothing happens.

The Internet can lead to changes in customer behaviour, products and services, market reach, and, consequently, organizational changes. This complex of change makes it no longer acceptable for organizations to use the Internet casually. The strategic choices concerning the Internet must not be left to the IT specialist, who will approach the issue on the basis of technological criteria, nor to the marketing experts, whose allegiance lies with market needs and customer relations. Instead, the strategic decision-making process relating to the potential opportunities and impact of the Internet requires a multi-disciplinary approach, with equal attention paid to technology, marketing and organizational aspects. Since technology only facilitates the change process, the decision-making process should focus, first and foremost, on markets and customers. For this reason, it is fair to suggest that the marketing discipline should play the lead in shaping the organization's Internet strategy. Thus, the strategic choices discussed in this chapter are approached from that angle.

Basis of change

The basis of the change process has three core elements:

● change from physical to virtual products;
● change by direct communication;
● change by new technological possibilities.

The change from physical products to virtual products and services was described by Negroponte[18] in 1995 as a change from atoms to bits ('being digital'). The transformation from atoms to bits, it was held, would eliminate all physical restrictions. The philosophy was that virtual information and the virtual world were boundless. The underlying concept of the change was that people experienced physical boundaries as restrictive; consequently, the new world, that had no limits within the imaginable, would be a more enticing place. Inspired by this thought, new companies sprouted up in all sorts of places, offering new services and digital products. The world was their market place. The 'think global' principle was embraced with passion. The new enterprises eagerly seized the opportunities that came with the change. In the world of the imaginable, cyberspace was the limit. It was the young creatives who set the pace for change. Creativeness and originality were seen as the ingredients for success; old-world constrictions, values and standards were thrown overboard.

Yet, looking around, we are still surrounded by restrictions, and there is a new awareness that our traditional norms and values were not invented merely to make life hard for businessmen and women. We still buy physical products, and many of us still prefer buying in old-fashioned, non-virtual shops, and choose doing business with trusted partners. Shopping preferences aside, investments in the virtual economy, too, must eventually pay themselves back, and at some point the money companies can spend is simply gone. What stays is the realization that one cannot simply discard the values and rules forged in the past in favour of alluring prospects created by technology. Nevertheless, the Internet has galvanized a new way of thinking that can lead to important new opportunities.

A second core element of the change lies in the direct communication enabled by the Internet. In R. Levine *et al.*'s *The Cluetrain Manifesto*,[19] communication is taken as the starting point for change. Communication provides knowledge, makes consumers better informed, and changes their buying behaviour. Mass marketing is based on a message; the Internet on communication. To enable this communication there must be contact between the sender and the receiver; a direct contact between suppliers and receivers. In this way, the communication – or interaction – becomes the basis for doing business. This direct form of communication enables suppliers to respond better to individual requirements, stimulates supplier-customer bonding, and is a more efficient way of putting a message across. Organizations must therefore pursue a policy that supports this direct communication, and

> **Mass marketing is based on a message; the Internet on communication**

which allows the business processes to be guided by that communication. Alvin Toffler talks about an 'invisible wedge' between products and consumers. A similar divide exists between customers and organizations, and between suppliers and buyers. Communication and consultation can help tear down this divide and enable new forms of cooperation. Based on this orientation model, the 'clue train' message is that organizations should adopt marketing policies that are based on the network orientation, and that they should accept the organizational consequences (network organization).

Essentially, the business of doing business must be reviewed on the basis of how people behave in the physical, real world. In the same way that the market place provided an opportunity for personal contact between buyers and sellers, and in the same way that a spoken agreement, clinched by a physical handshake, has long provided the basis for business transactions, so too must direct communication between people once again become the basis for business transactions. Trust, once more, should be earned on the basis of mutual respect and direct, interactive communication. Traditional values and norms are not obsolete; on the contrary, they are the basis for successful change.

The third pillar of change is the use of technology. Technology clearly holds the key to many possibilities and will lead to changes in organizations and their relationships with customers, suppliers and personnel. However, what is technically possible is not always necessary or the best way.

The changes that are happening around us today relate to:

- extended limits in relation to business, organizations, personnel, structures and markets;
- new market structures and different relationships with market players;
- new forms of competition and changed competitive advantages.

Due to the information explosion – and possibly because of imploded organizational structures – it has become necessary to separate the information processes from the physical flows. Organizations are compelled to reappraise the information value chain independently from the physical value chain.

The information value chain regulates information flows between organizations and markets, and within organizations. The explosive growth of information that came with the vast expansion of information sources and better accessibility has made markets more transparent. Organizations today know more about customers, mutual relationships and market relationships than at any time before. This knowledge has led to increased mobility of personnel, customers and suppliers. It has also become easier to collect information on remote markets, while the information obtained can be transferred much faster and independently of time or place. In light of these developments, new choices must be made that are based on the possibility of separating the physical flows from the non-physical ones (information flows). Evans and Wurster,[20] in their book *Blown to Bits*, talk of a choice between reach (market reach) and richness (complexity of the product). In their view, there is a correlation between both, therefore the decision process will be based on two principal alternatives, as shown in Figure 8.1.

The philosophy behind the reach-versus-richness concept is explained in *Blown to Bits*. The use and interpretation of the concept does not necessarily have to correspond with the authors' interpretation; however, their line of thought has been followed here in order to impart structure to the strategic choice process. By linking the concept of reach versus richness to marketing orientations and marketing models and to physical flows and information flows, it has been possible to construct a strategic cube model. In the process, a certain freedom of interpretation was needed in approaching the issues of market reach and product complexity.

Figure 8.1   *Market reach versus product complexity*

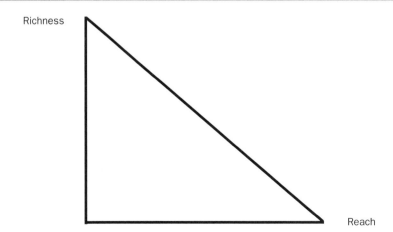

Richness

Reach

Richness is the complex of values and features that surround a product. This includes physical values, e.g. colour, scent, design and options for use, as well as information values. The information values include sales support, awareness of the product or service, and the interaction that is required in the buying process. In other words, richness is the totality of factors associated with the purchase of, for example, a computer system or pension insurance. 'Reach' denotes market reach, i.e. the number of markets covered. In *Blown to Bits*, the authors conclude that an evaluation is necessary that acknowledges that relatively simple products require less sales support and are more easily recognized and therefore easier to sell in a large market (the world). The more complex the product and the buying process become, the more difficult it is to sell the product in a large market. By using the possibilities enabled by technology in marketing, market reach can, however, be increased (see Figure 8.2). Previously, this occurred using direct communication tools, e.g. direct mail; later, telemarketing was introduced as well. Later still, telephone marketing became an important element in the market approach.

The more complex the product and the buying process become, the more difficult it is to sell the product in a large market

The telephone makes it possible to communicate with a number of customers individually within a short time span, and enables different markets to be reached. In the US, the effect of this approach has been far greater than in Europe, thanks to the fact that the same language is spoken throughout the country. In Europe, problems were encountered when it came to providing sales support in national markets in the local language. Increasingly, this is tackled by setting up centrally located call centres that employ native-speaking staff for telephone sales support. Many of these centres are established in countries with a relatively large non-native population, or where a relatively large part of the population speaks more than one language. The Netherlands is seen by many as an important place for international call centres, providing a home base to corporations such as Hewlett-Packard, Holiday Inn and Mercedes. Other conditions, e.g. infrastructure and tax law, also play a role in electing to establish a call centre in a particular country.

Ireland has set its sights on playing a pioneering role in Europe in this area of specialization, providing it with a strong basis for employ-

Figure 8.2   *The use of technology in marketing activities related to market reach and product complexity*

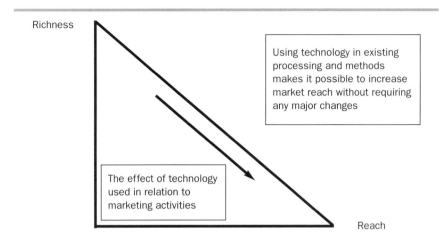

Greater market reach by technological applications within existing processes and methods

ment growth and attracting related industries and services. In return, the country is prepared to provide the necessary technological, social and legal infrastructures. In this way, it can play an important role in Europe, even though it is situated on the fringe of the continent. In Finland, there has been a similar development. When the country lost its largest export partner (Russia), this had a dramatic effect on the country's economy, compelling it to re-examine its strengths and weaknesses. In essence, it was a nation with a complex language, situated far from Europe's centre of gravity, and with a relatively small industry. However, combining electronics with a strong domestic market, it was able to play a leading role in mobile telephony (Nokia). The cellular phone was quickly accepted by the Fins as a part of everyday life. It clearly satisfied a dormant need in a thinly populated country with vast expanses. Thus Finland was able to reassert its competitiveness by responding to the needs of the home market, an emerging market for mobile telephony, and the specific advantages associated with economic recession.

Both countries have demonstrated that there are new advantages associated with technological developments. Both countries had few natural resources, both had relatively small but flexible markets, and both had physical restrictions in terms of climate and geographic location. However, none of this played a role because of the strategic choices they made. What is true for countries is also true for organizations.

Market reach and product complexity

The Internet is a new medium enabling organizations to reach a large number of markets. In addition, its interactive features can help reach larger groups of potential customers. However, the Internet has certain limitations. Factors that have a negative effect on market reach include:

- complexity of products and services (richness);
- different standards and diversified markets;
- different legal frameworks and tax laws;
- local cultural differences.

A smaller market reach often implies a need to offer more individual products (targeted at a smaller group of potential buyers), more complex products, or products requiring a relatively large amount of sales support. Thus, a correlation emerges between product complexity and potential market reach. As the complexity of the product increases, its market reach decreases, and vice versa. Therefore, an organization that wants to increase its market reach must find ways to reduce the complexity of its products and services. Based on the options described, it could achieve this by:

- simplifying the buying process and/or sales support;
- simplifying communication with the market by brand projection;
- simplifying/standardizing the products and services.

The complexity of the product or service can be reduced by making use of the new media or other structures, e.g. by using new communication techniques in market communication, as described. In addition, a product concept can be changed by reducing its information content. This was done, for example, with software intended for both private consumers and companies (PC software). By providing automatic installation routines and set-up functions, it was no longer necessary to provide user support or detailed user instructions. The simplification enabled suppliers to extend their market reach.

Another option is to introduce a higher level of product

standardization – a tactic that can increase product recognition importantly. This development has been seen in the computer industry in recent years. The production of different computer systems, operating systems and standards led companies to seek niche markets for selling their products. The niche strategy was very popular throughout the 1980s, as companies were trying to gain a strong position in certain markets (countries) and certain application forms (users) only.

> **Because the niche strategy was a sure impediment in terms of market reach, it was bound to limit suppliers' potential market volume**

However, because the niche strategy was a sure impediment in terms of market reach, it was bound to limit suppliers' potential market volume. With the advent of computer networks and the popularization of the Internet, the merits of the niche strategy rapidly declined.

To be successful in an economy of standard products, economy of scale was a precondition. At the same time, organizations were forced to pursue communication-based and customer-focused strategies. The basis for the new strategic choices lay in an intensive market approach, extensive marketing communication and support, and an effective use of the Internet. The only suppliers that were able to compete successfully in the new markets were those that could supply uniform products for a uniform market which did not require intensive support. The market by then had become much larger due to increased transparency. Players that were unable to meet the new criteria in terms of standardization and economy of scale either disappeared or were bought up. An organization such as Apple computers, for instance, was able to survive in the eleventh hour by offering a universal platform for universal use. After this, the competition was not about content but about design. While every product was designed for universal use, the various target groups were approached on the strength of particular exterior features.

Adjusting market communication

Having created uniformity, the organization's communication policy can be adjusted accordingly. If global markets are to be reached, an effective communication policy must provide the basis. The substantial cost of marketing communication campaigns, an increasingly difficult climate for drawing the attention in local markets, increased market transparency, and the earlier noted need for uniformity, have required the manufacturing industry to re-examine its market reach ambitions. By rephrasing the information message time after time to appeal to different target groups and different markets, market reach is restricted to the extent that it changes competitive relationships. In other words, the huge cost of communication undermines the competitiveness of suppliers in various markets. Because organizations are required to communicate in different markets, the expense of marketing, in the traditional media structure, is growing beyond their means.

An efficient transfer of information and putting a simple message across stimulate product/brand recognition. Thus, many suppliers have had to reconsider the composition of their products and services (more standard products and a uniform brand for various markets), the composition of their product portfolio (fewer global brands), and the role of the distribution channel and local branches. An organization such as Unilever, for instance, has adjusted its marketing policy for the same reasons. With fewer global brands, the organization could communicate with global markets on a cheaper and more effective scale. Market transparency and new communication technologies enable more product contacts and more uniform product recognition. In addition, there are important cost savings to be earned. A simple, uniform message can be communicated at less cost and to a greater extent in many markets. In adopting this strategy, Unilever chose to increase market reach by reducing product complexity.

At the same time, special products or products that satisfy a local demand can still be carried with a view to serving local or smaller markets. These products might be more complex, also to enable the supplier to set himself apart. Universal products, designed for global reach, are generally less suitable for smaller markets, with their more specific local needs and preferences. Although technology enables products to be manufactured in variable appearances – close to the point of individualization – the problems noted earlier in the area of communication and market transparency encourage companies to seek a more universal use of the product and a broader recognition. As a result, a paradox emerges that importantly determines an organization's strategic choices, and, ultimately, its chance of success.

Technology and market reach

The case of Dell computers serves to demonstrate that changing a market approach can work. Dell was able to increase market reach by selling only via certain communication media. Sales were effected initially by telephone, and later through the Internet as well. Telephone sales enabled the company to provide a high level of service (7×24 hours) and direct sales support, and in that way expand its market reach. The company was able to develop and consolidate this strategy with the aid of Internet technology. Dell computers are manufactured on the basis of several standard models, which can be modified and extended to meet customers' requirements. Customers who visit the Dell Web site or phone the company receive immediate service, and are able to directly order the computer of their choice. What appears to be a customized product in fact comprises several simple modules or even a standard computer with options for upgrading. This is a good example of a supplier which simplified the choice of computer (reducing product complexity) while increasing its market reach by using the Internet and telephone communication.

Dell in fact introduced a change in the personal computer market. It was no longer necessary to choose between complexity and market reach, between supplying simple products and market volume. Instead, by using new technology to communicate with customers, the company achieved both. It could continue supplying a reasonably complex product, yet at the same time, being able to provide a high standard of sales support it could also reach a larger market. This translates in Figure 8.3 as a shift in the coordinate system, changing a fundamental market principle by demonstrating that market reach can in fact be increased for complex products.

The same trend can be observed in relation to the use of Internet communication. Until recently, financial advice and investment products, for example, were the domain of personal sales (via banks and intermediaries). Offering direct sales support via the Internet, organizations can provide customized products with a larger market reach, offering what is basically a complex product on a global scale. As a result, markets are changing. Customers have come to expect similar service and support from the traditional distribution channels, and therefore expect more from the existing distribution system. If the old channels cannot offer what is experienced by the customer as important added value, customers will sooner use a telephone or Internet service.

Figure 8.3   *How technology affects market reach and product complexity*

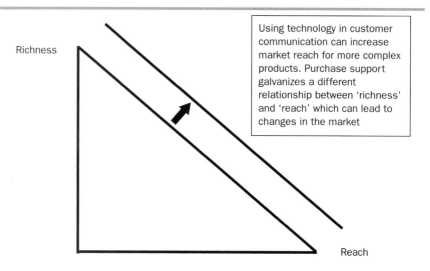

The suppliers that operate on the Internet aim to reach new markets, which potentially leads to market changes brought about by newcomers

Furthermore, the suppliers that operate on the Internet aim to reach new markets, which potentially leads to market changes brought about by newcomers (see Porter's competition model). As the traditional market conditions and structures change, so does the balance of competition. The developments described here are therefore highly relevant for the established market parties. In fact, they have no choice but to:

- simplify their product range by offering comparable services;
- generate sales through comparable channels and use their position in the present market;
- offer additional services, based on their market position and knowledge of local markets and customers.

What happens here is a counteractive movement, whereby the more established suppliers are required to adjust, both in terms of product and service, as well as in the area of customer communications. If they provide the same services as the Internet newcomers, an established market position can support this. If use is made of existing distribution forms and available customer knowledge, the customer orientation will increase, providing a stronger basis for customer relationships and customer loyalty. In that case, a deep-seated CRM strategy would be the best option. (See Table 8.1.)

Table 8.1

Effect of strategic choices

Strategic choices	Change: *New suppliers change existing market conditions by reducing product complexity and increasing market reach (e.g. by using the Internet)*	
Defensive	Providing the same options as the newcomer or innovator to protect market position	Too compliant; will be seen as slow and conservative. Will eventually lose market share and market position. *Negative scenario*
Offensive	Offering extra services by combining existing distribution channels and new options for telephone and Internet sales. Multi-channel is the leading strategy	Enables various customer groups to be reached, but will lead to problems in structuring the organization optimally. The information policy should be based on the principle that the information is available wherever and whenever a company is in contact with a customer. Far-reaching changes in the organization are a precondition for success. *Internally focused scenario*
Active	Depending on value and individual customer needs, offering a customized package responding to personal needs. Consolidating established customer relations; CRM as the leading strategy	Enables established position to be used to consolidate market position, and to increase market reach on that basis. *Powerful scenario*
Passive	Pursue the same approach, using the new media only to facilitate/support the existing operating methods	Customer range will gradually shrink, resulting in loss of market position. *Sure-death scenario*

Marketing orientations and market reach

The above model serves to demonstrate the relationship between market reach and product complexity. The relationship that emerges equates product complexity with limited market reach. However, product complexity and related market reach also play a role in determining the organization's marketing orientation. The aspired market reach will reflect in the organization's marketing activities – after all, if the organization is active in certain markets, it will have a policy for working those markets. The problems associated with extensive marketing efforts have been responsible for the difficulties experienced by start-ups that have chosen the Internet as a distribution channel. In many cases, the required investments and marketing communication efforts to reach a large number of markets were seriously underrated. Again, this example demonstrates that there are more factors at work in the market reach mechanism than product complexity alone. (Like the different flows of information and goods.)

In Chapter 2, the various marketing orientations were discussed that lie at the basis of the marketing choices. The orientations described reflect the inherent possibilities of the organization, the dynamism of markets, and the extent to which the demand for a certain product is homogenous. In addition, a marketing orientation will reflect the level of product uniformity. On the basis of the various marketing orientations and the complexity of products, as explained earlier, a three-way relationship can be identified between product complexity, market reach and marketing orientation. The more complex the product, the more market-focused the marketing orientation must be. With a simpler product, a more internally focused orientation could be very effective, as it enables a better control of the business processes, while the more traditional, hierarchical organizational structure provides for very effective financial controls. A target group or customer-oriented marketing approach will require a different organizational structure, enabling much more intensive market and customer communications. This will tend to restrict market reach. The product will be more tailored to meet specific market needs, possibly individual requirements. The correlation between market reach and product complexity, as in relation to marketing orientation, can be illustrated as in Figure 8.4.

The model can be used to draw connections between the traditional choices of organizations, the marketing orientation of organizations,

Figure 8.4 *Correlation between market reach, product complexity and marketing orientation*

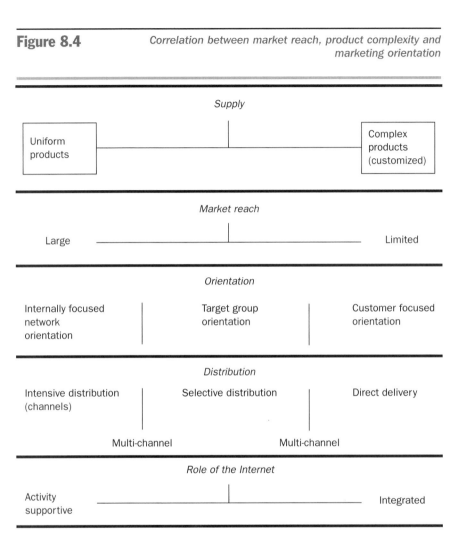

and the use of the Internet. Many choices made by organizations in the past were inspired by their ambition to achieve market reach by offering a uniform product that was communicated to the market by way of a uniform message. For this, the brand concept was used, which enabled the supplier to impart a uniform charge to all market communications. The brand concept, specifically associated with that product, enabled the company to communicate a simple, uniform product concept, in a uniform manner. Everybody knew what the product was, and what to expect from it. Using mass media communication, the same communication could be addressed to a large audience. Using the knowledge of markets and customers accumulated over time, the same (marketing) campaign was used in many markets, requiring only a language change (voice-over). Market reach was achieved by communicating a recognizable product based on a standard format and by selling the product through a distribution network.

The traditional marketing discipline has the following functions:

- marketing management;
- product management;
- communication management;
- channel management.

Each of these functions serves the overriding objective of creating market reach. In markets where demand is relatively homogenous and market conditions are stable, the traditional approach has advantages in terms of creating market reach and implementing a marketing policy. Therefore, this structure and systematics are frequently used in organizations with an internally focused marketing orientation. Today, however, due to important changes in markets, market dynamism, market players and customer preference, many organizations are forced to review previous choices in relation to marketing and market reach. As many markets are becoming increasingly dynamic, companies are more and more under pressure to keep abreast of the changes and respond effectively. For this, more direct contact with markets and customers is required, and market reach, consequently, will decrease. At the same time, greater product diversity will be introduced.

As many markets are becoming increasingly dynamic, companies are more and more under pressure to keep abreast of the changes and respond effectively

Changing trends and time-to-market are ever more important, and marketing efforts will increasingly centre on smaller groups of potential buyers. Sales must be closely monitored, and organizations must respond as astutely and timely as possible to the changes described above. To be successful in each of these aspects, the organization needs to adopt a more externally focused approach. This, in turn, requires a different marketing orientation on which to build the marketing, information and management activities. In a more dynamic market, the complexity

Figure 8.5 *Product and distribution channel choices*

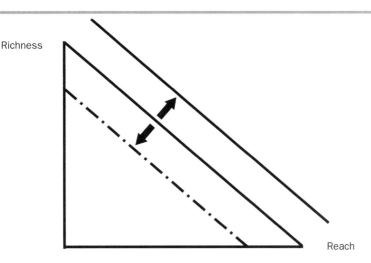

Richness

Reach

of the product will increase, and market reach will decrease accordingly. This mechanism pressurizes sales and profits, thus requiring a review of the marketing strategy.

Market dynamism exercises an effect that is contrary to the effect of the use of technology (see Figure 8.5). Timing and strategy are increasingly important. To meet the challenge, organizations must be closer to their markets than ever before, which requires an effective CRM strategy.

The organization could, for example, choose to focus more on a specific target group. In the case of Nike, this led to a re-energized marketing orientation on athletes, as well as addressing the young and trendy. Unilever elected to compete worldwide with selected brands only. In doing so, it chose to pursue market reach. It adopted that strategy for a limited number of brands only, so that it could approach those markets more intensively. For this, brands were used that had a global image and a uniform product concept, and which projected a simple message that was simple to communicate (homogenous product/universal demand). In each case, the traditional marketing activities and instruments were adapted to serve the objective of increasing market reach. This required choices to be made in order to change organizational structures and harmonize the marketing orientation. In both cases, this process could have resulted not in a uniform marketing orientation but in different orientations for various markets and product groups, possibly identified per market, per product or even per department. The marketing orientation and derived marketing activities for Liptonice, for example, are very different from the marketing strategy used, for example, for selling Omo, another Unilever product.

The conflict between market dynamism (more players, more competition, rapidly changing demand) and larger market reach, enabled by technology, requires organizations to make very clear strategic choices. It is important to know exactly what market trends and developments are happening at any given time, so as to be able to respond adequately to them. In relation to marketing orientation, this calls for a more broad-based and more intensively market-oriented approach. An organization with a customer orientation or a network orientation will be better equipped to respond to change than an internally focused organization. Because time-to-market is crucial for survival, organizations must accept that changes and a possible reallocation of responsibilities are inevitable. The closer the organization is to the customer, the more able it is to collect detailed knowledge of customer requirements and market dynamism, and the more important it is for it to use that information in the decision-making processes.

The power of a 'first mover' like Amazon lies in that change of orientation. By changing the market conditions, the organization placed itself in the driver's seat, enabling it to influence new structures and changes. Slow, lumbering organizations, which often have an internal orientation, e.g. publishing houses and manufacturers of 'fast mover' goods, will increasingly feel the hot breath of the dynamics and rapid changes that are happening in today's markets. The changes that Amazon forced upon the established publishing houses and bookstores have led to irreversible changes. The role of Amazon in that market afterwards is, in fact, no longer relevant.

The role of the Internet can be supportive only. However, the Internet can be used to exercise direct influence on product complexity and potential market reach. If used mainly to support the company's regular activities, the Internet will probably be used to increase the efficiency and effectiveness of those processes. To bring about change, however, the Internet must be used in a more pro-active manner. The changes it can bring about primarily concern products, the way products are sold (distribution channels), and the way an organization responds to customer needs. In a next stage, there may be consequences in the area of market reach and reduced product complexity. With regard to the strategic choices, it is essential to first decide what you want to sell, why you want to sell it, and, finally, how you are planning to sell it. This choice process has three important dimensions:

- products and services;
- distribution channels;
- customer needs.

Products and services

Products and services were approached on the basis of their complexity, enabling a relationship to be established with market reach. This complexity can be expressed in terms of how far there is question of a personal approach or personal preference. The relationship between marketing orientation and product complexity is reflected in the extent to which the product is a standard product (simple product, uniform product communication) or a customized product (individual approach). Based on the two extreme ends of the scale, the organization will decide on a product concept, combining physical, service and perception elements. This will result in a product which may or may not require some degree of customization. (See Table 8.2.)

The extremities in terms of product complexity – standard product or concept product – at once provide an indication of the service elements associated with the product. With a standard product, there is usually a universal product, manufactured in a standard version, with a standard service pattern. In most cases these are physical products, sold through a distribution channel. Product recognition and product

With a concept product, the supplier is looking to respond to a total spectrum of customer needs

bonding (customer loyalty) are important. With a concept product, the supplier is looking to respond to a total spectrum of customer needs. This could, for example, be an entertainment package or a home insurance package. The entertainment deal might be 'a night down town'. This concept could comprise several elements, e.g. taxi down town, dinner at a restaurant, a theatre visit and a disco afterwards. Each element could be offered separately, whereas the integrated

Table 8.2   *How the product concept influences sales support*

Product concept and sales support				
Product/service form	Sales process	Product value	Sales support	Marketing orientation
Standard product	Simple sales process	High physical value	No interaction with sales process. Product support is clearly focused on contact	Internally oriented, mass-market approach. Market reach through distribution channel
Target group-focused product	Empathy with target group	Perceived value	Target group adjusted/ empathy oriented	Target group orientation
		Individual value	Direct communication and interaction	Customer orientation
Perceived personalization	Customer knowledge	High 'virtual' service value	Intensive sales support, aimed at generating trust and providing information	Network orientation
Customized product/ integrated product concept	Individual sales process			

The relationship between the extent of product standardization and marketing orientation

package would reflect the customer's personal preferences. Therefore, although the customer might purchase individual services, the supplier could also offer a total concept. Customer communication, the role of the distribution channel, customer knowledge, and the function of the Internet will vary within the two ends of the spectrum.

How the Internet influences the change process bears directly on the level of standardization and derived values. In order to choose the most appropriate organizational structure, it must therefore be decided whether to focus on a standard product, whereby the Internet can be used to provide information and as a distribution channel, or to deliver a customized product, using the Internet as a distribution channel for intensive interaction. This choice essentially decides the organization's distribution policy. (See Figure 8.6.)

Figure 8.6

Relationship between the Internet and product concept

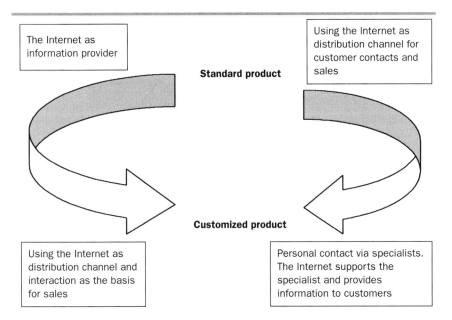

The role of the Internet is not a dominant factor in the strategic choice process. What matters is what the organization wants to achieve with its products and services, and what kind of customer and market relationships it wants to build. Market conditions, market dynamism and organizational possibilities also play an important role in the choice process.

Distribution channels

Based on the choices in relation to product and service concept, the distribution channel is more or less implied. If market reach is the object, an intensive distribution policy is the logical option; *being there, in as many places as possible.* If the product or service is marketed for a specific target group, a selective distribution policy will be the most effective; if building close customer relationships is the object, a multi-channel policy or direct distribution channel would be chosen (see Table 8.3). Possible choices in relation to product policy were discussed previously. The associated choice of distribution channel reflects the relationship the organization wants to build with the customer and the market.

Table 8.3   *Relationship between distribution concept and Internet use*

Distribution	Focus	Objective	Orientation	Internet
Intensive	Market reach	Increasing market share	Internally oriented	Information function
Selective	Target group reach	Market leader in target group	Target group focused	Information and communication function
Multi-channel/ direct	Customer contact	Large 'share of wallet'	Customer oriented, network oriented	Additional transaction function

Using the Internet requires certain organizational provisions to ensure correct e-mail response time, processing speed and timely dispatch of items purchased

Based on the above connections, the role of the Internet is also indicated. It is important in the choice process to be aware that the product concept has consequences for the distribution concept, and for the way in which the Internet could be used. This is a particularly relevant aspect, due to the fact that there are certain limit conditions, e.g. concerning the layout of the Internet site, the navigation model, and the allocation of responsibilities for Web site direction and maintenance in the organization. Using the Internet requires certain organizational provisions to ensure correct e-mail response time, processing speed and timely dispatch of items purchased. If the organization is either unable or unwilling to deal with these consequences, it would be wise to choose a different form of distribution, instead of trying to increase its market reach via the Internet.

The problems many Internet companies have experienced with regard to order handling trace back to this choice process. Having been successful in the first stages (designing a nice Web site, drawing customers, even persuading them to buy), many Internet start-ups have failed to take the necessary organizational measures to enable them to meet customers' expectations. Because fulfilment – a back-office function in most companies – was not sufficiently integrated in the front office, the effort resulted in dissatisfied customers and loss of turnover. Consequently, they would have had to reconsider the way the Internet was used and the distribution policy followed. For direct customer contacts and direct distribution, the front office must have a fulfilment function to control and direct all customer-related processes. The rest of the organization must follow, and must therefore be willing and able to implement the consequences.

Besides enabling direct customer contact, the Internet can play a facilitating role in the relationship between other parties, e.g. playing a broker's role. In this case, the front office does not have a fulfilment responsibility but a 'switchboard' task that extends to communication, information provision and customer relations. The actual transaction work is passed on to the supplier. Order fulfilment should be a core competency of this supplier. This approach can be seen, for instance, at investment sites, where the Web site owner does not conclude the actual transactions. Buying collectives use a similar system, whereby the task of the buying combination is limited to maintaining customer relations, and bundling the demand on behalf of the manufacturer (supplier).

Customer needs

What exactly do customers want, and can one still predict their behaviour? Using today's advanced technologies for building customer know-how, it should still be possible to collect sufficient information and on that basis respond adequately to customer needs. However, this calls for direct customer communication and information on customer behaviour. But is that what customers want? It probably is, at certain times, but surely not always. Customer needs, too, can be distinguished in terms of the specific and the individual. The distinction applies to groups of customers, as well as on an individual level. People are not always in the mood for going out to dinner and selecting a menu. Sometimes they prefer a quick meal. Therefore, both a standard product and a customized product must be offered to them. (See Figure 8.7.)

In many cases, the choice will depend on a time factor or other circumstance. Factors of influence include:

- personal details: age, sex, education/training, marital status;
- location: distance to shop, distance from home to work, mobility;
- product features: what products are offered, support required, customization (product complexity);

Figure 8.7   *Strategic choice process, based on product and/or service supply*

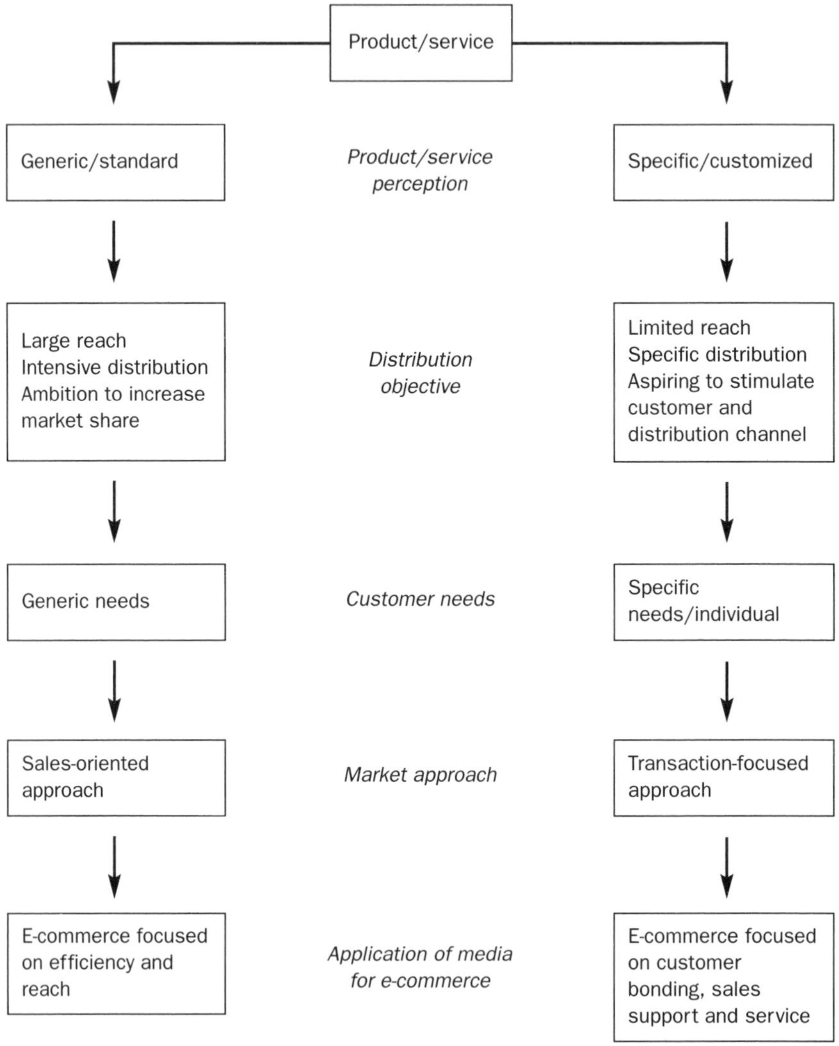

Generic/standard	Product/service perception	Specific/customized
Large reach Intensive distribution Ambition to increase market share	Distribution objective	Limited reach Specific distribution Aspiring to stimulate customer and distribution channel
Generic needs	Customer needs	Specific needs/individual
Sales-oriented approach	Market approach	Transaction-focused approach
E-commerce focused on efficiency and reach	Application of media for e-commerce	E-commerce focused on customer bonding, sales support and service

- distribution features: how far to nearest distribution point, how fast can product be delivered?

Based on the above criteria and individual needs, the customer chooses either a standard product or a customized product, home delivery or collect from store.

Strategic cube model

In all of the above factors, there is a common dimension: choosing between a standard and an individualized product. This dimension is equally important in relation to customer needs, products and services, and the chosen distribution channel. Based on this common factor, we can build a three-dimensional model serving as a basis for the decision-making process. This model has the following dimensions:

● customer needs;

● products and services;

● distribution channels (see Figure 8.8).

Taking the strategic cube model as the point of departure, we can take a closer look at the most relevant elements. To begin with, there must be a clear understanding of the various dimensions of the cube, the possibilities in relation to each dimension, and how to use them. The following questions must be answered:

● What are the needs of the customers?

● What exactly do our customers want from us?

● How can we get to know our customers better?

Figure 8.8 *Strategic cube model*

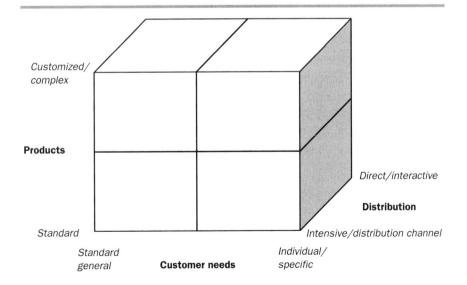

● Do we know why our customers buy from us?

Based on these core questions, we can then proceed with making choices with regard to product supply and the required distribution form.

In relation to product, the choice is whether to supply a standard product or a customized product. But the decision must also be between a simple product (e.g. standard product) or a complex product (e.g. product concept), in which case a number of standard products can be combined to offer a complete service package. This choice also implies the level at which service elements must – or might – be added to the product. Providing service elements can enable suppliers to set themselves apart from the competition and respond better to customer needs. On the basis of identified customer needs, service modules can be added to enable customers to make certain individual choices, e.g. extended service period, maintenance within a day or within the hour, or product user support.

If the organization has an intensive customer orientation, it will be looking to provide a total product/service proposition

A product concept is a combination of products and service elements, delivered to meet individual customer requirements, or satisfying an object-based, integrated demand. To supply a product concept often requires cooperation with another partner or partners in order to be able to provide a total offer. If the organization has an intensive customer orientation, it will be looking to provide a total product/service proposition. Consequently, an organization that delivers to this group of customers will, almost inevitably, opt for a network orientation. A network orientation is strongly focused on the interests of the various partners, in relation to satisfying customers' requirements.

The options for distribution must be evaluated in a similar way. If a distribution channel is chosen, this will probably reflect the organization's ambition to maximize market reach. On the other hand, a distribution form could also be chosen specifically to enable product-based customer bonding. Customer communication is handled by the distribution channel. The supplier can stimulate the desired product positioning and recognition so that the customer will be persuaded to buy their product or acquire a preference for it. If a service product is supplied, it is still possible to use a distribution channel, since this enables advice to be added using the intermediary's expertise, network and position in local markets.

If direct customer communication and interactivity are required, the supplier may choose to handle customer communication under his own roof. This can be done by developing an in-house distribution channel, using the telephone as distribution medium, or supplying via the Internet. Each approach has specific advantages, depending on the required customer contact immediacy. If direct contact is required or preferred, the supplier may wish to operate his own sales points. If support is needed only with non-standard questions, or if trust is to be built through perceived personal contact, telephone communication may suffice. If the supplier wishes to be able to respond to anticipated questions, and if an information structure can be determined, the Internet is an option. Because customer requirements will differ individually, and seeing that customers may require information at any time of the day, enabling the customer to choose their own distribution channel is a good idea. For this, a multi-channel strategy can be used. The distribution channel will focus on a specific function: sales or service provision (service desk) or a specific target group. This has the advantage that customers have various options for communicating with the organization.

In determining a strategy, the possibilities of each of the three dimensions must be considered carefully and independently before drawing cross-connections. Finally, the choices can be determined, including possible use of the Internet.

The choices made are based on the principles of the strategic cube model. Tables 8.4 and 8.5 outline possible product directions and examples.

Based on the above analysis of the various dimensions of the cube,

Table 8.4

Possible product choices, demand-based

	Standard needs	Specific needs
Customized products	Insurance, financial products. Internet for information and communication	Investment products, healthcare, accommodation, education. Internet for interaction, i.e. information and communication, possibly transaction
Standard products	Food, housing, security. Internet usable to an extent, possibly for information only	Entertainment, holidays, music, books. Internet for information provision, possibly for transaction also (e.g. wine, vegetarian products)

Table 8.5 *Products and distribution choices*

	Intensive distribution	Direct/interactive distribution
Customized products	Insurance products, financial products. Internet for information and communication	Pensions, building materials, complex products, e.g. machinery and customized software. Internet notably for information, communication and transaction
Standard products	Food, reading, music. Internet usable to an extent	Computers, PC software, books. Internet for information and transactions

the optimal use of the Internet is determined in respect of each of the four functions of the Internet, i.e. information, communication, transaction and infrastructure (see Figure 8.9).

The choice of whether and how to use the Internet will reflect the extent to which product customization is required. The more specific the product or service concept, the more information must be supplied, and the more interaction will be required by customers in the orientation phase of the transaction process. Whether or not the customer will actually buy on the Internet will depend on the chosen distribution strategy.

The infrastructure function of the Internet is used especially in

Figure 8.9 *Relationship between strategic choices and Internet use*

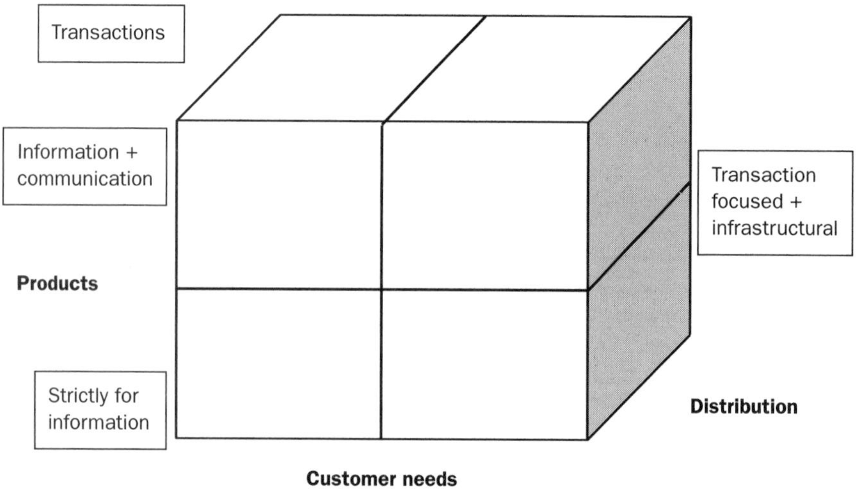

Figure 8.10   *Using group concepts with strategic choices*

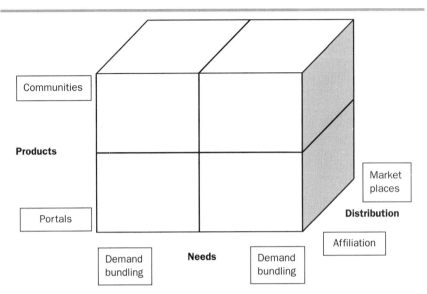

situations where there is a very specific demand, a very specific product and a direct distribution channel. Particularly with repetitive buying patterns, automatic recognition functions are useful aids.

The innovative developments of the Internet, based on products, demand and distribution channels, have led to other market forms, such as portals, market places and communities.

This innovative process is shown in Figure 8.10, specifically in relation to demand bundling. As a result, there is a shift in the buyer-supplier power balance. A possible form of demand bundling is first to find out what customers want to buy, and then to negotiate a special price on that basis. Suppliers may buy in bulk for a certain group of buyers and resell at a discount. Finally, suppliers can work together with others on a permanent basis, as happens in the business-to-business market. The most important changes relate to increased cooperation between individual buyers.

For suppliers, there is the possibility of cooperating with portals to communicate a message to a specific group of customers, or

> **The infrastructure function of the Internet is used especially in situations where there is a very specific demand, a very specific product and a direct distribution channel**

to offer products on the basis of consumer preferences or behaviour (communities). The changes in relation to product dimension reflect the possibilities of the Internet. The Internet enables messages to be directed and offered to a general audience (portals) or to focus on target groups (communities). In the area of distribution, there are options for cooperating at a conceptual level. This could be in the form of affiliated cooperation (click-throughs) or by offering an integrated product package in conjunction with others. In addition, the Internet offers opportunities for market place cooperation and direct sales. In either case, cooperation with other suppliers is required.

Integrated model

The integrated model (Figure 8.11), which expresses the relationships between strategic choices and how these are given shape on the Internet, demonstrates that the 'interface' between the strategic choices and Internet use is found in the way customer communications are handled and customer data are interpreted.

Figure 8.11   *Integrated 'business' model*

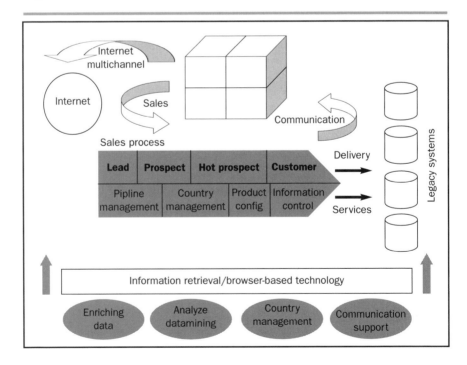

Web site dialogue support, customer recognition and anticipating customer behaviour are the basics of Internet use. The integrated model demonstrates how all components of the business process should be perfectly harmonized. This starts at the strategic choices, in line with the principles of the strategic cube. This choice process largely shapes the way the organization will handle customer communications: individual, target group focused or generic. Based on the desired market position, the Internet can be deployed and the 'look and feel' of the Web site can be determined. Finally, it can be decided whether or not certain (parts of) transactions are to be outsourced to business partners. This could even include total subcontracting (infrastructure function) or an affiliate agreement, whereby a certain part of the supply is handled by the partners.

Summary

In deciding on the possible use of the Internet, and the effects of this on the existing business processes, clear strategic choices must be made with regard to the marketing of the products and/or services (see Figure 8.12). Special consideration must be given to the issue of market reach versus product complexity. On the basis of this, it can be decided to what extent the Internet could contribute to increasing market reach and reducing product complexity. The choice is mutually effective. Once these issues have been decided, the business processes can be adjusted accordingly, paving the way for using the Internet in the most effective manner. The decision-making process has three dimensions:

● The supply dimension: which products are we selling on the Internet and how?

● The demand dimension: what are the needs of customers and how do customers express those needs?

● The distribution dimension: how do we want to sell our products and services; do we want to cooperate with others to increase market reach or tighten our customer relations?

The choice process as a whole is decisive in terms of how effective customer contacts and information support (ICT) will be handled. Since all issues involved in the choice process are interdependent, the question of whether or not to use the Internet is not an isolated matter but one which requires an integrated approach if the Internet is to be used as effectively and competitively as possible.

Figure 8.12   *Strategic choice process, based on market approach*

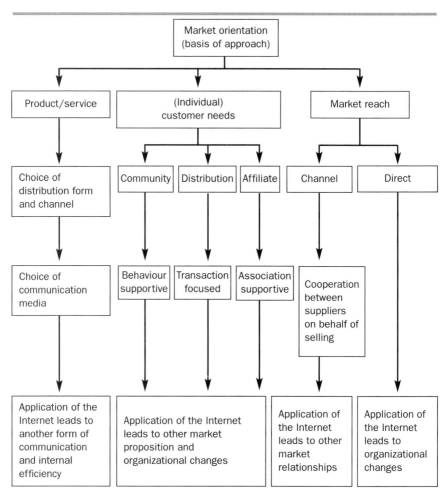

Notes

18 Negroponte, N. (1995) *Being Digital,* Alfred A. Knopf, New York.

19 Levine, R. *et al.* (2000) *The Cluetrain Manifesto,* Perseus Books, Cambridge, Massachusetts.

20 Evans, Paul and Wurster, Thomas S. (2000) *Blown to Bits,* Harvard Business School Press.

9

■ ■ ■ ■ ■ ■ ■ ■ ■ ■ ■ ■ ■ ■ ■ ■ ■ ■

Think it: do it

The pain is in the doing, not in the talking.

On the basis of the changes identified and the strategic choice process, decisions have to be taken in relation to the envisaged strategy. Because these decisions will be far-reaching and because, in order to maintain credibility in the market, it would probably not be good policy to implement the desired restructures overnight, most organizations will opt for a phased change process. However, before making any strategic decisions, the organization must have a clear vision of where it stands today and what the basic conditions are for the market position it has established. It must also have a clear picture as to the feasibility of the desired changes. Therefore, it must first be determined where the limits of the playing field are in relation to product, distribution and demand concepts, following the strategic cube model. So doing, an overview is acquired of the limit conditions and playing field size of:

- the present product concept and the potential demand for it;
- current and potential needs of customers;
- the present distribution concept and other possible distribution concepts.

Business concept

The various scenarios are described in the form of a proposal, identifying the desired changes and possible strategies for achieving those objectives. The implementation process will have a phased structure, as follows:

- *Business concept*
  - describing the current business concept;
  - determining possible business concepts;
  - strategic choices.

- *Conceptual framework*
  - describing the current conceptual framework;
  - determining the desired/required conceptual framework;
  - changes.

- *Realization and implementation*
  - realization in line with time, function and application requirements;
  - reiteration, evaluation and adjustment.

With regard to the strategic changes, it is necessary to determine, on the basis of the strategic cube, what objectives are to be achieved, and how these are to be achieved. The strategic cube model enables various scenarios to be developed, based on the three dimensions identified earlier, i.e.:

- the possible potential of products and product concepts;
- the needs and requirements of customers and markets;
- possible channel strategy.

It is necessary to determine, on the basis of the strategic cube, what objectives are to be achieved, and how these are to be achieved

Following the strategic cube model, a change scenario is developed for each of the above elements. These scenarios will reflect the organization's current position, maximum potential and optimal position, expressed in a sliding scale of potential. In this way, it is possible to determine the choices on the basis of the consequences identified in terms of realization and anticipated market developments.

Product concept

In the process of formulating the desired business concept, the existing concept, possible change scenarios, and the best possible concept are reviewed. This means that, using the strategic cube, the possibilities for adjusting the product concept are reviewed. This includes an evaluation of the advantages of increased product standardizing, adopting a more target group-focused approach, or supplying a more customized and individualized product. These choices will be influenced by the possibilities of the Internet, since the Internet enables a higher level of perceived customization and customer interaction.

This puts some pressure on the various scenarios. On the one hand, the organization wants to extend market reach, which implies delivering a more or less standard product. On the other hand, the Internet enables a higher level of interaction, which is important in supplying more personalized products. The latter, however, implies that specific service elements may need to be added. Essentially, there is friction between the two opposing movements, whereby a balance must be found in the choice process between the possibilities of the organization, and the needs and wishes of the market(s) it wants to serve (see Figure 9.1).

The schedule shown in Figure 9.1 outlines the choice process in relation to product. The first step is to decide whether to supply a customized or standard product. The implications of this in terms of market reach are identified. This requires reviewing the various consequences, also in light of the chosen strategic objective. In principle, the intensity of customer communications and the limit conditions of the chosen orientation determine the possibilities for offering a more or less standard product. In developing the product concept, it is important to determine to what extent the organization wants to cooperate with other market parties (see Table 9.1). This could be with a distribution channel (to sell the goods), but it could also take the form of supplying a complete, integrated product concept. With the

Figure 9.1   *Choice process*

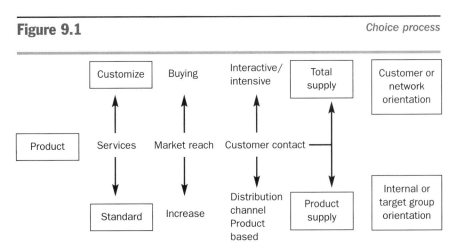

latter, the organization would participate in supplying a total package, which implies a close form of cooperation with others. Finally, an integrated plan is prepared, outlining:

● product proposition;

● cooperation with other parties;

● extent of customer contact;

● the vision of the organization in relation to customer communication policy.

Table 9.1 *Consequences of product choices*

Proposition	Cooperation	Customer relations	Internet	Information requirements
Standard product	Collaboration in the distribution channel	Limited customer contact	Internet for market reach	Product information
Customized product	Possible collaboration for integrated concept	Intensive customer contacts	Internet for interaction and transaction	Customers and contact information

Demand concept

It is important for the decision-making process that a clear picture is formed of customer needs. These may be generic or more specific, they may be universal for the whole market, but they could also be time-bound or situation-bound for the individual customer. The decisive factor in the choice process and approach taken to specific customer needs is the market approach: sales oriented or purchase oriented (see Figure 9.2). If sales oriented, attention will centre on generic market needs and specific product qualities. The match between generic market needs and product qualities determines the organization's ability to respond to assumed needs. Communication will tend to be directed at a large audience, connecting to perceived behaviour and customer needs. This market approach relies predominantly on push.

If the organization is looking to respond to more specific customer needs, it must focus more on the buying process. This type of approach

Figure 9.2   *Sales process versus buying process*

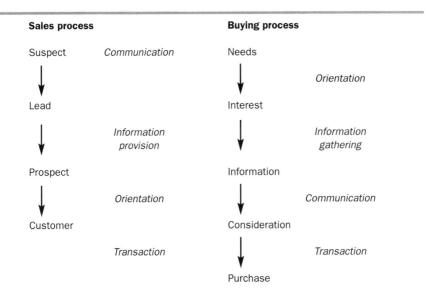

has a post-active, facilitating character.

In the schedule shown in Figure 9.2, orientation, information, communication and transaction are directed by the customer. It is important to know who influences which phase of the buying process. Is it the customer or a decision maker? Is it the product user or someone else? This is important because the supplier's (sales) arguments must connect to the needs of the customer at every stage of the buying process. Hence, the supplier must have an understanding of the (specific) buying process, and therefore will require specific customer information. In many cases, customer needs are time-bound (when?) and/or environment-bound (where?). Ultimately, it is individual customer needs (or aggregated customer needs) that determine the offer which the supplier is able and willing to make, and how the supplier communicates his offer to the customer or the market. (See Table 9.2.)

Based on the specifics identified in relation to the organization, the communication

Ultimately, it is individual customer needs (or aggregated customer needs) that determine the offer which the supplier is able and willing to make

Table 9.2 *Consequences of the demand concept*

Needs	Focus	Sales approach	Market approach	Communication
Generic	Market approach	Sales driven	Push approach	Mass communication
Specific	Customer approach	Purchase driven	Pull approach	Interactive communication

provision and the information provision, connections can be established between the demand concept and the product concept (see Table 9.3).

Table 9.3 *Relationship between product concept and demand concept*

Product/ needs	Standard	Adapted	Customization	Information
Generic	Distribution channel. Large range	Distribution channel. Services direct or service centre	Interactive, support channel	Product oriented
Target group	Multi-channel. Internet supported	Selective distribution. Internet for communication and information	Interactive, multi-channel. Internet for all functions	Target group focused
Specific	Multi-channel. Interactive. Direct distribution	Support distribution channel. Internet for all possible support	Direct interactive contacts. Limited market reach	Customer focused
Organiz-ation	Hierarchical	Matrix, business units	Horizontal/ network oriented	

Distribution concept

Following the same systematics as used in determining product and demand concepts, a framework is devised for the distribution concept (see Table 9.4). At the extreme ends of the scale, the options are outsourcing all distribution work to a distribution channel, or keeping all distribution activities within the organization. Then it must be decided whether to operate as manufacturer or supplier only, or to handle customer communications as well. If the organization settles for the role of supplier, it will have no customer relationships, and its use of the Internet will be limited. The role of the Internet, and thus the extent of the changes associated with the use of the Internet, will be limited. Market reach will be decided by the distribution form and distribution channel chosen.

At the opposite end of the spectrum, it may be decided to handle all activities in-house, as well as maintaining direct consumer relations. This type of organization is often used by suppliers in the business-to-business market which offer a complete product and services package in close consultation with the customer. For organizations that operate on the basis of 'just in time' management, this structure is in fact a precondition. Cooperation between the two parties will be intensive, and may include participation in each other's business processes. Here, too, a matrix can be made of the extreme ends of the scale.

Table 9.4   *Consequences of the distribution concept*

Distribution	Focus	Measuring point	Objective	Internet application
Generic	Product based	Sales	Large market reach	Infrastructure
Specific	Interactive	Relationship	Limited market reach	Interactive medium

Once the limits for these dimensions are set, the maximum factors and optimum possibilities can be determined. In combination, these will render the blueprint for the desired business proposition.

Based on the customer needs identified and the specific possibilities of the organization, the above approach enables a business proposition to be developed that is built on the organization's specific strengths and competitive advantages. The proposition is assessed against prevailing market conditions in relation to:

● competition: any changes adopted by the competition and/or changes in competition structure;

Figure 9.3   *Technological developments that can induce market changes*

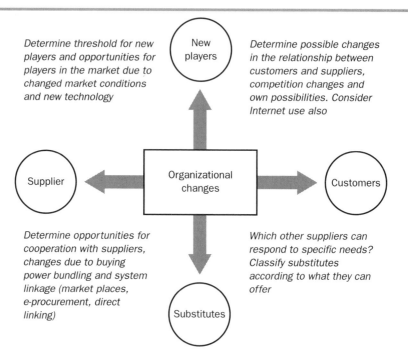

Determine threshold for new players and opportunities for players in the market due to changed market conditions and new technology

New players

Determine possible changes in the relationship between customers and suppliers, competition changes and own possibilities. Consider Internet use also

Supplier

Organizational changes

Customers

Determine opportunities for cooperation with suppliers, changes due to buying power bundling and system linkage (market places, e-procurement, direct linking)

Which other suppliers can respond to specific needs? Classify substitutes according to what they can offer

Substitutes

Source: Porter, M. (1980) *Competitive Strategies*, The Free Press, New York. The central block for market conditions has been adjusted to indicate the value of organizational adjustments in terms of competition relationships

- any changes in markets brought on by product substitution and distribution changes.

The changes identified can be positioned in the model of Porter (see Figure 9.3).

The result of the strategic orientation on the business concept will translate as an analysis of the desired concept and the current concept. This analysis serves as the basis for the change process, by confronting the organization's current possibilities with its ambitions.

Conceptual framework

The conceptual framework reflects the functional requirements for the business concept, covering the following aspects:

- organization;
- information provision;
- communication;
- product policy.

The requirements in each of these areas must be identified in relation to the desired business concept. From there, it can be determined where the organization stands now, and what changes are necessary. These changes will be derived from the marketing orientation model, whereby the change process and possible scenarios will reflect the possibilities for using the Internet. The conceptual framework will dictate specific choices in relation to the elements above.

Organization

If a company aspires to increased market orientation, this implies that direct customer communication must be facilitated. Thus, an organization form or structure must be chosen to enable this. This organizational structure can be central (hierarchical) or it can be an organizational form that enables decisions to be decentralized. The chosen organizational structure will depend also on the aspired (or current) marketing orientation, i.e. the extent to which the organization is focused on the customer, or whether it is internally oriented. Each organization has basically two components: an external (sales-focused) component (see Table 9.5) and an internal (production-focused) component (see Table 9.6).

Because both components are usually only loosely connected, there is a potential conflict. This could surface in the area of internal information provision, or in the way that the various functions are harmonized. This is why many organizations prefer to use a centrally controlled structure, whereby all the important instructions are issued top down. The rest of the organization is required to follow the instructions and to conform to the going norms and standards. This type of structure characterizes internally focused companies whose principal objective is to keep all processes and

Many organizations prefer to use a centrally controlled structure, whereby all the important instructions are issued top down

Table 9.5   *The externally oriented component*

	Internally focused	Change	Highly customer focused
People	Conservative, experts, procedure focused	From internal to external, from technical expert to communicator. From function oriented to team oriented	Strong communicators and improvisers. Open, sociable, customer focused. Flexible
Products/services	Standard	From standard to individual	Customized, responding to individual needs
Processes	Standard, focused on production and supporting departments/functions	From internal efficiency focus to customer focus: from inside-out to outside-in	From externally focused to internally focused, from customer to production. Customer value and customer features/indicators are important
Resources	Strongly focused on cost reduction and efficiency. ERP systems	Strong focus on information provision surrounding the customer entity	Supporting customer communication, focused on pro-active approach. CRM systems
Communication	Mass communication. Limited internal communication by memos and meetings	Pro-active, interactive and individually focused	Individual, mostly based on historic customer data

functions under control. The way the Internet is used in such organizations will focus on stimulating efficiency, and achieving better communication between staff.

The key elements in the externally focused functions are:

● the products and services offered;

● sales methods, sales strategy (direct or indirect, role of ICT and the Internet);

Table 9.6 — *The internally focused component*

	Internally focused	Change	Strong customer focus
Control/ management	Centrally directed, leader/board sets the limits	Decentralization of authorities, management and control, different power structure	Decentral, autonomous customer units, directed at a distance, close to the market
Culture	Conservative, central decision making and power. Compliant	Less focused on the process, more on the individual	Open, approachable, friendly, service-oriented, warm
Structure	Hierarchical, divided into functional groups	Separate units. Self-directed	Decentral units or customer-focused units, large measure of authority
Competency	Efficient production, high quality, strong emphasis on product	From technique to customer knowledge. From product management to knowledge management	Flexible, alert to market changes, listening to customers
Mission	Strong focus on the organization	From internal to external, from production to demand	Strong ideals, strong focus on customer needs

- commitment of personnel;
- tools and resources;
- the way of communication with the market.

In relation to the internal organization, the key elements are:

- culture;
- structure;
- competence (knowledge and skills);
- control;
- mission (objective of the organization).

The way in which each of the above elements is approached, and the requirements and possibilities of the organization, will reflect the extent to which the organization is either internally focused or customer focused.

The extent to which an organization is internally focused largely determines its flexibility and speed in responding to changes, and the requirements with regard to direct customer communications. If an organization wishes to be closer to the customer and the market, the externally focused functions become more important, including the authority and powers of those who fulfil those functions. The information provision in a more externally oriented organization will be more focused on supporting and facilitating that communication. This includes recording moments of customer contact, advice given and decisions made. For an internally oriented organization, the ERP platform will dominate the information provision. In a customer-oriented organization, the CRM platform will be more important.

An organization that has a specific external orientation will have a more horizontal structure, enabling other functions to be involved in the customer communication process. Clearly, the changes between the two organizational forms are inspired by the wish to create a more level organization, where power lies in flexibility more than efficiency (see Figure 9.4). The management structure chosen for an internally oriented organization will therefore be a different one than that in an externally oriented organization. Likewise, both organizations will have different managers, leadership and corporate cultures.

The change from an internally to an externally oriented organization must lead to a renewed harmony between the elements described. How effectively this happens largely determines the limits within which an organization can change.

Having set one's sights on the desired change process, it must first be determined which of the elements noted above the organization wants to and can change. Concerning product policy, the choice is between a standard product or a customized product and corresponding variants, as shown in the strategic cube model.

The information provision element can be categorized into three main groups (see Table 9.7).

Depending on the level of market orientation, the customer contacts will be decisive in relation to the system requirements (CRM). With an internally directed orientation, the efficiency requirements of the internal processes (ERP) will be decisive. (See Figure 9.5.)

Figure 9.4   *Organizational change*

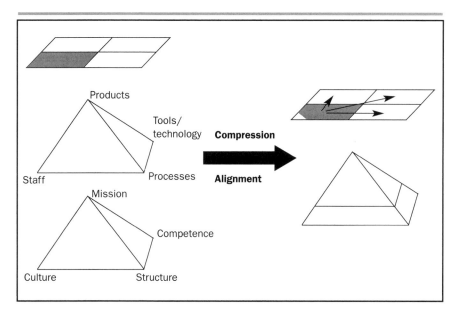

Table 9.7   *Information clusters*

Customer contacts	Products/production	Buying
Supporting	*Forming part of*	*Application*
Account management	ERP systems	Electronic market places
Distribution channel		Buying function
Telephone		Linked systems
Internet		E-procurement
Other		

Communication

The core question is what, how and with whom must the organization communicate? In formulating a communication strategy, it must be decided, once again, whether to apply direct communication or mass communication. The choice is made on the basis of the marketing orientations and the strategic choice process, following the principles of the strategic cube model. The function of the communication is to facilitate the interaction with the market. The communication

---

Figure 9.5   *Integrated system set-up*

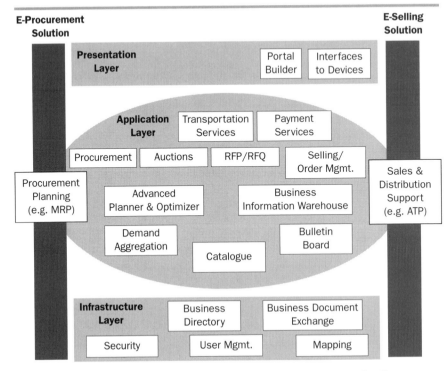

Source: MySAP.com. Integrated system set-up showing the functional components, as well as the combination of strategy, buying and commerce

instruments decide how communication is effected. This can be:

- direct forms of communication, such as direct mail or telemarketing;
- mass communication instruments such as television commercials, brochures or advertisements;
- interactive ways of communication, such as CD-ROM and the Internet.

The communication instruments are chosen on the basis of the:

- desired level of interaction with the market and individual customers;
- available budgets;
- envisaged objectives.

A customer-oriented approach requires information to be collected on the customer, which is why a customer database is required.

> Besides the communication form, the message is important: *what* does the organization want to communicate?

Besides the communication form, the message is important: *what* does the organization want to communicate? Likewise, it is important *how* the message is communicated: non-committal or direct, informative or matter of fact. Choosing *what* to communicate *about* is important too: the company, a specific product brand, or a way of fulfilling a need. The subject determines the actual contents of the communication message. Finally, the organization must be keenly aware of *with whom* it wants to communicate: the market (generic), a target group or individual customers. Knowledge of the target group and an understanding of how to reach this group is an important condition.

The choices made with regard to communication are based on the business concept and the scope of the conceptual framework, e.g. IT support and organizational possibilities. These are the peripheral conditions for the communication, and provide an indication of the feasibility of the (marketing) objectives formulated in the business plan.

Realization and implementation

Finally, once the objectives and limit conditions are determined, implementation can commence (see Figure 9.6). At that point, a platform structure is determined, and it is indicated how the changes are to be implemented, the timeline, and milestones for further development. The consequences outlined are cast in a timeframe, accounting for mutual inter-dependence of the various aspects. Based on this planning framework, budgets are allocated, measuring points determined, and the realization process can actually be supported. Because in preparing the plans three different scenarios were outlined (ideal situation, attainable situation, current situation), a projection can be made, which is superimposed on the ideal scenario, and from there led back to the current situation. In this way, a spectrum of changes transpires, each affecting the other. The spectrum divides into timeframes and functional phases.

Figure 9.6

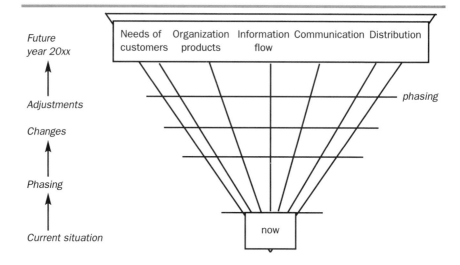

Integrated change model, showing the current and future situation and indicating a phased approach to the various sub-areas (platform based)

Summary Based on the strategic options, a plan is prepared which describes *what* the organization wants to achieve, *how* it plans to achieve this, how this needs to be *phased*, and what *changes* are necessary. The realization and implementation scenario will reflect, to an extent, the limitations of the organization and the available resources. Furthermore, the motivation for accelerated implementation plays an important role. In many cases, the prospect of change may impede efficient implementation of the most optimal change scenario. Change is often perceived as threatening, and this is a hurdle, which is in fact recognized by many organizations. People tend to reject change if it gives rise to uncertainty or reduces their authority. Therefore, an incentive is needed to encourage them to accept change. Inability to keep up with the competition if nothing changes could be such an incentive. In other words, no change means less profit. But there may be other economic motives, e.g. if nothing changes, the customer will take his business elsewhere, where his individual wishes *are* satisfied, or where he *can* shop around the clock.

Essentially, in order to determine an e-strategy, the organization must review its commercial objectives, and it must know its possibilities and limits for change. Finally, it must let itself be inspired by customer needs, since it is the customer, ultimately, who provides its raison d'être, and who brings in the profits. Therefore, it is essential that the organization can respond to the needs and wishes of the customer. ICT, the Internet and other technologies have provided the tools to work more efficiently and effectively, and the means for more efficient and interactive communication with other market players, including customers. In fact, one could argue that the world, in many ways, is again becoming the place it once was. A community where everybody knew everybody and everybody listened to each other. A place where people were socially concerned, and economically motivated. A world that was small and comprehensible. A society that was far more transparent than ours. As our vision of the world expanded over the past two centuries, inspiring individuals and organizations to want to be part of that world, it became less and less transparent, and less and less comprehensible. Current technological achievements in the area of ICT may hold the key to restoring some of the transparency of the pre-industrial world, where people communicated directly with each other and knew what was happening around them.

Technology facilitates the changes that are happening around us, but people influence the pace, scope and necessity of those changes. It is not technology but people who decide which companies are successful, which developments are important in fulfilling consumer needs, and in which way they want to buy a product or service. Business, after all, is still a people's business, or, perhaps more aptly, a customer's business. So the future of marketing is in understanding each customer, knowing all individual needs and making sure that each individual customer experience is positive.

Index